# Football Italia

Globalizing Sport Studies

Series editor: **John Horne, Professor of Sport and Sociology, University of Central Lancashire, UK**

Public interest in sport studies continues to grow throughout the world. This series brings together the latest work in the field and acts as a global knowledge hub for interdisciplinary work in sport studies. While promoting work across disciplines, the series focuses on social scientific and cultural studies of sport. It brings together the most innovative scholarly empirical and theoretical work, from within the UK and internationally.

**Books already published in the series:**

*Global Media Sport: Flows, Forms and Futures*
David Rowe
ISBN 9781849660709 (Hardback)
ISBN 9781849666756 (Ebook)

*Japanese Women and Sport: Beyond Baseball and Sumo*
Robin Kietlinski
ISBN 9781849663403 (Hardback)
ISBN 9781849666688 (Ebook)

*Sport for Development and Peace: A Critical Sociology*
Simon Darnell
ISBN 9781849663441 (Hardback)
ISBN 9781849665919 (Ebook)

*Globalizing Cricket: Englishness, Empire and Identity*
Dominic Malcolm
ISBN 9781849665278 (Hardback)
ISBN 9781849665612 (Ebook)

*Global Boxing*
Kath Woodward
ISBN 9781849668101 (Hardback)
ISBN 9781849667999 (Ebook)

*Sport and Social Movements: From the Local to the Global*
Jean Harvey, John Horne, Parissa Safai, Simon Darnell and Sébastien Courchesne-O'Neill
ISBN 9781780934143 (Hardback)
ISBN 9781780935560 (Ebook)

**Forthcoming:**

*Localizing Global Sport for Development*
Davies Banda, Ruth Jeanes, Tess Kay and Iain Lindsey

*Sport and Technology: An Actor-Network Theory Perspective*
Roslyn Kerr

# Football Italia

## Italian Football in an Age of Globalization

Mark Doidge

Bloomsbury Academic
An imprint of Bloomsbury Publishing Plc

BLOOMSBURY
LONDON • NEW DELHI • NEW YORK • SYDNEY

**Bloomsbury Academic**
An imprint of Bloomsbury Publishing Plc

50 Bedford Square   1385 Broadway
London              New York
WC1B 3DP            NY 10018
UK                  USA

www.bloomsbury.com

**BLOOMSBURY and the Diana logo are trademarks of Bloomsbury Publishing Plc**

First published 2015

© Mark Doidge, 2015

Mark Doidge has asserted his right under the Copyright, Designs and Patents Act, 1988, to be identified as Author of this work.

This work is published subject to a Creative Commons Attribution Non-commercial No Derivatives Licence. You may share this work for non-commercial purposes only, provided you give attribution to the copyright holder and the publisher. For permission to publish commercial versions please contact Bloomsbury Academic.

No responsibility for loss caused to any individual or organization acting on or refraining from action as a result of the material in this publication can be accepted by Bloomsbury or the author.

**British Library Cataloguing-in-Publication Data**
A catalogue record for this book is available from the British Library.

ISBN: HB: 978-1-4725-1919-1
ePDF: 978-1-4725-1921-4
ePub: 978-1-4725-1920-7

**Library of Congress Cataloging-in-Publication Data**
Doidge, Mark.
Football Italia : Italian football in an age of globalization/Mark Doidge.
pages cm
Summary: "Football Italia examines the development of Italian football in relation to the wider global transformations impacting football, and addresses the reasons for Serie A's initial success and current malaise"– Provided by publisher.
ISBN 978-1-4725-1919-1 (hardback)
1. Soccer–Italy. 2. Soccer–Political aspects–Italy. 3. Soccer–Social aspects–Italy.
4. Sports and globalization. I. Title.
GV944.I8D65 2015
796.3340945–dc23
2015002912

Series: Globalizing Sport Studies

Typeset by Deanta Global Publishing Services, Chennai, India
Printed and bound in Great Britain

*For Luca*

# Contents

| | | |
|---|---|---|
| Series Editor's Preface | | viii |
| Acknowledgements | | x |
| 1 | The Rise and Fall of Italian Football | 1 |
| 2 | Italy in a Globalizing World | 13 |
| 3 | The Political Economy of Italian Football | 45 |
| 4 | Scandal | 67 |
| 5 | Stadiums | 95 |
| 6 | Policing | 123 |
| 7 | The *Ultras* | 141 |
| 8 | Other Forms of Fandom | 181 |
| 9 | 'Year Zero' | 197 |
| Glossary | | 213 |
| Methodological Note | | 215 |
| Notes | | 221 |
| Bibliography | | 225 |
| Index | | 239 |

# Series Editor's Preface

There is now a considerable amount of expertise nationally and internationally in the social scientific and cultural analysis of sport in relation to the economy and society more generally. Contemporary research topics, such as sport and social justice, science and technology and sport, global social movements and sport, sports mega-events, sports participation and engagement and the role of sport in social development, suggest that sport and social relations need to be understood in non-Western developing economies, as well as European, North American and other advanced capitalist societies. The current high global visibility of sport makes this an excellent time to launch a major new book series that takes sport seriously, and makes this research accessible to a wide readership.

The series **Globalizing Sport Studies** is thus in line with a massive growth of academic expertise, research output and public interest in sport worldwide. At the same time, it seeks to use the latest developments in technology and the economics of publishing to reflect the most innovative research into sport in society currently underway in the world. The series is multidisciplinary, although primarily based on the social sciences and cultural studies approaches to sport.

The broad aims of the series are to: *act* as a knowledge hub for social scientific and cultural studies research in sport, including, but not exclusively, anthropological, economic, geographic, historical, political science and sociological studies; *contribute* to the expanding field of research on sport in society in the United Kingdom and internationally by focusing on sport at regional, national and international levels; *create* a series for both senior and more junior researchers that will become synonymous with cutting-edge research, scholarly opportunities and academic development; *promote* innovative discipline-based, multi-, inter- and trans-disciplinary theoretical and methodological approaches to researching sport in society; *provide* an English language outlet for high-quality non-English writing on sport in society; *publish* broad overviews, original empirical research studies and classic studies from non-English sources; and thus attempt to *realize* the potential for *globalizing* sport studies through open content licensing with 'Creative Commons'.

As the first book-length sociological study of Italian professional football, *Football Italia* provides an analysis that charts the way in which a once powerful league has lost ground to rival national leagues in Europe.

In 1990 the FIFA World Cup Finals ('Italia '90') made a global statement about the superior infrastructure and organization of the Italian game. The state-of-the-art stadiums housed some of the greatest players and offered a sharp contrast to the rest of European (and arguably therefore world) football. English football, on the other hand was emerging from a period of crisis involving fan disorder and inadequate stadiums and policing that saw English teams being excluded from European competitions. The stadiums of Italia '90 reinforced the drastic decline of the English infrastructure and the need for a dramatic overhaul.

Since the early 1990s, however, elite Premier League English football has been transformed in terms of its commercial growth, attendances, redeveloped stadiums and global exposure, while football in Italy has been beset with entrenched problems of racism and hooliganism, financial irregularity and a relative lack of modernization of the sport's key structures and core facilities.

Mark Doidge's analysis of these reversals is grounded in a global political economy based on first-hand observation and research. He argues that globalization has seen a shift in power within Italian society that has been reflected in Italian football. *Football Italia* provides a much-needed analysis of specific problems in Italian football, including match-fixing, stadiums, and policing, as well as the way in which fans are involved in attempts to bring about a positive change.

John Horne,<br>
Preston and Edinburgh, 2014

# Acknowledgements

It was while sipping a nice glass of Primitivo in the courtyard of the British School at Rome that this book was envisioned. I had been studying sport and exercise in Ancient Rome as part of my Masters, and through a conversation with an archaeologist friend, it was concluded that Italian football would make an apposite subject of study for the PhD that preceded this book. The wheels were set in motion for a journey that would allow me to fulfil several personal ambitions.

Sir Isaac Newton remarked that his success was because 'he was standing on the shoulders of giants'. No journey can be completed alone and this book could not have been published without the support of a number of fantastic people. Without Anthony King taking a chance on an unknown, with no background in sociology, the PhD that preceded this book would not have been possible. As Series Editor of this book, John Horne has been a wonderful help and incredibly encouraging in getting this project get off the ground; his advice and support have been invaluable.

I have been privileged to work at the University of Brighton among some of the most outstanding academics in the field. They have provided an amazing intellectual space, outstanding support and incredible advice. Many thanks to Alan Tomlinson, Jayne Caudwell, Dan Burdsey, Belinda Wheaton, Megan Chawansky, John Sugden, John Nauright, Udo Merkel, Nigel Jarvis, Tom Carter, Gill Lines, Jack Wilkinson, Mark Perryman, Paul Gilchrist and Marc Keech. I hope this book is worthy of being linked to the University of Brighton. Thanks also to people in the wider sociology of the football community, particularly Pete Millward and Carrie Dunn. These acknowledgements would not be complete without a massive display of gratitude to Lara Killick and Ruth Lewis who have been so supportive since this journey began.

Obviously, this book would not have been possible without the warmth and generosity of the Livornesi. Many people travel to Italy for the weather, the architecture, the food, the wine, the art and the history. In concentrating on these factors they miss the warmth of the people who make up the individual cities and create the special culture that exists in Italy. Thanks to all the raggazzi in the *curva*. Thanks for letting me come to games with you, and most of all, for making me feel so welcome. Thanks especially to my 'Rosetta Stone', Riccardo Bertani, whose archives, personal history and interest in all things football, Livorno, England, and Italy, provided me with so much information.

*Grazie mille* to the members of Club Luca Rondina in Livorno. There is a reason this book is dedicated to Luca. You were amazingly generous with your time and contacts that provided me with so much information. I would also like to thank Sarah Thomson who runs the website livornonow.com. She gave me the contact of Elena Batazzi, who kindly interviewed me for the newspaper, *Il Tirreno*. These articles provided me with many contacts and allowed my research to flourish. Daniele Bavone deserves a special mention for helping me find somewhere to live. To Gabriella Bianchi, I would like to thank you for letting me into your home. I would also like to send my warmest regards to Dr Giuseppe Boni and Antonella Freschi, whose generosity, help and support provided a concrete foundation for my stay in Livorno.

I would also like to thank UEFA for their grant that supported a separate project on anti-racism in European football, and this enabled me to meet some important people, especially Carlo Balestri, Riccardo Bertolin and Lorenzo Contucci, in the wider fan movements across Italy and Europe.

I should thank my parents, grandparents, brothers, and numerous friends for providing me with the development and support to pursue this research. My parents, Corinne and Keith, have always advised us that 'anything is possible if you put your mind to it'. I hope this book is a testament to that.

# 1

# The Rise and Fall of Italian Football

As the BBC globe faded away, the camera panned across a renaissance fresco that was inspired by Classical art. The female chorus rose while the screen filled with an image of an opera house. The curtain rose and the iconic voice of Luciano Pavarotti began the final line of 'Nessun Dorma', from Giacomo Puccini's opera *Turandot*. As Pavarotti reached the climax of the aria, declaring, 'vincerò! vincerò, vincerò!' (I will win! I will win! I will win!), the video montage replayed iconic moments from World Cups of the past, starting with Pele celebrating his opening goal in the 1970 World Cup Final. This was followed by the Cruyff turn, through Maradona and ending with Marco Tardelli exploding with joy and emotion while celebrating Italy's second goal in the 1982 final. The opera, culture, footballing memories and visceral emotion combined to introduce Italia '90, the World Cup hosted by Italy. The tournament itself delivered its own iconic moments as Cameroon launched the tournament by defeating the reigning champions, Argentina, before Roger Milla shot to stardom by dancing with the corner flag. However, Cameroon's fairy tale was ended by England, who, lost to Germany in the semi-final, a defeat that famously left Paul Gascoigne – and with him all of England – in tears. Meanwhile, Argentina overcame their loss to Cameroon to reach the final with a victory over the hosts, Italy, in Naples. The Argentine captain Diego Maradona, who played his club football with Napoli, called on the Neapolitans to support him over the Italians who, he argued, looked down on his adopted city. And in a bad-tempered final, the victors over England, West Germany, defeated Maradona's Argentina. Despite the appeal to nostalgia and tradition presented at Italia '90, a new era of football was beginning.

Italia '90 was a defining moment for global football, and for English football in particular. It demonstrated, as King (1998) argues, the superior infrastructure and organization of the Italian game. The state-of-the-art stadiums housed some of the greatest players who had just graced the 1990 World Cup. Argentina's

Maradona and Careca played for Napoli, while their German adversaries, Rudi Völler and Thomas Berthold both played for Roma. Their German teammates, Jürgen Klinsmann, Lothar Matthäus and, the scorer of the winning goal in the final, Andreas Brehme, all played for Internazionale (Inter). Across the city of Milan, Inter's rivals, AC Milan included Marco van Basten, Ruud Gullit and Frank Rijkaard from the Netherlands. Italy's most successful team, Juventus, also boasted a finalist, in Thomas Häßler, one of Italy's emerging stars, Roberto Baggio and the leading scorer of the tournament, Salvatore 'Toto' Schillaci. The range of international footballing talent, alongside the outstanding stadiums, marked a sharp contrast to the rest of European football, and English football in particular.

English football was emerging from a sustained period of crisis. Although there was a long history of disorder associated with British football matches, hooliganism became entrenched in the 1970s. Sustained patterns of hooliganism culminated in the Heysel stadium disaster during the 1985 European Cup final between Juventus and Liverpool. An hour before kick-off, supporters of Liverpool rushed towards a section of Juventus fans. The antiquated and poorly maintained Belgian stadium was ill-prepared for the onslaught and a wall collapsed on the Italians. Thirty-nice Juventus fans were tragically killed. This resulted in English clubs being banned from European competitions for five years. In addition to the ignominy of being excluded for the first time since the competitions' inception in 1955,[1] English football suffered another stadium disaster at Hillsborough four years later. Poor facilities and policing at the Sheffield stadium left ninety-six Liverpool fans crushed on the terraces. Consequently, the government investigation led by Lord Justice Taylor instigated a period of sustained investment in stadiums and policing. In particular, the stadiums of Italia '90 reinforced the dramatic deterioration of the English infrastructure and the need for a drastic overhaul.

Italia '90, more importantly, highlighted a growing demand for football in England. The relative success of the England national team, combined with the celebrity status of Paul Gascoigne's tears, suggested that the wider British public were voracious consumers of football. The Broadcasting Act of 1990 had deregulated television, which opened up competition and permitted BskyB a broader remit within British broadcasting, enabling Rupert Murdoch to use sport as his 'battering ram' to enter British broadcasting and capture the lucrative football market (Rowe 2004, p. 100). The popularity of Italia '90 and the deregulation of television combined to ensure that BskyB could table an offer for the exclusive rights of the nascent Premier League, obliterating ITV's offer and 'blow them [ITV] out of the water', as Alan Sugar lobbied (King 1998, p. 110). Thus the elite division of English football broke away from the Football League and established the Premier League in 1992. Since then, the Premier League has become the 'Global Football League' (Millward 2011) and assumed a leading position in terms of media contracts, star players and advertising revenues.

At the same moment in history, the leading European clubs were campaigning for greater control over UEFA's elite cup competition. The president of AC Milan, Silvio Berlusconi, was agitating for a league structure that would give the larger clubs a greater chance of progressing through the competition. 'The European Cup has become an anachronism', Berlusconi argued. 'It is economic nonsense that a club such as Milan might be eliminated in the first round. It is not modern thinking' (King 2003, p. 14). Meanwhile, television audience became a major driving force for owners and federations. Deregulation of the television markets across Europe, and new satellite and cable technology, saw the emergence of transnational media companies such as Kirch in Germany, Sky in Britain and Mediaset in Italy. In the end, UEFA succumbed to club lobbying and the pressures of commercial and media expansion. They established the Champions League in 1992, the same year as the English Premier League was formed, and their rebranding exercise mirrored that of the Premier League. Exclusive media contracts were granted to the highest bidder from each nation and a suite of corporate sponsors were given the exclusive rights to align their brand with that of elite European competition, mimicking what had taken place with the FIFA World Cup and Olympics previously (Sugden and Tomlinson 1998; Horne and Whannel 2012).

The deregulation of players' contracts under the Bosman ruling also facilitated in transforming the European competition (Giulianotti 1999; King 2003; Goldblatt 2007). Consequently, those national markets that could accumulate the most resources from television and sponsorship could also accumulate the most playing resources. As King (2003, p. 83) highlights:

> The unification of the player market has facilitated a concentration of playing power in the core football markets of the New Europe – in England, Germany, Spain and Italy – because the clubs in these countries are financially better equipped than those in smaller leagues (now unprotected by national trade limitations) to buy players.

Those clubs within national markets that could leverage the greatest revenue could also further accumulate playing resources. Consequently, the elite clubs in England, Germany, Italy, France and Spain became central actors on the global network. They replicated wider transformations in global capitalism that witnessed global cities emerging as central nodes for company headquarters, while subsidiary companies were dispersed across the globe (Sassen 2001; King 2003). This permitted the paradoxical process of accumulation and diffusion.

The transnationalization of the game has resulted in a process of accumulation at the wealthiest clubs within the wealthiest national leagues of England, Italy, France, Spain and Germany. The economic deregulation of national economies and national leagues permitted this accumulation, as Goldblatt (2007, p. 696) argues:

> The logic of economic concentration has allowed the leading teams in Europe to assemble the global elite of football talent, drawing on players from every continent. Most teams in the final stages possessed a majority of internationals, the leading players from Africa and Latin America as well as the very best from Europe, the concentrated talent of which has been sharpened by the regularity of European games.

Deregulation had helped transform global football by permitting a coterie of elite clubs to accumulate and concentrate resources. These clubs use a variety of strategies to increase their revenue, including signing star players, merchandising, sponsorship, stadium redevelopment and media rights.

## The continued rise of Italian football

Independent of these changes, Italian football was building on the strength of Italia '90. Italy's elite league, Serie A, continued to attract a range of international footballing talent. Two years after the World Cup, AC Milan signed Jean-Pierre Papin and Zvonimir Boban to complement their Dutch trio of van Basten, Gullit and Rijkaard. In addition, they made the world-record signing of Gianluigi Lentini for £13 million. In Florence, Fiorentina signed Gabriel Batistuta of Argentina and Dunga of Brazil, while Taffarel, Dunga's international teammate, and Thomas Brolin of Sweden joined Parma. Faustino Asprilla, Fernando Couto and Hristo Stoichkov followed these international stars to Parma in subsequent seasons. In Rome, Aldair and Claudio Caniggia signed for Roma, while at Lazio, Aaron Winter and Karl-Heinze Riedle were joined by one of the stars of Italia '90, Paul 'Gazza' Gascoigne. Other English players, who often aren't noted for their willingness to play outside of England, followed 'Gazza'. David Platt signed for Bari in 1991 before moving to Juventus and then to Sampdoria. Des Walker also signed for the latter in 1992, while Paul Ince moved to Inter in 1995. As can be seen, Serie A was attracting some of the best players in the world and was increasingly being seen as the 'most beautiful league in the world' (Clegg 2010).

Much of this success was built on the money from television and the particular ownership model in Italy. For Porro (2008), the deregulation of television had a profound effect on the cultural medium of football as well as in providing increased revenues for clubs. Porro termed this new form of football, *mediacalcio* (media-football), to reiterate the importance of media to the economic transformations. Other Italian academics have also identified similar changes. Russo (2005) termed these changes *ultracalcio* (ultrafootball) to suggest that football had morphed into a different sport. This was echoed by Liguori and Smargiasse (2003), who argued that football was a postmodern version of its previous guise and had now become *neo-calcio* (neo-football). What unites all of these analyses on Italian football is the role that television (through finances and cultural impact) played in transforming the sport. Silvio Berlusconi and others, who were the driving forces of Italian football, helped put it at the forefront of world football in the early 1990s. Similar globalization processes were taking place in Italy as elsewhere in Europe.

The establishment of the Premier League, and its move towards satellite television, coupled with the transfer of English players to Italy, provided an opportunity for Channel 4. Two years after Italia '90, the British broadcaster launched *Football Italia*, which ensured that high-quality football remained on terrestrial television. Moreover, Italian football exuded glamour and this was reflected in Channel 4's production. The presenter, James Richardson, hosted the shows from a range of alluring locations – from Florentine piazzas to Roman cafes. The outside broadcasts in world-famous cultural locations were congruent to the image of Italian football; it exuded quality, culture and style.

The contrast with English football was stark. The Hillsborough tragedy capped a decade of conflict and decline in the English game. Organized hooliganism had blighted the sport since the 1970s. Spectator culture was aggressively young, masculine and exclusionary. Racism was prevalent on the terraces and violence characterized Saturday afternoons. The brutal decline of the culture surrounding the game was symbolized in the infrastructure. British stadiums had not been significantly upgraded since many of them were constructed at the start of the twentieth century. The only major improvements were related to violence containment or to the early cautious approaches to sponsors' boxes. The deterioration of the stadiums resulted in the major tragedies of the 1980s. The initial warning signs were not heeded even after the Ibrox Stadium disaster in 1971, when sixty-six spectators were crushed in a stairway while trying to exit the stadium. A month before the Heysel stadium disaster, a major fire engulfed the stand at Bradford City's Valley Parade Stadium. The stadium's wooden structure, discarded litter and locked emergency exits, together with the windy conditions, helped the fire to spread across the stand. Despite fifty-six spectators dying in the fire, major stadium regulation and reconstruction did not take place until after the Hillsborough tragedy where ninety-six fans lost their lives. The aftermath of Hillsborough combined with the euphoria of Italia '90 to create the conditions required for the restructuring of English football.

## The decline of Italian football

During the twenty-five years since *Football Italia* was first broadcast on British television, globalization processes have profoundly impacted the respective fortunes of Italian and English football. While the English Premier League has developed into the most successful league in the world, Italian football has experienced profound crisis. As Gould and Williams (2011, p. 587) highlight:

> Over the past two decades, it [The Taylor Report] has contributed to making English football something of a model, one that has been widely envied across Europe. Indeed, in terms of its commercial growth, rising crowds, redeveloped stadiums and its global reach – but also in its apparently effective response to a hooliganism problem that seemed endemic and almost beyond resolution in the 1980s – the top levels of English football have been transformed. By contrast, it is football in Italy today that seems plagued by entrenched problems of racism and hooliganism, by financial irregularity and by a relative lack of modernization of the sport's key structures and core facilities.

Even though Serie A was initially successful in adapting to the changing global political economy in the 1990s, it has not been able to capitalize on this early success. The turnover for Serie A in the 1996-7 season was second only to the English Premier League. By 2006–7 it was fourth behind Germany and Spain (Hamil, Morrow et al. 2010). Financially, this has impacted Serie A clubs' ability to compete over wage expenditure on players, and many clubs operated with significant debt. During this period, many of the top leagues in Europe made operating profits, whereas Serie A made an operating loss of €1355 m.[2] The financial crises have been compounded by a number of scandals relating to match-fixing and administration (which are explored in Chapter 4).

For decades, Italian football has also been blighted by fan violence. It reached its nadir in February 2007 when a policeman, Filippo Raciti, was killed during a riot between Catania and Palermo fans. In November of the same year, on his way to the game, a Lazio fan, Gabriele Sandri, was shot by a policeman. Violence has become a major aspect of the matchday experience. Not only do some fans engage in football-related disorder, but the police and politicians also use the symbol of violence to justify ever more draconian measures (which will be explored in Chapters 5 and 6). Alongside this, key fan groups, the *ultras*, have disrupted games, including Genoa fans invading the pitch in 2013 and forcing the players to remove their shirts, and more spectacularly, Napoli fans stalling the kick-off of the *Coppa Italia* final in 2014. With these dramatic incidents, there is a growing realization that such disruption and fan violence cannot continue. Contucci and Francesio (2013, p. 4) have argued that 'after the *annus horribilis* of 2007 … finally it was realised that the situation has become unsustainable'.

Crises in the Italian game have resulted in fan apathy and a decline in attendance at matches. As Merkel (2012, p. 364) argues, 'One of the most convincing indicators of football's popularity is matches' attendance figures. Fans often react promptly and unequivocally to changes.' The beginning of the 2012-13 season was notable for two games that were attended by a sole away fan. In October, Corrado Nastasio, a former Livorno player, was the only fan of his hometown team to travel to Messina, 500 kilometres from the Tuscan city (Barker 2012). A month later, Arrigo Brovedani made more headlines after he became the only Udinese fan to travel to Genoa for his team's Serie A match against Sampdoria (The Daily Telegraph 2012). Although these are extreme examples, they symbolize a wider malaise among football fans in Italy. Chapter 3 highlights how the over-reliance on familial and patrimonial networks has prevented the Italian clubs from understanding and exploiting wider global transformations. As demonstrated in Chapter 5, the infrastructure has not been upgraded to reflect the changes taking place elsewhere. Failure to upgrade stadiums and instigate effective business policies has limited the range of fans that clubs can attract. This has been compounded with continuing problems related to violence at football matches. Attempts to tackle hooliganism have resulted in all fans being treated as potential hooligans and this has, in turn, strengthened the position of the *ultras* and delegitimized the authorities (see Chapter 6). Draconian measures have been imposed, including the introduction of identity cards, which, as Chapter 9 argues, is making it increasingly difficult for fans to attend matches.

Attendances at Italian football matches contrast sharply with average attendances in Germany and England. After comparable average attendances in the 1970s between Italy and England, the two national leagues encountered contrasting fortunes. England faced continuing problems with hooliganism that resulted in English clubs being excluded from European competition after the 1985 Heysel stadium tragedy. Italian football began a similar decline at the end of the 1970s but sustained a rapid growth in attendances after Italy won the 1982 World Cup in Spain. A sharp decline began in the mid-1980s that was again halted by hosting a successful World Cup tournament. The transformation of Italian football, as illustrated in Chapter 3, led to Serie A continuing to have the highest average attendances in Europe at the start of the 1990s. However, this success was not capitalized upon. Elsewhere, in Germany, and particularly in England, stadiums were transformed, leagues were reformatted and wider business models were incorporated. The assimilation of football into the broader global economy facilitated the wider popularity of the sport. As a consequence, Germany and England experienced continued rise in average attendances, while Italy's continued to fall. Indeed, Teotino and Uva (2010) state that Serie A was the only European league to witness a fall in the average number of spectators over the first decade of the twenty-first century. After Udinese's lone fan travelled to Sampdoria, one of Italy's national newspapers, *La Repubblica*, reported that Serie A's average crowd was just 20,732, which represented only 48 per cent of the stadium's capacity. In contrast, Germany's Bundesliga had an average attendance of 42,257, utilizing 86 per cent of capacity, while the Premier League had an average attendance of 35,753, nearly 95 per cent of capacity (Bianchi 2012). Similarly, Contucci and Francesio (2013) have observed that while the average attendance of Germany, England and Spain has increased over the previous twenty years, the average attendance has fallen by 10,000 in Serie A and halved in Serie B. Ultimately, fans are being affected, which, in turn, is impacting Italy's standing in Europe.

The problems in Italian football are affecting not only attendances at stadiums but also its ability to capitalize on the new global market for football. The English Premier League has negotiated a range of contracts with international television companies that helped promote the English Premier League's global brand. Serie A has not been able to do the same as they individually negotiated their television rights (until 2010). As a consequence, they have not been able to turn their matches into global television events. By restricting their focus to the domestic market, the Italian clubs have not maximized their global image and are losing market share to rival leagues. The failure to respond to these transformations has affected the performances of the clubs outside their domestic league. After Italia '90, Italian football was seen as the epitome of European football; now it has joined the second tier of European leagues and its status is continuing to fall. The organizer of the Champions League, UEFA, determines the number of participants from national leagues based on their success in Europe. This is determined on a coefficient system that calculates national leagues results over a five-year period.[3] Higher-ranked national leagues have more representatives in the competition. Since the coefficient system's inception, England, Spain and Italy have been in the first tier, with each tier having four representatives in the Champions League. Italian clubs, however, have not maintained their previous standard. As a consequence, they lost their status in the top tier to the German Bundesliga in 2010. Four years later, Juventus lost to Benfica in the semi-finals of the Europa League. As a result, Serie A dropped in the coefficient table to the fifth, one place below Portugal.

The coefficient reflects the transformation of European football and the relative success and failure of various national leagues. In the last decade of the twentieth century, Serie A was the undisputed leader of the Champions League. It had seven representatives in the semi-finals, six of whom proceeded to the final. Of these, AC Milan and Juventus won the competition in 1994 and 1996, respectively. Of all the national leagues in the Champions League in the 1990s, Italy had more semi-finalists than any other national league. This led to them having more finalists, and consequently more winners. During the same period, the English Premier League managed just two semi-finals, with Manchester United being the only club to achieve that feat in 1997 and 1999. The last year of the decade saw Manchester United progress to the final and win the competition in the last minute of their game against the German side, Bayern Munich. This victory marked a turning point for the English Premier League in the following decade.

The twenty-first century has seen a dramatic reversal of fortunes for the respective leagues. Since 2000, Italy has maintained its standing at the semi-final level, by having six semi-finalists. Of these, four progressed to the final, with AC Milan winning the tournament twice, in 2003 and 2007. The former was an all-Italian final against Juventus. In contrast, the same period has seen a dramatic increase in the number of English clubs at the semi-final stage. In stark contrast to the two semi-final appearances of Manchester United in the previous decade, the English Premier League had seventeen representatives in the decade after Manchester United's 1999 victory. Eight teams had subsequently qualified for the final, which resulted in three clubs winning the competition: Liverpool beat AC

Milan in 2005; Manchester United beat their fellow English club Chelsea in 2008; and Chelsea beat Bayern Munich in 2012. In sharp contrast to the dominance of Italian clubs in the early years of the Champions League, representatives from the English Premier League now demonstrate their European dominance.

Teams from Germany and Spain have also dominated the Champions League. Whereas three clubs (Inter, Milan and Juventus) have dominated Serie A, only two Spanish sides have succeeded in Europe. Real Madrid are the most successful club in European competition, while Barcelona have captured the world's imagination with an aesthetically pleasing and successful style of football that has seen them win the Champions League in 2006, 2009 and 2011. An all-Madrid final in 2014 also highlighted the power of Real compared with the plucky Atlético. Despite a strong showing in the coefficient, teams from the Bundesliga have fared less well. However, Bayern Munich have built on their strong showing in the European Cup in the early 1970s and have won the Champions League in 2001 and 2013 (which followed three runners-up positions in 1999, 2010 and 2013). The losing finalists to Bayern Munich in 2013, Borussia Dortmund, have also won the competition in 1997. What the coefficient shows is that German sides generally are more successful and progress further in the competition than Italian clubs.

Italy's approach to the economic transformation of football represents an apposite case study. Contucci and Francesio (2013) suggest that this indicates 'last days of Italian football'. Meanwhile, Teotino and Uva (2010) say that Italian football needs to 'reboot'. This book will provide an analysis of Italian elite male football in order to contribute to debates in the sociology of sport in Europe and highlight how a once powerful league has lost ground to rival national leagues. The analysis will be grounded in the global political economy; through the complex transformations that have taken place it is possible to see the profound effect that these have had on the nation state. Globalization has seen a shift in power within Italian society and this is reflected in Italian football. The continued practice of patrimonial networks undermine the state and its institutions, which reinforce the hegemonic positions of already powerful groups and individuals.

The following two chapters will focus on the wider Italian political economy. Broadly, the continued fragmentation of the central Italian state has led to the formation of competing power networks. These combined to undermine local communities and fragment political engagement in Italian society. Chapter 2 will illustrate the historical development of Italy's national political economy. In particular, it will focus on the transition from the Keynesian state capitalism of the immediate post-war period to the more deregulated global economy of the 1980s and beyond. These globalized transformations are not uniform; in Italy, they have developed a specific characteristic because of the prior weakness of the state and the power of extensive patrimonial networks. This argument is explored in Chapter 3. The culture of mistrust in the central authorities and patrimonial networks has been replicated within the world of football. The weakness of the deregulated institutions has facilitated the emergence of strategic actors who can manipulate their networks for the benefit of the major clubs.

The subsequent three chapters focus on specific problems in Italian football: match-fixing scandals, stadiums and policing. These demonstrate how the personalized networks have been detrimental to the wider structural aspects of the game in Italy. Chapters 7 and 8 will focus on the role of the fans and how the wider crises impact upon them. Chapter 7 will trace the historical development of the *ultras* and how their social and political affiliations have fragmented and converged in parallel to the deregulation of the national political economy. The fragmentation of the fan groups has substantially weakened the position of the fans and facilitated the emergence of the strategic actors in football. Chapter 8 looks at a different aspect of football fandom in Italy. Although members of official supporters' clubs engage in forms of protest and debate politics, this is not automatically transformed into action. Supporters' trusts are new and heavily influenced by European trends of political activism among fans. These are attempting to engage politically in different ways, but they are in their infancy and have a significant battle to gain access to power. As with the *ultras*, the hegemonic patrimonial networks that operate across Italian football limit political engagement. Finally, the concluding chapter will return to the theme of Italian football in decline. It will assess the various aspects addressed throughout the book and consider whether Italian football stands at 'Year Zero', the starting point at which it can move into the future.

# 2

# Italy in a Globalizing World

Standing in the bedroom of his sumptuous Sicilian villa, Prince Fabrizio was shaving in front of the mirror. In the reflection, he saw his nephew, Prince Tancredi, enter the room. Tancredi has come to tell his uncle that he will be leaving and heading into the mountains to fight for Giuseppe Garibaldi. The 'red shirts' of Garibaldi had landed on the Sicilian coast and were fighting to unite the island with the new Italian nation. Sicilian aristocrats, like Prince Fabrizio, were being confronted with exile or death. Initially, there was familial concern for his nephew's well-being in the campaign. Tancredi allayed these fears and explained that the northern politicians will impose a republic unless the aristocracy takes control of the situation: 'If we want things to stay as they are, things will have to change.' Tomasi di Lampedusa's novel entitled *Il Gattopardo* (The Leopard) illustrated the turmoil of the *Risorgimento* during the mid-nineteenth century. unification required social elites to change their way of life or face extinction. Those that changed were incorporated into the new state, a phenomenon that introduced the term *gattopardismo* into the Italian language to illustrate the way that people and traditions remain continuous despite tumultuous change.

In 2011, Italy celebrated the 150th anniversary to mark its unification. Although it is a relatively young nation, it has encountered several diverse forms of government: from monarchy, through fascist dictatorship, to republic. As social elites remain, despite the apparent changes, the state has been unsuccessful in imposing itself completely. The incomplete nature of the Italian state has created intense cleavages and a profound crisis of legitimacy that undermines central authority. Its status as a young nation and its sustained crisis of legitimacy have permitted several pre-unification traditions and identities to continue, reinforcing the weakness of the state. Central among these is the reliance upon the family. Foucault (1991b) argued that the state imposed itself in the United Kingdom and France through population management, effectively breaking the family as a unit. In Italy, the continuance of traditional practices, and the failure of the state to impose itself upon its citizens, result have resulted in the family becoming the central unit of support. Family connections have superseded those of the state and have permitted the persistence of patrimonial networks of support (Banfield 1958; Ginsborg 1990; Cento Bull and Corner 1993; Sapelli 1995; Ginsborg 2003; Silverman 1975), which have resulted in a vacuum within public politics as family and personal connections provide the focus. This vacuum has facilitated the growth of charismatic leaders who exploit their patrimonial networks to provide a focus for political and national identity.

However, sport does not operate in a social vacuum. It is both a product of and a reflection of its social context. To present a background to *Football Italia*, this chapter will briefly outline the 150 years of Italian history. In doing so, it presents a broader historical and theoretical framework that underpins the remaining chapters. Through this outline on the nation's history, several recurring themes emerge. There is a strong regionalist identity throughout Italian history that contributes to a crisis of legitimacy of the central state. Local familial and patrimonial networks have strengthened as the central state failed to institute a legitimate alternative. In order to overcome the resultant factionalism, charismatic leaders emerged to temporarily unite the disparate groups. These charismatic leaders, however, operated within their own patrimonial networks, which further delegitimized the central state and perpetuated the crisis. The first section of this chapter will address the formation of modern Italy and its difficult transition from traditional communities to modern society. In order to understand Italian football, particular focus will be placed on Italy's post-war development to account for the transition from a protectionist national economy to a deregulated global economy. The collapse of the Fordist mass-manufacturing system facilitated the emergence of a new form of economy that flourished in the central regions of Tuscany and Emilia-Romagna. It also resulted in the continuance of existing patrimonial practices as *gattopardismo* remained. Patrimonial networks and deregulation have permitted the close networks between football, business and politics to be intensified. This has occurred spectacularly with Silvio Berlusconi, who became both the leader of a political party and prime minister, and the owner of a number of businesses, including one of Italy's top football clubs, AC Milan.

## Italian modernity

In order to understand Italian football, we must situate the sport within Italian society. Italy is essentially a modern construct that refers to the geographic peninsular south of the Alps. Until the mid-nineteenth century, the Italian peninsula was a historical oddity; it was still an assortment of regions with disparate forms of government, including the Doges in Venice, the Kings of Naples and Piedmont and the Papacy. The increased influence of the nationalist model spreading across Northern Europe, however, saw nationalistic sentiment grow across the peninsula, particularly in the north. Austrian political influence in this area resulted in strong anti-Austrian sentiments and fuelled the calls for an independent unified nation state. The charismatic leader Giuseppe Garibaldi became a focus for the political project of unification, the *Risorgimento* (Resurgence). Supported by thinkers and politicians such as Count Cavour and Giuseppe Mazzini from the northern region of Piedmont, unification effectively became a 'Piedmontization' of Italy (Arvidsson 2003). Through political machinations and conquest, the peninsula was declared a united kingdom in 1861. Anderson (2006) saw the growth of the nation as a cultural construct where participants with shared rituals and cultural traditions were considered part of an 'imagined community'. With disparate local traditions and identities, the new state has become the apposite example of an 'imagined community' (Dickie 1996). Consequently, successive governments have struggled to impose the unifying 'myths, memories and symbols' (Smith 1987) and the 'invented traditions' (Hobsbawm and Ranger 1983) on the nation state. Traditional practices continued after unification, creating a number of religious, political and geographical cleavages. Traditional identities conflicted with emerging national identities, with neither becoming truly dominant. As a result, the state struggled to impose itself over its subjects and faced a perpetual crisis of legitimacy.

The Catholic Church is central to the conflict between traditional practices and state control; it destabilizes the state from above and below. To unite the peninsula and the nation, the city of Rome had to be incorporated into the new kingdom. As a key symbol to a glorious past, Rome had been declared the capital of the new state even though it had not been physically incorporated into the nation. To unify the peninsula, Garibaldi had to invade Rome, leading Pope Pius IX to declare himself a 'prisoner in his own city'. As a consequence, the Pope refused to acknowledge the new state and forbade all Catholics, both at home and abroad, from participating in Italian politics, thereby effectively destabilizing the state at its inception (Wood and Farrell 2001). Meanwhile, local identity continued to remain strong. Catholic rituals that focused on the town's patron saints helped reinforce individuals' strong attachments to one's hometown or village. Localized festivals that worshipped the town's patron saint combined with annual festivals, such as Easter and Christmas, of the religious calendar. These fuelled local sentiments and contributed to strong feelings of attachment to the local town, or *campanilismo*. Literally, this means the love of one's bell tower. The bell tower, as a dominant urban symbol, could be seen and heard from all areas of the town or locality and came to symbolize the town and one's attachment to it:

> The *campanile* identifies the community of membership, in how its visibility delimits the community territory, that is the space becomes 'ours', of the well known, of the obvious, of the everyday; the *campanile* is a symbol of a '*appaesamento*' [a sense of belonging] that is not only physical, but is principally psychological (Sanga 1996, p. 36).

*Campanilismo* is also fuelled through local historic festivals. Throughout Tuscany, there are many folk games that reaffirm a localized, pre-unification activity, such as the *palio* at Siena, the *palio marinario* in Livorno and the 'game of the bridge' in Pisa. The paradox of conflicting symbols emerges through the folk game of *Calcio Fiorentino* that originated in Florence. Mussolini emphasized the links between the Florentine game and the new game of football. In doing so, he reinforced the Italian origins of the game while simultaneously reaffirming a localized, pre-unification activity (Doidge 2015).

The Church's focus on the role of the family provides an alternative challenge to the state. The Church stresses that the family is the only social unit, creating a strong kinship society. As the family constitutes the first and primary point of reference for individuals, this colours their interactions with others. During his fieldwork in the 1950s, Banfield (1958) highlighted the lack of civic association within a rural community in the south of Italy. He termed such focus on one's own family as 'amoral familism', since individuals would focus on assisting their immediate family rather than aspiring to a higher, civic ideal. Helping others would not only cause the individual a material or temporal loss but also potentially make rivals stronger than the immediate family. Those who were seen as helping others were seen as frauds or hypocrites (such as the Church or Communists) or they were doing so because it is their job (like council officials). These officials were seen as corrupt, whether they were actually corrupt or not. They were assumed to perform to the same cultural 'amoral familism' and favour their own family. With a weak state, without the legitimacy to overcome these challenges, the residue of 'amoral familism' remains within bureaucratic systems and everyday life.

Regional and family identification became a feature of the Italian media. The late political development of Italy prevented the formation of a national print capitalism that could unite the imagined community. Industrialization in Italy took place in the north and around certain ports in the early nineteenth century, that is, before unification. The lack of national industrialization inhibited the formation of a national consumer market. Manufacturers did not seek to expand their market by advertising nationally or provide additional economic stimulus to the newspaper industry (Nowell-Smith 1990). Ultimately there was a lack of independent newspapers that needed to derive their revenue from publishing and advertising. As a consequence, Italian newspapers are:

> owned by companies which exist for, and earn most of their revenue from, other activities, and for whom the newspaper is merely a tool for promoting those activities. (Wagstaff 2001, p. 297)

Although some independent publishers have emerged, such as Rizzoli (who owns the *Corriere della Sera*) and De Benedetti (who owns *La Repubblica*), many Italian newspapers have been incorporated into the wider business conglomerates of leading families.

Political affiliations were formed before unification in the same way as regional and religious identities. The Socialist Party and the trade unions represented workers before universal suffrage was extended to all males after the First World War (Sapelli 1995), highlighting a serious disjuncture between the social citizenship of most Italians and their political relationship. The political membership was further divided by religious membership that precluded political involvement. Political and religious discord divided the urban and rural bourgeoisie and prevented the formation of a middle-class party, such as the British-style Conservatives (Sapelli 1995). Such divisions inhibited the formation of mass political parties and created a fragmented political system. This contributed to a feature of Italian politics after unification, called *trasformismo* (transformism), where politicians would change political allegiances so as not to lose power or influence. Effectively, this created a consistent ruling political elite who exercised power for their own ends. *Trasformismo* continued the practice of *gattopardismo* where elites, despite changes, remained the same.

The prevalence and success of *trasformismo* helped the Marxist theorist Antonio Gramsci develop his theory of hegemony. He observed how the dominant power incorporated opponents into its sphere of influence through a process cooperation and coercion. The practice of negotiation and persuasion ensured that ruling bodies governed with the consent of the public. The result was 'the permeation throughout civil society ...', as Gramsci stated, 'of an entire system of values, beliefs, attitudes and morals that is in one way or another supportive of the established order and the class interests that dominate it' (Gramsci 1971, p. 39). Hegemonic groups have access to the legal system and establish or repeal laws to provide a wider legal–political framework. The police and armed forces are also utilized to uphold these laws and physically quash challenges to the hegemonic order. It is in the cultural sphere that consent is manufactured with allied groups, but it does so with the potential threat of coercion. Consent is, as Gramsci argued, 'protected by the armour of coercion' (Gramsci 2000, p. 235). Hegemony is not the simple act of forcing beliefs onto a group, but a process of persuasion. Access to material resources, whether privately or state-owned, can help with this process of persuasion.

The fragmented political system necessitated a charismatic leader who could use their negotiation skills and extend their patronage to unite the factions. Through patronage and negotiation, successful leaders could utilize *trasformismo* to alienate the extremes of the political spectrum and create a relatively stable centrist government. Giovanni Giolitti utilized this system with some success and acted as Italian prime minister five times between 1903 and 1921. However, the First World War led to the collapse of the liberal post-unification political system. Military failure in the war culminated in the humiliating Battle of Caporetto in 1917. The post-war territorial settlement resulted in Italy losing territory and gaining nothing of Germany's overseas colonies (which were divided between Britain and France). Fascism drew upon the embarrassing military defeat in the First World War in order to justify its nationalist project (Wilcox 2008). The weakness of the coalition government resulted in the emergence of a new charismatic leader to unite the nation. This particular context permitted Benito Mussolini and his Fascist Party to assume control in 1922. Mussolini proceeded to impose a centralized bureaucratic state and reinforced national identity through carefully invented traditions. Mussolini invoked the image of Rome and the Renaissance to reassert Italian national identity. Football subsequently became central in Mussolini's strategy. Italy hosted and won the second World Cup in 1934, before successfully defending their title four years later in France.

## The 'Miracle': Italy's post-war political economic development

The fall of fascism in 1943 and the post-war reconstruction of Italy retained many pre-fascist features. Cooperation between the Catholics and the Communists during the Resistance resulted in an agreement to support parliamentary democracy and the birth of the first Italian republic. Despite this cooperation, the Vatican entered politics and actively supported the *Democrazia Cristiana*, the Christian Democrat Party (DC), to prevent the Communists taking power. To assist, Pope Pius XII excommunicated all members of the *Partito Comunista Italiano*, the Italian Communist Party (PCI). The Church's support for the DC reinforced key aspects of Italian society. The DC fought to have the rights of the family guaranteed in the Constitution. As Bernini states, this resulted

> in the Constitution, the rights of the family as an institution superseded the rights of its individual members, and the protection of the family as a whole took priority over the guarantee of the 'legal and moral equality' of the spouses. (Bernini 2010, pp. 74–5)

Consequently, the DC reaffirmed the role and influence of the Catholic Church in Italian society. It also reinforced the centrality of the Italian family that precluded identification with wider associations or the state. Vatican support also operated to alienate the PCI and maintain a Catholic hegemony.

The emergence of two mass parties did not prevent political fragmentation. Proportional representation permitted many localized, independent parties to emerge, whereas factionalism remained within the DC and PCI. In order to maintain parliamentary democracy and prevent the PCI from obtaining power, the DC utilized its patrimonial influence to maintain its hegemony. The negotiation practised through clientelistic relationships and *trasformismo* continued. In order to control the factions and independent parties, the mass parties retained localized patrimonial networks and used these to distribute resources quickly and readily to supporters. Italy continued, as in other southern European countries, to be 'governed more by the division of the spoils by the parties than by legal and bureaucratic rationality' (Sapelli 1995, p. 115). Through effective control of government and distribution of the resources the DC prevented the Communists from forming a government. As a result, Italy became a one-party state, or *partitocrazia* (partyocracy) (Della Porta 1995; Ginsborg 1996). The *partitocrazia* and factionalism reinforced the need for charismatic leaders to control the patrimony. Alcide De Gasperi was the founder of the DC and led the party since 1945 for eight successive years. De Gasperi was instrumental in negotiating the terms of the Marshall Plan that provided American aid for European reconstruction. American support through the Marshall Plan provided the political capital for De Gasperi to reinforce public opinion against the communists, as the PCI became the largest Communist Party outside Eastern Europe. American aid provided economic capital to lubricate the system of patrimony and financial reward for DC supporters, which further alienated the PCI.

The patrimonial system under the *partitocrazia* was assisted by state control of the economy. As a result, Keynesianism in Italy was distorted to facilitate clientelism (Della Porta 1995; Farrell 1995). Consequentially, Italy has retained a large nationalized industrial sector into the twenty-first century. Mussolini set up the Instituto per la Ricostruzione Industriale (ISI) to retain certain industries under national control. The ISI's involvement in Italian industry was so great that, by 1962, it became the second largest industrial group in Europe – only the Royal Dutch Shell group was larger (Sassoon 1986). ISI was augmented in 1953 with the Ente Nazionale Idrocarburi (ENI), the state oil and gas company, that (literally) provided the energy to support Italy's post-war recovery. Another agency of the state was instigated to overcome the 'southern question'. The Cassa per il Mezzogiorno was set up in 1950 to provide state support for development in the south of Italy. The fragmented political system, and hegemonic power in the north, had contributed to a piecemeal industrialization that had left the south significantly underdeveloped. The Cassa, ISI, ENI and similar government bodies became vehicles for clientelism as public money was used to facilitate existing patrimonial networks. Patronage was embedded in the system to such an extent that a process called the Cencelli Manual was implemented in 1968 to allocate ministerial positions (Foot 2003). Massimiliano Cencelli, a DC undersecretary, devised a mathematic formula to calculate the number of factions and ministers and allocate ministerial positions according to the number of supporters within a faction. A further example of patronage can be demonstrated within the state-controlled television station, RAI. By the 1960s, state control, and therefore control by the DC, was contested by the other political parties. A form of political deregulation occurred with the *lottizzazione* (Ginsborg 1996; Hanretty 2010). The two television stations were divided between the DC and the *Partito Socialista Italiano* (PSI), Italian Socialists. A third channel, *RAI Tre* (RAI Three), was added in 1979 to provide a station for the PCI. Despite putatively relinquishing control, it still reinforced the hegemonic position of political elites.

The dominance of a single political party in the *partitocrazia* politicized much of society. As the DC maintained hegemonic control, public appointments from teachers to council workers became acts of political patronage. This led to the formation of a state bourgeoisie; a compliant network of public officials who relied on the patronage of the DC for their jobs and were incorporated into the hegemonic group. As opposed to the independent, rational and efficient Weberian bureaucracy, the Italian system stagnated; it necessitated the need to utilize personal and family contacts in order to circumvent bureaucratic processes. This was exacerbated by jobs being filled by a system of *raccomandazione* (recommendations) (Zinn 2001). This ensured that the patron could provide favours to their clients by recommending them for a job. Other clients dispensed their obligations by hiring the recommended individual. This became an important aspect of the patron–client relationship network.

The clientelistic relationships in Italian society encouraged 'people to become negotiators. Because everything is fluid, everything may also be considered negotiable' (LaPalombara 1987, p. 59). In American society, Riesman (1961) argued that during the 1950s, individuals started to become 'other-directed' and focused on their interactions with other people. Italy also developed 'other-directed' individuals who utilized their social networks and, through negotiations, developed ways to improve their position. Gundle and Parker (1996, p. 23) argue that 'the speed and efficacy of a bureaucratic act depended to a great extent upon the pressures that a citizen could exert upon the administrator'. Consequently, the personal connections of an individual became a vehicle for patrimony and resulted in a variety of practices being used, ranging from a network of contacts to systemized corruption.

State support and Fordist manufacturing facilitated the 'economic miracle' that originated around Milan and the north. During the 1950s, large-scale mass production provided the catalyst for this 'miracle'. The concentration around Milan and Turin intensified the contrast between north and south. This was exacerbated by extensive internal migration as young workers from the impoverished south migrated to work in the northern factories. Alongside the demographic transformation within Italy, consumption dramatically changed. Increased prosperity led to a growing demand for (Italian made) consumer items such as televisions, white goods, scooters and cars. Large-scale manufacturing was central to this boom in consumption. This was dominated by the car industry and ancillary companies, such as road building, rubber, oil and steel manufacturing. Fiat controlled 90 per cent of the national market and its dominance turned many small and medium-sized enterprises into dependent companies (Sassoon 1986). These industries remained, and remain today, resolutely family owned. Fiat was established by Giovanni Agnelli in 1899, and the Agnelli family have become synonymous with the company ever since. In 2010, Giovanni Agnelli's great-great-grandson, John Elkann, became chair of the company. Similarly, the current president of Pirelli is Marco Tronchetti Provera, who is married to the granddaughter of the founder of the company.

What is significant for a book on Italian football is that family business groups incorporated football clubs into their business empires. The Agnelli family have owned Juventus in Turin since 1923; their current chair is Andrea Agnelli. In Milan, Pirelli and Olivetti were involved with Inter and AC Milan, respectively, in the 1930s. Pirelli continue to be involved with Inter and have sponsored them since 1995. As football became the most popular pastime of the more affluent Italian society, these large companies could improve staff morale by financially supporting successful local teams; industrial patronage became the norm. The Italian economy's reliance on large family businesses afforded their owners political power and saw Italian industry become an extension of the political patrimonial system.

## Economic crisis and deregulation

The industrial success that fuelled the growth in consumption started to collapse in the late 1960s. Economic recession, state inefficiency and dramatic cultural changes caused by the Miracle culminated in the 'hot autumn' of 1969. The increase in trade union power led to widespread strikes across the country. Italy's economic problems were exacerbated during the decade as their inflation and balance of deficits grew. Low wages saw Italy increasingly at the bottom of the division of labour, as high technology remained with the United States, Germany and Japan. Further changes in international trade left Italy open to increased foreign competition, and its low technology base meant that it could not compete. These transformations were heightened with the devaluation of the dollar and the oil crisis in the early 1970s. Large mass-manufacturing companies had to adapt themselves to compete. Fiat, which epitomized the large Fordist mass-manufacturing of the 'Miracle', was forced to restructure with redundancies and outsourcing. Under these economic pressures, Italian society began to politicize around earlier historical traditions.

Political turmoil culminated in terrorism during the 1970s, termed the *anni di piombo* (years of lead) (Wagstaff 2001; Foot 2003; Bartali 2006; Cooke 2006; Ignazi 2006; Ginsborg 1990; Wood and Farrell 2001). The period saw the emergence of a number of invented traditions that harked back to the Resistance. With memories of the war and fascism fading, the 1970s saw the re-emergence of the extreme right in Italy. Groups such as the *'Ordine Nero'* and *'Squadre di Azione Mussolini'* created a historical link back to Mussolini's black-shirted fascist *squadristi*. Bombings at the Piazza Fontana in Milan in 1969 and at the

Bologna Railway Station in 1974, were the neo-fascists' attempts to create a 'strategy of tension'. In the same way that the *squadristi* caused chaos in the 1920s, the neo-fascists hoped that creating disorder in the 1970s would allow a strong, Mussolini-like figure to emerge from the chaos to unite the nation and restore order. More insidious was that this 'strategy of tension' was initially blamed on left-wing anarchists by the government and police. Investigative journalists uncovered details, however, which highlighted that neo-fascists were to blame and that they were in contact with Guido Giannettini, the head of the Italian secret service. Much of this was facilitated through the secretive masonic lodge, P2 (Ginsborg 1990). State complicity in terrorism left a scar in the national memory that has not been successfully reconciled (Cento Bull 2010).

Parallel to the growth of right-wing political movements in Italy was a similar communist identity. The 1970s saw an increase in popularity of partisan songs from the Second World War. Political groups used names that were deliberately evocative of the Resistance movement such as *Stella Rossa* (Red Star), *Volante Rossa* (Flying Star), and most importantly, the *Brigate Rosse* (Red Brigades). In 1978, the *Brigate Rosse* became infamous for their kidnapping and assassination of Aldo Moro, the DC president. Moro was a key proponent of the 'historic compromise' between the DC and PCI that maintained the PCI's commitment to civic participation through parliamentary democracy rather than through revolution. The *Brigate Rosse* felt that revolution was the only way to overthrow the corrupt elites. Moro symbolized the 'historic compromise' and was kidnapped and assassinated. The legacy of the Piazza Fontana bombing, however, ensured that conspiracy remains. Variously, the P2 masonic lodge, the secret services and the Mafia have all been accused of organizing or supporting Moro's assassination.

The intense politicization within Italian daily life impacted football. The politics of the *piazze* were transferred to the stadium. This led to a politicization of fan groups and the emergence of the *ultras*. Although this will be discussed in more detail in Chapter 7, it is important to stress the wider sociopolitical processes influencing football fans. *Ultras* groups took the flags and chants of the protests into the stadium. The names of groups reflected this political influence. One of AC Milan's *ultras* groups called themselves the *Brigate Rossonere* (Red-black Brigades) to reflect the colours of the team and the colour of their politics. In this way they combined local identity with national politics.

Local political agitation resulted in the Italian regions winning significant autonomy in the 1970s. Fifteen regional governments were established to provide increased regional representation. After an intense political struggle, these regions were provided with increased autonomy in 1976. This provided a fine benchmark for Robert Putnam's initial study of political and economic success in Italy. Putnam et al. (1993) argued that regions in Northern and Central Italy had experienced significant economic success after winning more autonomy, while those regions in the south were less successful. Putnam argued that those regions with traditions of civic engagement were more successful, both politically and economically. Participating in civic associations led to greater interaction with a wider network of individuals, what Putnam (1993; 2000) terms 'social capital'. These networks of 'social capital' led to greater involvement in local and national politics, which bred economic success. What Putnam overlooked is that social networks are a significant feature of Italian sociopolitical life anyway. As argued previously, they lubricate the bureaucracy, industry and politics. Rather than 'making democracy work', they feed patrimonialism and corruption. Indeed, two of the biggest corruption scandals in Italy, *tangentopoli* and *calciopoli*, originated in Milan and Turin, which are located in the more 'civic' north. Deregulation removed any pretence at national stability and objectivity. Personal networks of 'social capital' merely facilitated corruption and the fragmentation of the state.

Increased autonomy and politicization resulted in a wave of invented traditions as regions sought to impose their identity. Monuments were built to commemorate local figures and events, while street names were renamed in honour of local luminaries. Many traced a historical lineage back to the Resistance. For example, a monument was erected in Bologna after two demonstrators were killed when a Carabinieri car mounted a pavement. Their epitaph was inscribed as: 'Fallen Partisans of the new Resistance' and 'now and always Resistance' (Cooke 2006, p. 172). The contestation between national and regional identification continued in 2010, with the cities of Florence and Rome contesting for the national ownership of icons such as Michelangelo's statue of David and the Colosseum.

These social and economic problems saw the development of a distinctly Italian brand of post-Fordist manufacturing. Regional autonomy and family businesses combined to create the appropriate environment for successfully adapting to the emerging global marketplace. A new geographical distinction emerged in Italy between the industrial Northern region and the impoverished South. The central regions of Tuscany, Umbria, Emilia-Romagna and Le Marche became known as the 'Third Italy' (Bagnasco 1977). In particular, the Emilia-Romagna region gave its name to a new type of manufacturing system called the 'Emilian Model' (Brusco 1982; Piore and Sabel 1984). Increasingly, flexible consumer markets combined with excessive unionization in larger firms like Fiat saw many of these companies subcontract their production. This necessitated a new form of dynamic small business that could respond quickly. Family orientation also provided the economic capital as support and security during the early years of the company. In addition, tax exemptions for small businesses with fewer than fifteen employees facilitated their survival. The newly autonomous regional authorities assisted with support for new industrial zones that permitted the creation of extensive cooperative networks that reinforced the social capital of the families. More significantly, globalization permitted these organizations to capitalize upon historical trade networks direct to foreign markets. As a consequence, Italian family businesses, such as Benetton, Armani and Gucci, became iconic global names.

Transformations in the global and Italian political economy necessitated a new type of charismatic leader. The economic shift from mass-manufacturing to flexible specialization was not restricted to manufacturing. Post-Fordist services, like advertising and finance, expanded to augment the changing economy. Together, these resulted in Italy overtaking Britain in 1987 to become the fifth largest economy. Increasing affluence introduced a new middle class of consumers. New charismatic leaders directly appealed to this emergent group of consumers. As Sapelli (1995, p. 116) notes:

> The roots of this [new charismatic leader] can be found in the fact that, in the 1980s, the electoral growth of all the parties was due to the leaders' ability to attract the new middle classes, only too happy to receive the resources dispensed by the party system of government that controlled the state.

For the political parties to continue to function as before, they had to extend the patrimonial system to the new middle classes. Post-Fordist consumerism, however, constituted an ideological issue for the mass parties of Catholicism and communism. State control and regulation could uphold traditional virtues without succumbing to the unconstrained vices of consumption. Italy's third party, the PSI, was less ideologically restricted and openly appealed to the emergent middle classes. Bettino Craxi was the leader of the Socialist Party and capitalized on divisions in the DC to negotiate his way to becoming Prime Minster between 1983 and 1987. Although he represented an ideological break from the two mass parties, he still operated within the political patrimonial system. Craxi was a new charismatic leader for the consumer age and attracted new middle-class voters through deregulation. Under Craxi, 'A whole army of careerists, social climbers and yuppies entered the PSI, and used it as an instrument of political and economic promotion' (Padellaro and Tamburrano 1993, p. 35). Unencumbered by ideological issues, as the DC and PCI were,

Craxi simplified politics and made it more media-friendly. He embraced the post-Fordist, deregulated changes taking place in other Western democracies and this facilitated the growth of the 'Third Italy' and the resultant economic boom.

Craxi's reforms were driven by political expediency rather than ideology. A key element of the New Right of Thatcherism in the United Kingdom was the notion of a 'free economy/strong state' (Gamble 1994). The State had to be strong enough to disentangle state involvement in the market, while at the same time retaining legitimacy to police the new economic order through effective regulation and contesting the vested interests of the previous Keynesian regime. In Britain, Thatcher undertook a series of contests with trade unions and other vested interests to end protectionism in the state-controlled market. Rolling back the state in Britain paradoxically re-legitimized the state as it relatively successfully disentangled itself from the economy and reinforced the role of central government. The factional nature of Italian politics meant that government measures always risked defeat in parliament. Consequently, vested interests and state involvement in industry were not disentangled by Craxi. Likewise, the battle with the trade unions was not undertaken in Italy as it was in the United Kingdom. Successful challenges to the unions at Fiat, for example, was undertaken by Gianni Agnelli, rather than the state. In a further distinction from Britain, the key Thatcherite policy of reducing taxes for larger businesses were not replicated by Craxi. When combined with the tax exemptions for smaller companies this facilitated the growth of the smaller business within the Emilian Model. Most significantly, there was no systematic privatization in Italy, as the ISI and ENI retained a number of nationalized industries.

## Berlusconi enters the field: The emergence of the new industrialists

Craxi's significant contribution to deregulation in Italy occurred in the world of television through his friendship with Silvio Berlusconi, a fellow Milanese. Berlusconi symbolized the new affluence in Italy and represented a significant shift from the traditional industrial families like the Agnellis and Pirelli. Furthermore, Berlusconi embodied the notion of the 'other-directed' individual (Riesman 1961). He was acutely aware of his public image and developed extensive social networks (Ginsborg 2004; Andrews 2005; Jones 2007; Foot

2003; Lane 2004). Through his friendship with Craxi, Berlusconi represents a shift towards neo-patrimony – networks based on personal connections (Eisenstadt 1973; Sapelli 1995). Craxi was godfather to Berlusconi's daughter Barbara who was born out of wedlock to his mistress Veronica Lario in 1984. Craxi subsequently acted as Berlusconi's best man at his marriage to Lario six years later. Berlusconi started his career as a singer on a cruise ship before capitalizing on his personal contacts in 1961. He persuaded the manager of the bank where his father worked to loan him the money to build an apartment complex. Showing his entrepreneurial spirit, he sold these apartments through adverts in the local newspaper. Three years later, Berlusconi used a further guarantee from his father's bank, and money from a Swiss bank with unknown proprietors, to build another residential complex (Lane 2004). It was with his third venture, however, that signalled the arrival of Silvio Berlusconi.

Berlusconi's third construction project signalled the emergence of a postmodern, individual consumer-orientated business in Milan. Entitled Milano 2, it was built throughout the 1970s and represented an early Italian example of bounded space, with resident-only access and security guards. Its location in the outskirts of Milan, close to Linate airport, meant that Berlusconi had to sharpen his negotiation skills and persuade various administrative bodies, such as the council, magistrates and unions, to receive the approval for its construction. He also persuaded the airport authorities to change their flight paths so that they would not disturb residents. The complex was marketed to the new affluent, yet individual, middle-class family and had to appeal to every generation of the family. Many green spaces and sports facilities were preserved by underground parking and were combined with schools, a church, shops and bars to provide an environment for the emerging consumer-orientated residents of Milan. Most significant for Berlusconi's future was that each apartment within the Milan 2 complex was provided with pre-installed cable television. One of these channels was supplied by TeleMilano, the cable company set up by Berlusconi in 1974 to provide local news and entertainment for the Milano 2 complex. This independent postmodern approach to residential complexes marked a profound departure from the Fordist residencies of the past. For example, the Mirafiori Sud apartment blocks for workers that were located next to the Fiat plant in Turin had communal heating systems rather than individual control.

Deregulation of the state broadcaster, RAI, by his friend Craxi, presented Berlusconi with an opportunity to expand his media enterprise. In 1975, parallel with the increased autonomy of the Italian regions, attempts were made by a parliamentary commission to make local television and radio more regional in outlook. A year later, the constitutional court decided that the state broadcaster, RAI, should no longer hold a monopoly of radio and television within the regions. This led to the development of a number of local networks and presented Berlusconi with an opportunity to expand TeleMilano. Berlusconi acquired many of these regional stations and changed the name of his media company to Mediaset. Through Mediaset, Berlusconi actively challenged the regulators and RAI, undermining their legitimacy. He circumvented regulations by pre-recording entire schedules and sending them to each regional station for concurrent transmission. This gave, in Berlusconi's own words, 'the illusion of a network' (Schlesinger 1990, p. 273). With these transmissions, he deliberately targeted the weak spots in RAI's scheduling, using American imports such as *Dallas* to increase audience share. *Dallas* was the focus of another battle with the regulators. The regulators wanted to control commercial programmes and banned Berlusconi from showing consecutive episodes of *Dallas and Dynasty*. To circumvent this, he showed them concurrently on different channels. Eventually these clashes culminated in 1984 when three magistrates from Rome, Pescara and Turin decreed that these regional television networks were for regional, not national broadcasting and ordered his channels to be suspended. This coincided with broadcasts of some of Mediaset's most popular programmes, *Dallas, Dynasty, the Smurfs and High Noon*. Unsurprisingly, Berlusconi gained much public sympathy and the matter had to be resolved by a special decree from his friend, Prime Minister Bettino Craxi.

Berlusconi's friendship with Craxi facilitated his contest with the regulators. As prime minister, Craxi could pass an emergency decree to temporarily permit the national broadcasts of Mediaset. However, Craxi's 1984 decree was soon declared unconstitutional. Craxi leveraged all of his political support to pass a new law that effectively deregulated Italian television. The Mammi Law, named after its author Oscar Mammi, was eventually passed through parliament six years later. The Mammi Law ended the unregulated free-for-all that existed since the emergency decree. Yet, rather than create a regulatory framework to ensure pluralism, the law confirmed the duopoly between RAI, the state broadcaster, and Berlusconi's Mediaset. Although the law was drafted to look like Berlusconi had made sacrifices, it still looked tailor-made for the media magnate. It maintained that no one could own more than three stations, yet also stated that the owner of the commercial television stations could not also own stakes in satellite stations or newspapers. Berlusconi sold the daily newspaper *Il Giornale* to his brother, Paolo, and his stake in a pay-TV satellite channel to a group of investors to whom he lent the money. The friendship between Berlusconi and Craxi facilitated new forms of patrimony based on personal contacts.

## Neo-patrimonialism: Development and change of Italy's patrimonial system

This new patrimony of Craxi and Berlusconi operated on a personal quid pro quo basis. These 'neo-patrimonial' networks (Eisenstadt 1973; Sapelli 1995) relied on personal contacts, rather than on a simple distribution of the resources; political support was granted in return for favours. Mauss (1967) has highlighted how gifts build solidarity between recipients. These gifts build reciprocal relationships that establish future obligations; the receiver of the gift is under a duty to return the favour at a later date. After the Mammi Law was passed, allegations surfaced that Fininvest, Berlusconi's umbrella company, paid 'consultative fees' to the government office that drafted the law. This was amplified when Fininvest employed one of the key authors of the Mammi Law shortly after he left the ministry. Similarly, Berlusconi had offered Craxi political support during the politically delicate takeover of the publisher Mondadori. Berlusconi already had a stake in Mondadori and had bought the ailing television station Rete-4 from them in 1984 (the same year as Craxi's emergency decree). In 1989, Mondadori merged with the L'Espresso group, which publishes the left-leaning newspaper, *La Repubblica* and the weekly magazine, *L'Espresso*. The anti-government chairman of Olivetti, Carlo De Benedetti, owned the group. Berlusconi entered the takeover to ensure that he gained control of Mondadori, while De Benedetti was left with the L'Espresso group. Although Berlusconi won access to another media outlet, by taking on the powerful anti-governmental L'Espresso group, he also provided political support to Craxi.

Italy's neo-patrimonial system was spectacularly exposed in the *tangentopoli* scandal of 1992. *Tangentopoli* (Bribesville) originated in Milan, the same city as the 'Economic Miracle' of the 1950s and the fashion and finance boom of the 1980s (Foot 2001; Foot 2003; Ginsborg 2003). Milan is also based in the region of Lombardy, which Putnam (1993) classed as 'civic' and more likely to be economically successful. Its 'civic' nature, however, did not prevent widespread political scandal. The scandal came to light on 17 February 1992 when the PSI politician Mario Chiesa was arrested for accepting a bribe. Chiesa was also the president of an old age home and frequently received *tangente* (bribes) in return for providing cleaning contracts. Chiesa was ostracized as a 'rogue' by

Craxi and the PSI, which led Chiesa to recount the widespread systemized corruption that was taking place in Italy. Pandora's box had been opened and revelations of bribes between businessmen and politicians proliferated. The magistrates intensified investigations and arrests, which magnified media interest. The investigations became known as *mani pulite* (clean hands) and profoundly affected the Italian political system.

Widespread public disenchantment with politics was compounded by the murder of prominent people by the Mafia. The Maxi Trial into various Mafia activities commenced in 1986. Led by Giovanni Falcone, it took nearly two years and led to the indictment of nearly 500 alleged members of *Cosa Nostra*. Despite this, Corrado Carnevale, a judge who was suspected of being paid by the Mafia, overturned many of these convictions (Dickie 2013). Falcone had been promoted to Rome and was able to have Carnevale removed for the final appeals that concluded in January 1992. The convictions against leading *Mafiosi* were upheld and the families took revenge. In March 1992, two months after the conclusion of the Maxi Trial, one month after Mario Chiesa's arrest set forth *tangentopoli*, and one month before the general election, Salvatore Lima was shot by the Mafia. Lima was a prominent Sicilian politician and member of the ruling party, DC, as well as being a friend of the then prime minister, Giuio Andreotti (who was also alleged to have Mafia connections). Lima was alleged to have been a 'man of honour' for one of the leading Mafia families. Following the result of the Maxi Trial, he was deemed to have outlived his usefulness and assassinated. The Mafia's reprisals continued. On 23 May 1992, Giovanni Falcone and his wife were killed, along with three bodyguards, in a bomb blast. The Mafia detonated a bomb that blew up their car as they drove to Palermo airport. Two months later, Falcone's friend and fellow anti-Mafia magistrate, Paolo Borsellino, was killed in another bombing, along with five bodyguards.

The general election in April 1992 marked the beginning of the end of Italy's First Republic. Craxi and the PSI were heavily implicated in the *tangentopoli* scandal. Craxi initially dismissed Chiesa as a 'rogue' before acknowledging that corruption was widespread. He acknowledged that corruption was inherent in the political system, when he stated that: 'We are all guilty. We all knew.' (Gundle 1996, p. 88). Craxi went into exile in Tunisia. The loss of their charismatic leader resulted in the PSI disintegrating. The DC were also heavily implicated in *tangentopoli* and polled their lowest ever share of the vote. Parallel to *mani pulite*, there was the ongoing Mafia trial. After the assassinations of Falcone and Borsellino, Tomasso Buscetta, the most prominent *pentito*, or informant, highlighted the close connections between the Mafia and politics. Giulio Andreotti, the DC leader who had acted as prime minister on three separate occasions, was heavily implicated in his connections to the Mafia, as was the assassinated Salvatore Lima. It was alleged that the DC could garner more votes through the Mafia, which, in turn, helped them maintain the balance of power within parliament. After being tried for collusion with the Mafia, judges declared that 'He [Andreotti] fully understood that his Sicilian associates had amicable relations with Mafia bosses, and he cultivated, therefore, amicable relations with the same bosses ... he asked them favours and he met them.' (Popham 2003). However, no proof of collusion could be proved after 1980 as the law outlawing association with the Mafia only came into force in 1982. The PCI was least tainted by scandal but could not capitalize upon the weakness of the other two parties. The crisis of Eurocommunism and the fall of the Berlin Wall in 1989 had substantially weakened the PCI. The symbolic discrediting of communism led to a period of introspection for the party. By 1991 the party had split into the centre-left *Partito Democratico della Sinistra* (PDS) and the *Rifondazione Comunista*. The weakness of the PCI also substantially weakened the DC who had established themselves as a bulwark against communism. With the continued scandal and the defeat of communism, the DC was further discredited and its factions split into various minor parties.

## The cultural impact of deregulation

Before detailing the outcome of *tangentopoli* and *mani pulite*, it is necessary to make a brief excursus to illustrate the effect deregulation had on Italian society. These changes facilitated the political transformations that took place after 1994 when Silvio Berlusconi dramatically entered politics. Deregulation transformed the structure and focus of the Italian economy; it shifted from production to consumption. This permitted the emergence of a new business elite who operated consumer-orientated businesses. They continued to operate within the patrimonial system, however, as personal relationships blurred the boundaries between politics and business. Football continued to be incorporated within the wider business groups of the new business elite. Silvio Berlusconi, for example, purchased and transformed AC Milan. The impact of deregulation on the development of Italian football will be considered in the following chapter. It is also important, however, to consider football within the wider political economic transformations that took place in Italy during the 1990s. In particular, football facilitated Berlusconi's move into politics. Therefore, aspects of Berlusconi's utilization of football will be covered within this section as it is instrumental in understanding the move. This section will also detail the impact of deregulation on television and consumption before assessing their influence on Berlusconi's dramatic emergence in Italian politics.

A central feature of Italian deregulation under Bettino Craxi was the support provided to Silvio Berlusconi. As the owner of Mediaset, Berlusconi fundamentally changed the role and approach towards television within Italy. Under the state monopoly, RAI was regulated to provide a public service, in the same way that the original BBC mission was 'to inform, educate and entertain'. In contrast, Berlusconi's strategy was simply 'to entertain'. This led to a dramatic shift towards what Eco (1990) calls 'neo-television'. There was no ideology underpinning Berlusconi's neo-television; it simply needed to generate audience figures. Indeed, it was not until 1991 that they complied with the law and broadcast a news programme, and news was only broadcast across all three of Mediaset's channels a year later (Menduni 1996). As mentioned in the previous section, Berlusconi's networks bought cheap American imports, like *Dallas* and a number of Hollywood films. These were supplemented by extravagant variety shows with popular presenters, some of whom were symbolically signed from RAI. Through these variety shows Berlusconi helped to reinforce gender divisions. Female presenters continue to be invariably decorative to the more commanding presence of the central, male presenter. In addition, Canale 5 was constructed as a feminine-friendly station to appeal to the new consumer-orientated housewives. Football also constituted a large aspect of Berlusconi's neo-television and will be covered in the following chapter.

Neo-television provided large audiences with which to advertise new consumer products and identities. In 1979, Berlusconi created an advertising company, Publitalia, in order to exploit the new commercial television that he was introducing. Through control of his television stations and Publitalia, Berlusconi dramatically reduced the costs associated with advertising. In doing so, he opened up many new commercial avenues for consumer-orientated companies. The increased exposure to consumer culture coincided with the post-Fordist changes taking place under Craxi's reforms. Through Publitalia, the Italian population became acculturated into this new post-Fordist consumer culture. Consequently, this new consumption took on a political agenda. As the boom was driven by Craxi and supported by the DC, it was fiercely contested by the PCI who followed the Frankfurt School of Marxism and saw excessive consumption as an erosion of traditional class boundaries. This would inevitably lead to the formation of a 'mass culture'. Despite recognizing this transition, the PCI didn't respond to these changes in their traditional support, and this contributed to their weakness after *tangentopoli*. With the mass political parties highly ideologically committed to either Catholicism or Communism, Fordist consumption could be heavily regulated. With the removal of television and advertising regulations, ideological morality could be eroded and a consumer culture created. In doing so, it opened the wider population to other aspects of Berlusconi's empire and ambitions.

Deregulation of television facilitated the transformation of commercial neo-television and transformed television into a spectacle presented to entertain. The collapse of the political system after *tangentopoli* presented an apposite opportunity of a new form of media spectacle. Berlusconi was central to the polarization of information and entertainment throughout the scandal. As Robinson observed in relation to the Watergate scandal and political news broadcasting in general, network television has the power 'to make the issues of our times those issues which best accommodate the medium' (1976, p. 431). Mediaset began broadcasting the political events as they unfolded and turned the scandal into public information and entertainment. It created a soap opera. The scandal created characters and plots as the drama unfolded. This was in sharp contrast to the state broadcaster, RAI, who presented in a 'dry' informative style. The result was a polarized audience between Mediaset and RAI viewers.

The spectacle of *tangentopoli* also created a strong feeling of 'anti-partyism' (Lipow and Seyd 1996, Axford and Huggins 1998). This feeling among the electorate led to resentment towards the traditional mass parties of the Christian Democrats (DC), the Socialists (PSI) and the Communists (PCI). Anti-partyism also led to a growing antipathy towards political parties more generally. This facilitated an interest in alternative political movements. More importantly, the feeling of 'anti-partyism' was fuelled by Berlusconi's media organization. It was in this political maelstrom, fuelled by his own companies, that he 'entered the field' of politics in 1994.

Berlusconi utilized his full range of business and media operations to assist his political emergence. Berlusconi built a broad business portfolio that was incorporated into an umbrella company called Fininvest. The company included Mediaset and Publitalia, in addition to AC Milan, Mondadori publishing, cinemas, supermarkets and financial services. Fininvest was founded in 1979 and entrusted to Marcello Dell'Ultri, Berlusconi's friend and confidant. Dell'Ultri was subsequently convicted of collusion with the Mafia and imprisoned for six years before having his conviction overturned in 2010 as the judges could find no evidence of collusion after 1992 (Ginsborg 2004; Lane 2004; Hooper 2010; Farrell 1995). A further arrest warrant was granted in April 2014, and Dell'Ultri fled to Lebanon. Despite this, Dell'Ultri was instrumental in planning and packaging Berlusconi's political presentation.

Berlusconi made full use of his Fininvest executives to construct and present a new political party called Forza Italia (FI). Publitalia chose the parliamentary candidates and charged them 500,000 lire (approximately £250) per day for their media training. All policies were market tested on voters by the market researcher Diakron, another Fininvest subsidiary. This market research permitted Berlusconi to communicate directly with the voters without the ideology of the traditional mass parties. As Habermas (1989) argues, as the electorate becomes fragmented and less cohesive as a 'public', the mass media are able to advertise the leader and his or her party to that section of society that is least engaged with the political process. Berlusconi treated the electorate as consumers and successfully utilized his media empire to target these crucial voters.

Berlusconi's media ownership facilitated direct communication. Neo-television had blurred the boundaries between news and entertainment. Berlusconi's political emergence further distorted the boundaries as 'the distinction between TV advertising, party political broadcasts, current affairs programmes and even light entertainment was de facto abolished' (Farrell 1995, p. 47). This was demonstrated when Berlusconi announced he was 'entering the field' through a television address broadcast live across all three of his networks. His direct televisual style utilized simple language and allowed him to develop his populist, anti-party appeal. During the factional days of the *partitocrazia*, political language, dubbed *politichese*, was opaque and cryptic as politicians tried to avoid revealing too much (Croci 2001). With his media and football background, Berlusconi began speaking in a clearer, more open style, *gentese*. This style facilitated the television-orientated approach of Berlusconi and helped present him to Mediaset viewers as a sharp contrast to the traditional parties. For example, housewives, the target market of Canale 5, were more likely to vote for Berlusconi's political party than for the traditional parties (Farrell 1995). They remain the only group that has not deserted Berlusconi after a series of scandals (Anderson 2014).

His media and football image combined to carefully symbolize his populist, man-of-the-people image. His choice of 'entering the field' is a direct reference to footballers running onto the pitch. Yet, despite his anti-partyism, he still created a political party, FI. This was another direct reference to football as it was taken from a chant sung by Italian football fans at international matches. In addition, Berlusconi also referred to his cabinet, as his 'team', and FI's political associations as Azzurri Supporters' Clubs (Porro and Russo 2000). This made another explicit reference to the Italian national team who are nicknamed the *Azzurri* after the colour of their shirts. Fininvest also used the transformation of AC Milan as a paradigm for FI. Following his success with AC Milan supporters' clubs, the Azzurri Supporters' Clubs were constituted in the same way. He used targeted advertising to attract new members and provided incentives and discounts to join. Members were offered vacations, financial services and discount language courses. The correlation between football and politics was complete when he used the Milan supporters' clubs to directly recruit *Forza Italia* members. The two-and-a-half thousand supporters' clubs of AC Milan recruited nearly 200,000 FI members.

Distinctions between politics and football became increasingly blurred through Berlusconi's media engagements. During the 1994 election, Berlusconi was campaigning against the economist Luigi Spaventa and quipped, 'This Spaventa, how many championship cups has he won?' (Porro and Russo 2000, p. 365). Berlusconi himself takes part in chat shows in his guise as an owner of a football club. This allows him to present his populist image and make political points. Much media attention is also created when Berlusconi visits the changing room of AC Milan to chat with the star players, or when visiting other squads. During the 2008 electoral campaign, Berlusconi visited the Juventus squad to encourage them to beat Fiorentina, so that AC Milan could qualify for the Champions League. This trend is not restricted to television, or the media controlled by Berlusconi. The boundaries are also blurred in the print media as the *Corriere dello Sport* ran a headline 'confidence vote while score 2-0' which referred to Berlusconi facing a confidence vote in parliament at the same time as Milan was playing Barcelona in the Champions League final, a match they subsequently won 4-0 (Porro and Russo 2000). Elsewhere, Berlusconi has further blurred the boundaries between football and politics. Despite his position as prime minister and upholder of law and order, Berlusconi frequently attacked magistrates for being communist. In a similar fashion, Berlusconi also criticized a referee after Milan lost to the newly promoted Cesena in September 2010, because 'the problem is that often Milan get left wing referees' (*La Gazzetta dello Sport* 2010a).

The fractious nature of Italian politics means that even Berlusconi cannot win enough votes to maintain power without support. Since the inception of FI,

Berlusconi maintained a delicate balance of power with the two right-wing parties which hold very different ideologies: *Allianza Nazionale* (National Alliance) and *Lega Nord* (The Northern League). Both parties make strange bedfellows, yet they both owe their proximity to power to the profound global transformations which took place at the end of the twentieth century. Both the *Lega Nord* and *Allianza Nazionale* appeal to popular, anti-party concerns and typify the postmodern, anti-party shift from traditional mass parties. They also represent another major paradox of Italian politics. Despite both campaigning for more autonomy and immigration controls, they represent two very different aspects of Italy. The anti-fascist composition of post-war Italy not only created the polarity of the DC and the PCI but also excluded the fascists. Mussolini's heirs continued under the neo-fascist party, the *Movimento Sociale Italiano* (Italian Social Movement). Led by Gianfranco Fini, they took the opportunity that *tangentopoli* presented them to embrace democratic government and reconstituted themselves in 1995 as a centre-right political party, the *Allianza Nazionale*. Following in the Mussolini tradition they remain staunchly in support of a strong centralized state and gain most of their support from the south of Italy. Their move towards the centre was complete when *Allianza Nazionale* merged with FI in March 2009 to form a new centre-right party called *Il Popolo della Libertà* (The People of Freedom). Fini cemented his position at the heart of government by acting as deputy prime minister for five years since 2001 before being elected as president of the Chamber of Deputies (the Speaker) in 2008. After feeling marginalized by his leader, Fini led a breakaway faction from *Il Popolo della Libertà* to form *Futuro e Libertà* (Future and Freedom) in 2010. This ultimately led to the reforming of FI in 2013. Thus, despite the anti-party populism of his rhetoric, Berlusconi continues to utilize the model of the political party. However, in contrast to this southern, centralizing influence, Berlusconi's other coalition member comes from the north and is resolutely secessionist.

*Lega Nord* represents an apposite example of a new social movement that has developed a significant political following. Its populist rhetoric typifies the anti-party, single-issue politics of contemporary Italy. *Lega Nord* grew out of the Lombard League which was started by the charismatic Umberto Bossi in 1984. It developed throughout the 1980s as increased economic success in Milan, combined with increasing regional identities, brought a stronger affiliation for the pre-Italian regions. *Lega Nord* itself represents the imagined nation of Padania in the north of Italy. Despite Putnam's (1993; 2000) assertion that civic associations contribute to national democracy, the

*Lega Nord* has resolutely regionalist outlook. Secessionist policies are fuelled by strong anti-state sentiments, echoed in chants of '*Roma ladrona*' (thieving Rome). These sentiments were confirmed during the *tangentopoli* scandal, even though the scandal originated in Milan itself. This also didn't stop scandal engulfing the party in 2012 when Bossi resigned as leader after allegations he was appropriating party funds for his family (Ferrarella 2012). Despite *Lega Nord*'s strong anti-state and anti-party rhetoric, they became key allies of Berlusconi and FI, although they have remained independent and did not join *Il Popolo della Libertà*. Bossi and *Lega Nord* not only combined anti-centralization and local identity rhetoric but also exhibited strong anti-southern and anti-immigration tendencies. Bossi orchestrated one of the most punitive immigration laws in Europe by effectively criminalizing immigrants, as well as being quoted as saying that officials should open fire on boats of immigrants to prevent them landing, 'I want to hear the roar of the canon. The immigrants must be hunted down, for better or worse ... At the second or third warning – boom! Fire the canons at them! Otherwise this will never stop' (Andrews 2005, p. 56). Fragmentation of the traditional mass parties has provided the right conditions for the emergence of Berlusconi and his allies.

Political support and mediatized populist rhetoric have combined to enable Berlusconi to act as prime minister on three separate occasions. His first coalition after *tangentopoli* lasted a year. However, he was the first prime minister to serve a full five-year term after the 2001 elections and narrowly lost the 2006 elections (by 0.1 per cent). The centre-left union party was unable to maintain control and subsequently called an election in 2008, which Berlusconi won with his new *Il Popolo della Libertà* party (PdL). Berlusconi eventually left office in 2011 when a technocratic government under Mario Monti was installed to deal with the economic crisis affecting Italy. Anderson (2014) suggested that this was not due to the political weakness of Berlusoconi *within* Italy, even though he was having problems with Fini and factionalism. It was his weaknesses in Europe that led to Mario Draghi, the head of the European Bank, and Italy's president, Giorgio Napolitano, effectively ousting Berlusconi and installing a technocratic government. After Monti was unable to hold onto power, another general election was called in 2013. Despite the leader of the PD, Enrico Letta, becoming prime minister, Berlusconi still retained the balance of power as the PD and PdL entered into coalition. In contrast to the *partitocrazia* of the Christian Democrats, the new Italian political settlement rests with charismatic leaders like Silvio Berlusconi. The following section will discuss the reasons and implications for this political transition.

## Postmodern populism: The continuance of Berlusconi

Postmodern politics sees the transition from modern mass-association political parties into a new form of political approach. The crisis in global communism and the *tangentopoli* scandal saw the decline of traditional mass parties within Italy. This has coincided with the rise in anti-partyism where voters withdrew their support to the traditional mass parties and began to focus on single-issue movements of personal identification. Axford and Huggins (1998) define this situation as 'postmodern populism'. Yet it is not just the dissolution of traditional boundaries and frustration with the previous system which accounts for this. Changes in consumption habits have shifted the traditional left-right politics centred on class and moved to politics of identity. In addition, as Castells (1996) suggests, society is increasingly becoming framed by electronic media. As a consequence, politics is becoming increasingly mediatized and being fused with the culture industry. Berlusconi's broadcasting of *tangentopoli* turned the scandal into a soap opera. The time-space compression facilitated by the media has transformed the public sphere into regional and virtual spaces, as well as creating a new 'immediacy' to politics as politicians seek to build their public image quickly.

The new social movements of the 1970s have developed into the 'anti-partyism' of the twenty-first century. These new forms of association are characterized as single-issue movements, with a more inclusive approach (Touraine 1981; Melucci et al. 1989). In Italy there has been an increase in popularity for anti-Mafia movements in the south as local issues become paramount. Other movements are adjusting to global transformations, such as the Slow Food movement, which was born in Italy as a reaction against fast food and McDonalds. It campaigns for locally sourced produce, rather than mass-produced 'fast food'. The *Lega Nord* represents another form of regional new social movement. It campaigns against state interference and immigration for the imagined nation of Padania. Under the leadership of the charismatic Umberto Bossi, it has been transformed into a powerful political party that embodies postmodern populism.

Like Bossi, Berlusconi utilizes the anti-party rhetoric of postmodern populism. He has fused football, politics and media into a populist anti-party movement (Andrews 2005). Through ownership of various media platforms, as his 'entering the field' showed, Berlusconi can operate quickly and efficiently. He can access many television networks to make political addresses use his populist football appeal to participate in many 'non-political' broadcasts. In addition, he draws political candidates from television and football. In 2008, he appointed the former model and winner of Miss Italy, Mara Carfagna, as Equal Opportunities Minister. Likewise, candidates for the 2010 European elections included another Miss Italia contestant, Italia Caruso, a former dancer from Mediaset's variety shows, Nicole Minetti and Giorgio Puricelli, a physiotherapist at AC Milan. Populist candidates are combined with continued anti-party and anti-state rhetoric; for example, Berlusconi continues to decry the influence of the independent magistracy. This has coincided with extensive investigations into the Berlusconi's financial affairs and has resulted in charges (and acquittals) of corruption, fraud, false accounting and bribery. Many cases have expired because of the case running out of time under statute of limitations laws, many of which were shortened by Berlusconi's governments (Ginsborg 2004; Lane 2004). As a consequence of his postmodern populism, Berlusconi continued to undermine the central state even though his role as prime minister symbolized the governance of the state.

Berlusconi has come to embody and symbolize 'postmodern populism'. Postmodern politics is increasingly personalized and constructed around charismatic leaders (Von Beyme 1996). Berlusconi mobilized a part of the population as a client in opposition to the state and political opponents. *Forza Italia* and Berlusconi were indivisible as there was no process within the party's constitution that allowed members to remove him. Berlusconi carefully crafted his public image to distance himself from the corruption of *tangentopoli* even though he was a good friend of Craxi and personally profited from this relationship. His party represented the neo-patrimonial nature of Italian politics. The corrupt links between political parties and industry were replaced with personal ties. As Farrell (1995, p. 41) states:

> Berlusconi talks of creating a new democratic order, but his own approach is czarist. His movement is a personal clique rather than an orthodox party – it is composed of followers and dependents rather than members or equals and has more in common with a court than with a democratic functioning organisation.

Under the statute of *Il Popolo della Libertà*, the president of the party became an elected post. In spite of this democratic shift, the postmodern populism of Berlusconi was still based on the cult of personality of its leader. In the summer of 2010, Berlusconi's key ally in the PdL, and speaker of the lower house of the

Italian parliament, Gianfranco Fini, led a faction away from the party. Fini wanted more internal democracy within the party and greater sanctions over those found guilty of corruption. It is illustrative that Berlusconi demanded that Fini step down as leader of the lower house, despite it not being within the purview of the prime minister.

Despite various personal and political issues, Berlusconi remained publicly popular. Even scandals in his personal life did not impact his popularity significantly. In 2009, Berlusconi became embroiled in a series of sex scandals. In May, Berlusconi attended the eighteenth birthday party of an aspiring model, Noemi Letizia, who he claimed was the daughter of a family friend and he presented her with an expensive necklace. However, his wife, Veronica Lario, stated that he did not attend his own children's eighteenth birthday parties and filed for divorce stating that he 'spends too much time with minors' (Kington 2009). The following month, photographs were published in Spain of semi-naked guests, including the former Czech Prime Minister Mirek Topolánek, attending a party at Berlusconi's Sicilian villa (Sarzanini 2009). In July, it emerged that a businessman from Bari had paid for female escorts to attend parties with Berlusconi in order to receive favourable business decisions. One escort, Patrizia D'Addario, released tapes intimating that she had spent the night with the prime minister (Tonelli 2009). She decided to release the details after she claimed that Berlusconi's promise of support for a hotel planning application was not fulfilled.

Berlusconi was embroiled in another sex scandal the following year. In May 2010, a seventeen-year-old Moroccan nightclub dancer called Ruby Rubacuori (Ruby the heartstealer) was arrested for theft. Berlusconi called the Milan police to pressure them to release her by saying that she was the niece of the then Egyptian president, Hosni Mubarak (Guastella 2011). Berlusconi asked for Ruby to be taken to Nicole Minetti, a former dancer on Mediaset. Minetti subsequently became a dental nurse, which brought her back into contact with the prime minister in December 2009. At a political rally that Berlusconi held in the square alongside Milan cathedral, Massimo Tartaglia, an engineer with a history of mental health issues, threw a marble replica of the cathedral at Berlusconi which broke his nose and two teeth. During this reunion with Minetti he proposed that she stand as a parliamentary candidate for the PdL. Berlusconi was prosecuted and found guilty of paying for sex with Ruby, a minor, pending appeal. Despite these allegations, Berlusconi remained a powerful symbol for his supporters. In a political rally in September 2010, Berlusconi joked of his sexual prowess as he suggested that a way for young people to escape the recession was to marry into money. His man-of-the-people charisma appeals to that section of society that is incorporated into his patrimonial network, and isolates his political opponents.

Political debate has been reduced to opposition of Berlusconi. Despite Berlusconi's power, he has become a potent symbol for opponents. For example, Antonio Di Pietro was a leading prosecutor in the *mani pulite* corruption trial into *tangentopoli*. During Berlusconi's first tenure in 1994 a number of counter-investigations were started against Di Pietro and were deemed to be politically motivated. Subsequently, he founded the anti-corruption party called Italia dei Valori (Italy of Values). This party demonstrates the personalized and mediatized nature of new political movements. Di Pietro has made extensive use of information technology to highlight corruption and continues to publish a blog and weekly vidcasts to communicate directly with his supporters. Even though Di Pietro has a broad political remit, the personalized nature of Italian politics has resulted in many attacks on Berlusconi.

Potentially the most dramatic political movement to have emerged in recent years is led by the comedian Beppe Grillo. Cutting his teeth on satirical shows in the 1980s, he was banned from television after making a joke about the Prime Minister Craxi and the PSI stealing (long before *tangentopoli*). Instead he turned his comedic and political skills to touring theatres and piazzas across the peninsula. Like Di Pietro, Grillo makes extensive use of new forms of media to reach a different demographic from Berlusconi. Echoing the new social movements of Touraine (1981) and Melucci (1989), Grillo campaigns against corruption and for environmental issues, rather than traditional left-right political ideologies. In 2007, he initiated a V-Day (Vaffanculo or 'Fuck Off' Day) to persuade people to sign a petition to prevent people with criminal convictions from standing for parliament. Grillo is also part of a collective of bloggers, citizens and celebrities who call themselves *Il Popolo Viola* (The Purple People). They have designated 5 December as 'No Berlusconi Day' after Berlusconi tried to pass an immunity from prosecution for the heads of government, which would effectively make him immune from prosecution. *Il Popolo Viola* have organized several more anti-Berlusconi rallies where participants all wear a purple item of clothing to symbolize their participation.

More significantly for the future of Italian politics, Grillo also started a political movement called the *Movimento 5 Stelle* (Five Star Movement or M5S). It was initially formed to fight the 2010 regional elections on a range of issues:

> The stars stood for the key issues they intended to raise: water (under threat of privatisation), environment, transport, connectivity and development.

> Candidates of the M5S who ran for election had to pledge themselves – uniquely anywhere in the world – not to appear on television, and if they were elected, to reduce their parliamentary salaries to the median wage, assigning the rest to public purposes. (Anderson 2014)

*Movimento 5 Stelle* dramatically increased its popularity among the electorate. In 2012, M5S won its first municipal government in Parma. A year later, they won 25 per cent of the vote in the general election and held the balance of power in the initial discussions to form a government. But, Grillo's unwillingness to enter the government effectively opened the door to Berlusconi and the PdL to go into coalition with the PD. Despite this, M5S still represents a dramatic new force in Italian politics and has become the largest party in less than three years. In 2014, it won the mayoral elections in Livorno, the spiritual home of the PCI. Simultaneously, 'Grillo's three-step motto for raising a popular revolt – laughter, information, political action – had proved stunningly effective' (Anderson 2014). The M5S represents a significant force in Italian politics, and potentially across Europe. While the populist right has grown in popularity across Europe (Wodak et al. 2013), environmental and solidarity movements have not. Grillo's M5S can be seen as a break from the old dynamics of the past – a lesson that Italian football fans can learn from.

When Berlusconi finally left office in 2011, it was not via an election. Despite the organization of anti-Berlusconi movements, and the large crowds in Rome celebrating his exit, the electorate had not voted him out of office. The growing global financial crisis was adversely affecting the Italian economy. The international markets were growing concerned at Italy's ability to cover its debts, which exceeded the national GDP. Despite electoral success, Berlusconi had not been able to achieve economic success. The upkeep of the neo-patrimonial network necessitated significant economic resources, which were shrinking in the global recession. Like Craxi before him, Berlusconi admired Margaret Thatcher in Britain, but did not engage in systematic privatization. The Eurozone's desire to impose austerity on Italy meant that Berlusconi's lack of commitment to neo-liberalism was an obstacle (Anderson 2014). For this reason, Napolitano and Draghi conspired to remove him and impose a technocratic government, led by Mario Monti, in order to appease the markets. A series of austerity measures were subsequently passed through parliament. After this Berlusconi resigned from office vowing to return and reiterating the fact that the Italian people had not removed him. Ultimately, global factors outside of Berlusconi's control proved to be his undoing. Yet despite further criminal convictions pending and additional sexual allegations, Berlusconi's party won 20 per cent of the vote in 2013 and held the balance of power behind the scenes.

## Summary

The unification of the Italian state has created an 'Italian solution' to the nation state. The lack of legitimacy derived from its political construction, led to the state evolving in a clientelistic way as individuals sought to maintain power through a patrimonial system of patronage and corruption. As a consequence, Keynesian economics became distorted and developed into systemized corruption that eventually brought down the First Republic. In order to navigate around the corrupt and inefficient bureaucracy, Italian firms developed small and flexible post-Fordist enterprises that remained under family control. These businesses were well placed to respond to global deregulation in trade and its subsequent consumer-driven economy. However, their rapid development and restrictive family control minimized the development of a separate business class. This was also constrained by the political and bureaucratic system that permitted the business families to operate within the political realm. Berlusconi represented the neo-patrimonial shift which took place in Italy after the 1970s. He fought the existing state regulation and capitalized on complete deregulation to build a personal empire in the new post-Fordist services. Yet this deregulation was done on a personal level, influenced by global processes, but only implemented through neo-patrimonial networks. Through media and football, Berlusconi embodied the shift from state control to power divested to individuals. However, he also exemplified a continuance with past practices as he utilized personal contacts to win governmental concessions, and has retained extensive personal and family control of his business empire. The family became the perfect image for Berlusconi, as Bernini (2010, p. 77) states:

> The family was used by Berlusconi as a useful metaphor to describe his own political and personal trajectory, as he presented himself alternatively as a father engaged in the rescue of his country, the offspring of a hard-working family, the devout son, and the patriarch at the head of a large family.

Berlusconi's transition into politics represents the fusion of these various postmodern aspects, but with the retention of individual and family control.

The new social movements of the 1970s have developed into the 'anti-partyism' of the twenty-first century. These new forms of association are characterized as single-issue politics with a more inclusive approach (including more female involvement). They encompass a wider range of issues, such as anti-Mafia, anti-globalization, slow food and anti-war. Despite the social capital accumulated with these movements, they are not contributing to national democracy. *Lega Nord* in particular actively undermines the state. Elsewhere, the M5S led by Beppe Grillo, campaign on an anti-party agenda. Potentially M5S could act as a reforming movement in Italian politics but will have to face the continued hegemonic power of the status quo. Parallelly, the fragmentation of politics has encouraged the emergence of the charismatic leader of Berlusconi who can utilize his control of the media, football and the political system to appeal to the widest audience and neutralize dissidence. The following chapter will show how these developments are reflected within Italian football, and more significantly, how Silvio Berlusconi contributed to the transformation of Italian football.

# 3

# The Political Economy of Italian Football

As Europe sat on the eve of a world war, *Il Duce* was being photographed in the ornate rooms of the Palazzo Venezia with the Italian World Cup-winning team. Around him were the stars of the tournament who had successfully become the first team to retain the trophy after their 4-2 victory over Czechoslovakia in the 1938 final in Paris. The distinctive bald head and square jaw of Mussolini are unmistakable. Standing at the centre of the photo, the stocky build of the dictator draws the attention of the viewer. In the photo, he is dressed in a distinctive white suit, where the only adornment is a dark pocket square. All of the players flanking the dictator, and those crouching down in front, are sporting the military uniform of the nation. Their dress is distinctive from that of the Italian leader. Reiterating the militaristic connections between sport and war in fascist Italy, Mussolini was highlighting how these successful players were both warriors and model Italian citizens. The photo was to be used as propaganda to celebrate the Italian victory, and for the dictator to be seen basking in their reflected glory. It also highlighted how he was central to their success. He had imposed an Italian identity onto Italian football and mixed this with fascist symbolism, even to the point that in the match against France in the 1938 tournament, the team wore black shirts and performed fascist salutes. *Il Duce* had managed to impose a sense of order and success onto Italian football.

Triumph and crisis have been regular partners in Italian football. Italy's short but colourful history has left an indelible mark on its football. Many of the social elites operate across the fields of politics, business and football. The over-reliance on familial and patrimonial networks can provide rapid outcomes, but can quickly collapse. Globalization, however, has seen other nations surpass Italy's industrial success. Global patterns of deregulation were initially successful within Italy as these networks quickly adapted to the new order. This pattern was replicated in football where the initial success of Italy has been surpassed by the English, German and Spanish. It is compounded by the central authority's failure to adequately impose the necessary requirements on the federations and clubs to rectify the issue. The vacuum in national politics is replicated even within the club structure as fans continue to remain outside the organizational hierarchy, yet still operate within the patrimonial system.

To enable the reader to witness these transformations within the Italian game, this chapter will present a history of Italian football to introduce the organizational structure of the Italian game. Several recurring themes lie within the context of football. In particular, there is a profound crisis of legitimacy of the central authorities that is undermined by widespread familial and patrimonial networks. These dense networks manifest in strategic cities, intensifying regional differences. Building on the theoretical frameworks illustrated in the previous chapters, this chapter will chart the development of football since its inception, from fascism to the Miracle, and into the 1970s. It will then chart the fragmentation that occurred after the 1970s and illustrate the transformations that occurred in the subsequent decades, the era of globalization. Italy's development and approach to these transformations helps explain the subsequent crises, which will be detailed in the following chapter.

## The development of Italian football

Football in Italy is entwined with the formation of the nation state and the global diffusion of the codified sport. During the nineteenth century, the modern nation state began to crystallize and the newly codified sports provided an apposite opportunity for identification for nations and citizens. As occurred elsewhere in the world, playing organized games of football dispersed from the ports. British sailors landing on the docks of Livorno, Genoa and Naples stimulated an interest in these cities at the same time they were undergoing extensive urbanization and industrialization. In keeping with the origins of the organized game, the English word *football* entered the Italian lexicon. As a result, the original governing body that was set up in 1898 adopted the name Federazione Italiana Football (FIF). The nascent governing body subsequently set up a national championship, which was won by Genoa Cricket and Football Club. Increasing internationalization of the sport led to the development of FIFA and UEFA, which Italy joined as a founding member.

The governing body in Italy has faced a crisis of legitimacy ever since its inception and struggled to impose national regulation. Conflict occurred over the foreign influence on the sport, establishing a love-hate relationship with its English roots. Early teams were established and populated by foreign players. The football section of Genoa Cricket and Football Club was founded by James Richardson Spensley in 1897. AC Milan was founded in 1899 by another Englishman called Herbert Kilpin. Elsewhere, Torino was formed by a collection of English and Swiss businessmen, whereas Internazionale was set up by Swiss and Italians. Meanwhile, in 1905 the first club formed in Livorno, Virtus Juventusque, was founded by Carmichael Montgomery, the son of the British vice consul in Livorno. Similarly, the English origins of Florence Football Club and Naples Football and Cricket Club can be traced in their names. The English influence of the game in Italy has resulted in the coining of the Italian colloquial term *Il Mister* (named after the first organized manager William Garbutt) for a 'manager'. Yet, this extensive foreign influence in the Italian game led to the first site of conflict as the FIF banned foreign players in 1908. This also provides the first significant challenge to the federation's legitimacy. Milan, in particular, felt that this ban prevented them from winning their third championship in a row. This success would have conferred the Spensley Cup upon them for winning three championships in a row. As a consequence, Milan, Torino and Genoa boycotted the tournament. With three of the larger clubs absent, the federation backed down and readmitted foreign players for the following season.

Conflict between burgeoning Italian nationalism and the sport's historical English roots re-emerged in the following season. Football in Italy provided an early opportunity for nationalist symbols to be constructed. In 1909, the governing body, FIF, changed its name to Federazione Italiana Giuoco Calcio (FIGC) to reflect the adoption of the Italian word *calcio*, rather than the English word 'football'. This made an explicit reference to the historic game of *Calcio Fiorentino* which had been played in Florence during the Renaissance. The historic version of the sport, what Hobsbawm (1983) terms an 'invented tradition', bore little resemblance to the organized game introduced by the English; *Calcio Fiorentino* was more akin to modern rugby and the hurling games of Britain. Mussolini continued this desire to Italianize the game. *Calcio Fiorentino* was reintroduced to Florence in 1930 to construct a clear link between the Medieval and modern games. Indeed, Foot suggests that the historic Florentine game 'has been adapted to *appear more like football* [original italics]' (Foot 2006, p. 3). In emphasizing this reinvented tradition, we see historical symbols of football being incorporated into the nationalizing tendencies of modern Italy.

Football in Italy quickly became incorporated into the industrial urban fabric. Industrialization and urbanization ensured a rapid participation rate in the new sport as the new urban working classes sought new pastimes. This is reflected in the clubs that found early success; the teams came from the port of Genoa and the industrial cities of Milan and Turin. Industrialists quickly adopted the game's popularity and incorporated football into their industrial network. The owner and founder of Pirelli was an early member of AC Milan and he was the president of the club from 1908 to 1929. Edoardo Agnelli, the son of Fiat's founder, became president of Juventus in 1923 and initiated the long and successful association between the club and the company that has continued into the twenty-first century with the club's current chair, Andrea Agnelli. Back in Milan, Inter's president from 1923 was Enrico Olivetti, from the typewriter manufacturers of the same name, before he sold it to Senatore Borletti from another leading industrial family.

The industrial growth of Turin and Milan led to political and economic conflict between the two cities. It was also reflected in the football clubs of these cities. Power struggles between the clubs took place within the corridors of the federation. The internal power struggle also undermined the legitimacy of the federation as it sought to appease Torino and Juventus on one side, and AC Milan and Inter on the other. The headquarters of the federation were transferred several times between the two cities as a strategy for appeasement. Yet, ultimately, it only weakened the federation's legitimacy and its ability to impose its authority.

The amateur ethos that was introduced by the English provided another site of conflict. The early game in Italy replicated its English forebears through the pursuit of amateurism. The kudos of victory and the reflected glory onto industrial patrons challenged this ethos. A sham amateurism emerged as patrons made clandestine payments to star players. For example, in 1913 Genoa's star play, Renzo De Vecchi was provided with employment as a bank clerk and also was reimbursed with 'travel expenses' (Foot 2006). The clandestine system was exposed in the 'Rosetta Case', which resulted in Juventus paying 50,000 lire for the Pro Vercelli player Virginio Rosetta in 1923. The president of Pro Vercelli, a lawyer called Luigi Bozino, was also the president of the FIGC and authorized the sale of Rosetta. The player meanwhile was an accountant and was set up with a new accountancy post in Turin, underwritten by Juventus (and by extension, Fiat, the owners of Juventus). The amount of money involved ignited the scandal and challenged the morality of the time. It also led to a number of resignations from the federation. Ultimately, the FIGC docked Juventus points that prevented them from winning the title and barred Rosetta from playing. The following season, however, he was allowed to rejoin Juventus and went on to win six championships with the club, as well as winning a bronze medal in the 1928 Olympics and the World Cup in 1934. Despite the dramatic showdown from with the federation, Juventus and Rosetta effectively carried on as before.

The federation's legitimacy has also been challenged in relation to match-fixing. The Allemandi scandal emerged in 1927 after Torino had just won their first *scudetto* (Foot 2006). A newspaper revealed that Torino had paid Juventus defender Luigi Allemandi 50,000 lire to underperform in the derby. The FIGC rescinded Torino's title and banned Allemandi for life. Yet the conflicted approach of the federation reaffirmed its crisis of legitimacy. The 1926–7 *scudetto* remained vacant, but Allemandi's ban was granted a pardon a year later after Italy won the bronze medal at the Olympics. Allemandi subsequently captained Italy and won the 1934 World Cup. Just as the Rossetta case showed, the initial show of strength from the federation was subsequently undermined.

Fascism attempted to assert a nationalist and centralized control over the national game. Mussolini saw football as the perfect way to create the necessary national symbols to unite the young nation. The last vestiges of English were removed from the sport. Foreign names of football teams were changed. Genoa Cricket and Football Club was renamed Genova 1893, while AC Milan was renamed Milano. Meanwhile, Internazionale changed its name to a more Italian-sounding Ambrosiana, after the patron saint of Milan. Alongside the reinvented tradition of *Calcio Fiorentino*, Mussolini also incorporated the powerful symbols of Ancient Rome, which included the notion of *mens sana in corpore sano* (a healthy mind in a healthy body) (Martin 2004). Mussolini supported the building of a number of municipal stadiums that would house the various sports clubs he initiated. This permitted Italy to host the second World Cup in 1934. Not only did they act as powerful symbols to the power of fascism but they also simultaneously harked back to Ancient Rome and looked forward to a Modernist future; the image of the Colosseum was incorporated into the smooth lines of Modernist architecture. As a consequence, many stadiums in Italy date from this period, in particular, the Stadio Olimpico in Rome, the Stadio Artemi Franchi in Florence and Stadio Armando Picchi in Livorno.

Fascist centralization and nationalism led to a major restructuring of football in Italy in 1926. The Viareggio Charter revolutionized football within Italy and instituted many of the features that exist today. The charter introduced a professional national league and set up Serie A and Serie B. This abolished the previous provincial leagues and likewise illustrated the boundaries of the Italian nation. The city of Trieste, acquired in the settlement of the First World War, could now be affirmed as Italian as it would play in the Italian national league (Foot 2006). Furthermore, the charter permitted professionalism that allowed for the best players to participate in these national leagues. Finally, echoing previous attempts to ban foreigners, the charter instituted a ban on non-Italians playing in the national leagues. Even under fascism, the illusion continued. Hungarians or Austrians were obviously barred from playing; however, players of Italian extraction (an *oriundo*) were permitted. Owing to large numbers of Italians immigrating to South America in the previous century, a number of *oriundi* transferred from South America to play in the new professional Italian leagues. Ultimately, some of these *oriundi* represented Italy in the national team and consequently won an Olympic gold medal in 1932 and the World Cups in 1934 and 1938.

Direct central fascist control did not minimize scandal within Italian football. Also, Fascism influenced the patrimonial structure of Italian football. For example, the leader of the Bologna Fascists (and future mayor of Bologna), Leandro Arpinati, took an active interest in the championship play-off between Bologna and Genoa in 1925 (Foot 2006). The federation's rules declared that when teams finished level at the end of the season, they should take part in a play-off. This was to be replayed in the event of a draw. In the 1925 play-off final, the two teams had already played two games and had them both end in draw. The third match was played in Milan, watched by 20,000 fans. Genoa proceeded to take a 2-0 lead before Bologna went on the offensive in the second half – the shot was made, the keeper dived and the referee indicated a corner. This resulted in a pitch invasion led by a group of 'black-shirts', delaying the game for fifteen minutes. The referee changed his mind and gave a goal – a 'goal' that Bologna subsequently doubled to force another draw. Under federation rules, the pitch invasion should have Genoa being awarded the championship. Arpinati, however, pressured the referee to attribute no blame for the pitch invasion. This permitted the federation to call for another play-off. The subsequent play-off, in Turin, was marred by gunshots being fired among fans at the train station after the match ended in yet another draw. Turin refused to allow another game to be held in the city, on the grounds of public order, so the following match was held in Milan two months later, a match Bologna duly won. Arpinati went on to become president of the FIGC and his tenure witnessed unprecedented success for the Italian national team and the Bologna football club. The control and influence exercised over football by Arpinati and Mussolini also led to a number of accusations being made regarding the 1934 World Cup final, hosted by Italy. Despite this, Italy successfully defended their title four years later in France after Mussolini sent the team a telegram saying 'win or die!'.

The FIGC has faced a long-standing suspicion of its central authority. The referees have come to symbolize this crisis of legitimacy. They became victims of abuse, violence and suspicion (Foot 2006). Through the 'deep play' of football, historian Paul Ginsborg (2003, p. 113) makes a clear comparison with wider society:

> Reactions to the game's rules and refereeing can be seen as a mirror of wider reactions to authority in contemporary Italian society. It is not difficult to discern ... a series of emotions – suspicion, contempt, cynicism, even hatred – that characterise the relationship between Italians and the state.

The pressure that Arpinati exerted on the referee in the Genoa–Bologna game in 1925 is merely an extension of this struggle for authority. The 1926 Viareggio Charter attempted to limit the opportunity for corruption by establishing a committee to select referees who were announced only on matchday. However, by the 1950s, this confidential information had become valuable to third parties who sought to gain an advantage. One such scandal involved the Catania football club. A local reporter claimed that while working for Catania, he bribed a referee and his cousin in order to gain access to the information (Foot 2006). In the following decade, the big clubs also tried to exert pressure on the selection of certain referees. In one case, Juventus threatened to go to court to bar a referee from officiating their matches and reinforced the lack of legitimacy of the central federation. This has continued into the twenty-first century as Silvio Berlusconi has frequently used the media to accuse referees of being left wing and biased against Milan.

## Italian football during the 'Miracle'

The economic 'Miracle' of the 1950s reaffirmed the hegemony of Turin and Milan. At the end of the Second World War, Torino emerged as the major force in Italian football. After winning the 1943 *scudetto* by one point over Livorno, the team won five consecutive titles and became known as the Grande Torino (Great Torino). The team created a number of records in Italian football and a majority of players represented the Italian national team. Tragedy struck on 4 May 1949 when a plane transporting the players encountered difficulty in fog around Turin and crashed into Mount Superga. All thirty-one passengers were killed. The catastrophe marked the decline of Torino (despite a brief resurgence in the 1970s) and permitted the consolidation of the three major clubs of Juventus,

Milan and Inter. The economic support provided by the industrial patronage of leading families ensured that these Italian clubs could afford to pay the highest transfer fees for players. Since 1952, the world-record for transfer fee was held by Italian clubs, and by Milan, Inter and Juventus in particular, for nearly fifty years. But the transfers of Johan Cruyff and Diego Maradona to Barcelona, Alan Shearer to Newcastle and Denilson to Real Betis dented the Italian monopoly. It's only in the present century that this domination was eclipsed by one club, Real Madrid.

The 'Miracle' allowed the three elite clubs to dominate financially. The rise of mass-manufacturing based on Fordist principles necessitated large numbers of industrial workers. The 'Miracle' also provided increased economic rewards with which the owners could reinvest in their team. Juventus, in particular, benefitted from the success of Fiat. The car giant contributed over 4 per cent to the Italian GDP and was the biggest employer in Italy; its staff canteen could host 10,000 employees. Consequently, Umberto Agnelli, the club's president during the 1950s and 1960s, has stated that 'The team has followed the evolution of the nation' (Alegi 2007, p. 79). Not only could the Agnelli family provide industrial patronage to finance the club's success but also the extensive internal migration caused by the Miracle could transform the supporter base of the club. Millions of workers left their hometowns, particularly in the south, and moved to Turin to work in the Fiat factories. The subsequent return of these workers to their hometowns has resulted in Juventus being the most widely supported football club in Italy, with every town and village having a Juventus supporters' club.

Financial support and industrial patronage also promoted the growth of the Grande Inter side of the 1960s. The oil magnate Angelo Moratti purchased Inter in 1955 and provided the financial support for the club to win three *scudetti* in 1963, 1965 and 1966, as well as to win consecutive European Cups in 1964 and 1965. Moratti's financial support was augmented by the club's Argentine manager, Helenio Herrera, who implemented a highly professional training regime to drill the players in a quasi-militaristic style. Herrera also bequeathed a lasting legacy on Italian football through his adoption and success of the *catenaccio* style of defence. Named 'door-bolt' in Italian, *catenaccio* was a highly defensive tactic that sought to nullify the opposition in attack and quickly counter-attack. The rigidity and discipline required to execute *catenaccio* emulated the Fordist principles operating within the factories of Milan and Turin.

Increased professionalism within football brought greater incentives to win. A number of teams became involved in doping scandals during the 1960s, which led FIGC to impose order through regular drug testing. In 1962, some minor members of the Grande Inter side were found guilty of doping (Foot 2006). The following year, five Genoa players were banned and the authorities decided to instigate a rule that any player who tested positive would see their team forfeit the match. Ultimately, this led to recriminations and a further demonstration of the crisis of legitimacy facing the FIGC. During the 1963-4 season, five Bologna players were tested positive for drugs following a game with Torino. Under the rules, the team from Emilia-Romagna should have forfeited the game and would have been three points behind Inter at the top of the league. Riots erupted in the streets of Bologna and the club's lawyers disputed the validity of the testing process. With Bologna and Inter tied on points at the end of the season, the authorities cleared Bologna amid stories of the possible switching of samples. As a consequence, the league declared that the title should be decided by a play-off – the only time such thing has ever occurred.

## The crisis of the 1970s

The global financial crisis of the 1970s directly impacted football. King (2003) has identified that European football went through a period of 'Eurosclerosis' during the decade as clubs faced a reduced economic viability that resulted in hooliganism, decline in playing standards and increase in incidents of match-fixing (King 2003). The period marked an end to the dominance of the top clubs. Both Milanese clubs failed to win a *scudetto* during the decade. Although Juventus remained dominant, provincial clubs won a number of championships. After the 'hot autumn' of 1968, Fiorentina won their second *scudetto* in 1969; Cagliari in 1970, followed by Lazio in 1973. Meanwhile, the year 1975 saw the brief re-emergence of Torino after the Superga tragedy. A similar pattern emerged in the early 1980s when Roma and Verona won titles in 1982 and 1984, respectively.

Footballers replicated the political militancy that transpired in the piazzas and the factories. The players became more political and demanded increased legal rights. In 1968, the Italian Footballers Association, the *Associazione Italiana Calciatori*, was created.[1] It called for greater freedom for players and instituted the Italian Footballer of the Year award to recognize outstanding players. In 1974, footballers protested by arriving ten minutes late for kick-off. The protest was to highlight the restriction of movement on players as they were forced to move to whichever team their club decided to sell them to. Players also reflected the extreme politics of the piazzas. For example, Paolo Sollier of Perugia was a visible supporter of far-left organizations (Foot 2006). Elsewhere, and the Lazio team of the 1970s exhibited fascist sympathies. Many of the *biancoceleste* players carried guns, which they took to training and away games. Their frivolous approach to their weapons resulted in the death of their midfielder, Luciano Re Cecconi, in 1977. As a practical joke, he pretended to rob a jewellery store and was shot by the owner.

The failure of the central authorities to effectively regulate the sport saw allegations of match-fixing re-emerge during the same period. In addition to the allegations of drug abuse detailed previously, the *Sunday Times* journalist, Brian Glanville, exposed, in 1974, a wide-ranging account of match-fixing of European Cup games by Italian clubs, called the 'Golden Fix' (Glanville 1999a; Glanville 1999b; Foot 2006; King 2003). The allegations centred on Italo Allodi, who was the sporting director at Inter in the 1960s before moving to Juventus in the 1970s. In the 1980s, he became the national team manager before moving to Napoli – the Napoli that contained Maradona and that finally wrested the title away from the powers in the north. Glanville suggested that Allodi used an intermediary to attempt to bribe referees. The intermediary worked for Allodi at both Inter in the 1960s and Juventus in the 1970s. In some cases, the bribe was deemed to have worked, such as with Inter in the 1960s, and allegedly with Juventus against Derby County in 1973. However, the allegations only came to light after a Portuguese referee, Francesco Marques Lobo, refused to be bribed the following year.

Another match-fixing scandal erupted in 1980 based on the Italian version of the Football Pools called Totocalcio. Two Roman shopkeepers attempted, unsuccessfully, to fix a number of games in a scandal that came to be known as *Totonero* (Foot 2006). The scandal included a number of players and coaches and led to seven clubs having points deducted while Milan and Lazio were relegated. The scandal also led to the suspension of several players, including the superstar of Italian football, Paolo Rossi. Rossi was suspended for three years, but in an act reminiscent of the Rosetta and Allemandi cases in the 1920s, the suspension was subsequently reduced to two years. This allowed him to take part in the 1982 World Cup final where he went on to become the leading scorer in the tournament as Italy won the cup for the third time. The inability of the Italian authorities to deal with the causes of corruption was highlighted six years later. *Totonero* was replicated on a wider scale in 1986. This time nine teams were relegated or deducted points and as many as seventeen coaches and thirty-four players were suspended.

## Deregulation in the Craxi years: The emergence of neo-television

The 1980s represented a significant shift in Italian football. Deregulation and changes to the Italian political economy facilitated a major transformation of Italian football. Significantly, deregulation of television directly impacted the presentation of football. This led to an increased popularity of the sport. The following section will illustrate the importance of television in the world of football. Significant focus will be placed on Silvio Berlusconi's contribution in transforming Italian television and football. Mirroring the continued challenge to the legitimacy of the FIGC, this section will show how Berlusconi continually challenged the legitimacy of the state, and the state broadcaster RAI. It will also demonstrate how connections between businesses and football intensified as leading organizations incorporated football clubs into their family of businesses. Despite the initial success, however, the system collapsed at the end of the twentieth century.

Global deregulation has re-articulated the interrelations between sport and industry. In contrast to earlier forms of industrial patronage, post-industrial patronage centres on services and information, particularly television. The resulting 'sport-media complex' (Maguire 1999), or *'media-calcio'* (Porro 2008), provides a mutually beneficial relationship. Football was the primary component of Berlusconi's programming despite regulations preventing the broadcast of live footage. Italy's victory in the 1982 World Cup led to an upsurge of interest in football. This coincided with the newly emerging commercial networks that were seeking to increase viewership and advertising revenue. Berlusconi announced his entry into football broadcasting in 1980 by purchasing the rights for £1 million to an international event called the Mundialito. This mini tournament brought together all winners of previous World Cups in Uruguay. Berlusconi's television networks would also broadcast friendly football tournaments so as not to conflict with RAI's monopoly of official tournaments.

Mediaset's style contrasted with the state-controlled and heavily regulated RAI channels. This fuelled consumer demand for televised matches and the shows focused on football. Owing to regulations preventing the broadcast of live images, neo-television led football debate shows to proliferate. The principal purpose of these programmes was to talk about football and the live matches became superfluous to the debate that was taking place in the studio. Outside broadcasts provided accounts of live matches, while back in the studio, the important features of the matches were simulated in various ways. Often, chalkboards were used to illustrate the players' position as the action unfolded. Telelombardia, for example, used ex-footballers to re-create the goals, often with more spectacular effects (Foot 2006). Computer-generated players have also been used to re-create the goals and have removed the human element altogether. When debating games, the *moviola* (slow motion replay) was extensively implemented to decide if a player was offside, if contact was made with a player in the penalty area or if a goal was actually handball. The *moviola* was also used to display other controversial events. For example, in September 2008, when the Milan and Italy midfielder Gennaro Gattuso was injured after falling backwards into the tunnel leading out from the changing rooms, the event was replayed and debated for several minutes, and the *moviola* was used more than twenty times to show how Gattuso fell into the tunnel.

Without any live footage of football, the debate becomes a fragmented collection of spectacles. Reflecting similar transformations in politics, a charismatic host helps to appeal to a wide audience and provide cohesion. Like the neo-television variety shows, football shows create hosts who are personalities. Foot (2006) dubs this phenomenon 'Biscardism' after Aldo Biscardi, the host of the longest-running football show *Il Processo* (The Trial). Personality hosts, like Biscardi, facilitate the emotion and spectacle of the debate. They are supported by partisan pundits who do not hide the fact that they are fans and show the excitement of the game taking place. They discuss the team, manager and performance and reflect the passion of the fans at home. The fan-pundits, such as AC Milan fan and pundit Tiziano Crudelli, have become celebrities in their own right. Crudelli has capitalized on this persona by making a series of adverts for the British betting firm Ladbrokes.

The debate in the studio is fuelled by audience participation. Many shows will have a studio audience who contribute opinions. Media technology also extends this debate into the homes of the viewers. Fans at home send emails, tweets and text messages, and these are read out by another (usually female) host. These actions stimulate a dialogue and emotional interaction that maintains interest in the sport. Football not just is played during the ninety minutes on a Saturday or Sunday but is replayed throughout the week in the conversations of fans (Nowell-Smith 1979). Television shows like *Il Processo* create and re-create the events throughout the week. They provide a space for debate to maintain the emotional involvement of fans. These shows are so popular that they account for the top twenty-five most-watched shows in Italy (Baroncelli and Lago 2006).

## Berlusconi enters the football field: AC Milan and the transformation of football

Alongside transforming the media presentation and popularity of football, Berlusconi transformed the operation of football. He introduced a 'business'-orientated, media-friendly approach to football that Liguori (2003) has called *neo-calcio* (neo-football) and Russo (2005) dubbed *ultracalcio*. AC Milan was one of the most successful clubs in Italy but had endured a difficult start in the 1980s. It was relegated for its role in the Totocalcio betting scandal of 1980, and despite winning Serie B the following year, it was relegated again in 1982. A second promotion saw them become a mid-table Serie A side and in serious financial turmoil. In March 1986, Berlusconi purchased the club he supported as a child, and commenced a major restructuring. Berlusconi signalled his intentions as he unveiled the team in July 1986. They arrived by helicopter to the stadium, to the tune of 'The Ride of the Valkyries' in front of 10,000 fans. Berlusconi then utilized his television channels to broadcast the event. Berlusconi was signalling a new approach to football. In his own words, he stated that 'I knew very well that people would laugh at me, even treat me with irony. But we needed to show that the whole way of thinking at Milan had changed' (Ginsborg 2004, p. 53). By turning it into a media-orientated spectacle, he was transforming the way the game was organized, not just at Milan but across Italy and Europe.

Berlusconi was initially successful at Milan as he combined his media panache and business acumen. He viewed the club as a business organization and placed the club under the management of some of his senior managers of his umbrella company, Fininvest (Poli 2001; Porro and Russo 2000). The role and importance of the Milan press office was transformed as Berlusconi carefully cultivated the image of the football club. To increase customers, Berlusconi targeted season ticket sales using television commercials created by his advertising company, Publitalia. He then broadcast these on his television channels. Automatic booking systems for the season tickets were introduced as well as designated seating. The popularity of football after the 1982 World Cup win saw Italy successfully bid for the 1990 World Cup. This led to a major state-funded renovation project of Italian stadiums. This saw Milan's San Siro stadium transformed into a world-class, all-seater stadium. The combination of a comfortable stadium, improved ticketing and extensive marketing saw Milan sell over 65,000 season tickets for the 1986-7 season (Ginsborg 2004).

Berlusconi also sought to increase revenue through merchandising. The range of the club's playing kits and other official merchandise were increased to provide more marketing possibilities. As a consequence, fans could use post-Fordist consumption to display their football identity. These identities were strengthened through the promotion of official supporters' clubs. Supporters' clubs were affiliated to the football club and provided additional benefits to club members. Official merchandising became available to club members, as well as to a new official Milan magazine, *Forza Milan*. This gave Berlusconi another platform to promote his personal and business interests. The covers of the magazine would depict the president in a variety of poses and refer to his channels when highlighting information regarding AC Milan. In addition, Berlusconi introduced other commercial initiatives, such as discounts on merchandise and events, that were advertised through his various media outlets. Brand loyalty was also fostered through events that players would attend, thus giving fans proximity to the stars of the club. As a result of these transformations, by the early 1990s, there were over 350,000 members in the AC Milan official supporters' clubs.

Television was central to Berlusconi's strategy. He took every opportunity to promote AC Milan on his channels by broadcasting a range of 'pseudo-events'. Team unveilings, such as his the team's helicopter entrance in 1986, were televised. Training sessions were broadcast, as well as the events where fans and players met. The club's annual budget was even televised on one occasion. He was careful, however, not to over-saturate the coverage of actual matches so that he could maintain a future market for pay-per-view. Friendly matches and international tournaments were transmitted, but Serie A matches were carefully controlled. With this coordinated use of television, commercial television rights became a central element of the club's income. In 1982, television rights provided $2 million to the clubs. This rose to $510 million by 1998 as pay-per-view and commercial television responded to the larger audience for football.

Deregulation of television broadcasting has directly impacted European and national leagues and has had a significant effect in Italy. As a consequence of complete deregulation of television and the weakness of the FIGC and *Lega Calcio*, the elite clubs successfully lobbied to negotiate individual television rights. This has permitted *all* matches in the top two divisions to be broadcast live on pay-per-view subscription channels. Unlike the more regulated English Premier League, which restricts the broadcasting of live football to three o'clock on a Saturday to encourage stadium attendance, any fan of Serie A and Serie B can watch their club every week without leaving their home. Combined with the problems affecting football in Italy, television deregulation is contributing to the decline in attendance in Italian football. This is impacting the club's ability to generate revenue from fans at the stadium.

Television has also impacted the revenue of Italian football clubs by strengthening the elite clubs. The English Premier League and German Bundesliga operate with collective television contracts. This ensures greater parity of income among clubs and provides for a more competitive league (Morrow 1999; Hamil et al. 2010). However, until 2010, Italian football clubs negotiated television deals independently. This gave more power and money to the elite clubs who could guarantee a larger television audience and helped reinforce their hegemony. These renegotiations contributed to the profound restructuring of the finances of Italian football clubs throughout the 1990s. For example, Juventus was the most successful and best-supported club in Italy, and in 2010, they derived 65 per cent of their revenue from television deals. The Italian giants could generate only 8 per cent from ticket sales on matchdays (Deloite and Touche 2010). Elsewhere, television revenue accounted for nearly 60 per cent of both Inter and Roma's income. Even with the more commercial approach of AC Milan, television revenue provided half of the club's income. In contrast, when Berlusconi purchased AC Milan in 1986, 92 per cent of its revenue came from ticket sales. With the full range of matches being broadcast live every weekend, as well as the over-reliance on television income, clubs were losing fans at the stadium, contributing to the decline in attendance.

The boundaries of spectacle and regulation in football were pushed by Berlusconi as he had previously done with television. In 1987, he deployed Arrigo Sacchi as coach, a man who had never played the game professionally but knew how to organize a team. Sacchi abandoned man-marking and introduced zonal defending, which allowed the team to play a high-tempo pressing game. This style of play was in stark contrast to the staid, *catenaccio* defensive style that typified many Italian sides in the post-war period. This style of play was well complemented by the signing of three of the best players in the world – the Dutch trio of Ruud Gullit, Frank Rijkaard and Marco van Basten. In keeping with many European nations, Italy placed restrictions on the number of foreign players who could play in each match. Throughout the 1980s the number of foreigners permitted in a team fluctuated between zero and three, before the Bosman rule in 1995 led to the suspension of quota for European players. In 1992, Jean-Pierre Papin was signed from Marseilles for a world-record fee of £10 million. This introduced the squad system to European football as Milan already had the full quota of foreign players. It prevented their rivals from having one of the best players in Europe and also provided a squad strong enough to compete on all fronts. It is also alleged that patrimonial practices were utilized at Milan in order to maintain a financial advantage. After the signing of Jean-Pierre Papin, Milan paid another world-record fee of £13 million for Gianluigi Lentini. Milan was accused of paying the Torino chairman £5 million outside of the accounts to obtain Lentini's approval (Lane 2004). As has occurred frequently in Berlusconi's legal career, the club was eventually acquitted in 2002 due to statute of limitations as the trial ran out of time.

Milan also implemented a professional training and recruitment programme to ensure that best players were signed. As Hoberman (1992) has argued, professional sport has become more influenced by sport science, which has turned athletes into 'mortal engines'. The MilanLab is based at the Milanello training facility of the club.[2] It utilizes extensive research to forecast physical and psychological aptitude. Through the PAS (Predictive Analysis Server) technology they predict the possible risks to the players. This allows the club to support their current players and predict which possible new players will be able to fulfil their role at the club. As the originator and head of MilanLab, Jean Pierre Meersseman states: 'If you can predict the possibility of injuries, you stop the player before it happens' (Wilson 2009). An apposite example occurred in 2009 when Milan wanted to sign Aly Cissokho from Porto. Milan's president, Adriano Galliani said, 'Our doctors found some problems with his teeth which cause muscular trouble, which he has and which could deteriorate' (Carminati 2009). Cissokho's dental problem indicated a potential spinal problem. The deal was subsequently rescinded.

Many other clubs have initiated medical support for footballers. In many cases support came from pharmaceutical products that were outside regulations. Star players of Napoli's *scudetto* winning team were found guilty of drug abuse. Notably, this included their talismanic captain and star, Maradona, who was addicted to cocaine and was banned for the use of ephedrine in 1991. Napoli later admitted that it circumvented the dope tests through the switching of samples (Foot 2006). In 1998 the Roma manager, Zdenk Zemen, suggested that 'Football must get out of the pharmacy' (Eve and Goodbody 2004; Alegi 2007; Goldblatt 2007; Malcolm and Waddington 2008). These allegations led to an investigation that found that Juventus had 281 different pharmaceutical products, although most of these were permitted prescription substances. Many players demonstrated evidence of increased red-blood-cell levels, suggesting the possible use of EPO (and at levels that would lead to bans in cycling). In a classic 'Italian solution', Juventus was found not guilty as it could not be proved that they had ordered the administration of drugs. However, the doctor, Riccardo

Agricola, was sentenced twenty-two months but was subsequently cleared on appeal. A further doping scandal emerged in 2001 when Dutch stars Jaap Stam and Edgar Davids and Fernando Couto of Portugal were found guilty of using nandrolone. Four years later, a startling footage emerged of the Parma player Fabio Cannavaro (and future World Cup-winning captain) injecting himself with a substance he later claimed as 'vitamins'. Despite increased testing from the authorities, the clubs were continuing to circumvent the regulations in order to achieve success.

The success of Milan's strategies was realized both on and off the pitch. Within two years of Berlusconi's purchases, Milan had won the *scudetto*, and the success was repeated the following year with the European Cup. In the six years between 1988 and 1994, AC Milan won four *scudetti*, three European Championships, two Intercontinental Cups, and three Supercups. They had been transformed into a financial and football global super club. The success of Berlusconi's model relied on continual on-field success and maximized television income. This meant that for sustained success in European competition, maximum revenue was required. The knockout structure of the European Cup meant that there was always a danger of large clubs, such as AC Milan, being knocked out by smaller clubs. In Berlusconi's own words, 'The European Cup has become a historical anachronism. It is economic nonsense that a club such as Milan might be eliminated in the first round. It is not modern thinking' (King 2003, p. 140). In addition to the clubs, the national broadcasters and UEFA would lose revenue through the early elimination of larger clubs. This was observed in 1986 when both Juventus and Real Madrid were eliminated before the quarter finals of the competition. As a consequence, UEFA introduced seeding to the competition, before introducing a coefficient system designed to calculate the success of individual clubs and individual leagues. As King (2003, p. 139) highlights, 'The seeding system was a conscious concession to the big clubs in the biggest markets.' By weighting the competition in favour of the larger clubs from the larger leagues, UEFA could ensure that they could participate longer in the competition. This in turn provided additional television revenue and greater exposure and revenue for the clubs, and which in turn helped maintain their hegemonic position.

Television revenue and market exposure was crucial for the transformation of the European Cup in 1992. Significantly, Silvio Berlusconi was a key driver of this transformation. In 1988, Berlusconi and the president of Real Madrid, Ramon Mendoza, proposed a new European competition based on the World Cup format of mini-leagues, with the winner of each group progressing to a knockout quarter-final. When UEFA rejected this idea, Berlusconi commissioned

Alex Fynn of Saatchi and Saatchi to propose a blueprint for the reform of European football. Although Fynn's proposal of a regional Super League was not implemented, it created the right environment for further debate. Two years later, Ramon Mendoza and the chairman of Rangers, David Murray, submitted another proposal for a mini-league that was adopted by UEFA for the 1991-2 season. The following year, UEFA rebranded the competition as the Champions League. The formation of the Champions League created a new brand that was used to market the competition to investors. Replicating similar commercial practices at the Olympics and the FIFA World Cup, UEFA created a 'family' of corporate sponsors who had exclusive rights to the Champions League. Meanwhile, television packages were sold to the highest bidder based on market share. Therefore, those nations with the largest television market, such as England, Italy, Spain, Germany and France, paid more for the exclusive rights to broadcast the competition. It also provided increased revenue to UEFA and the participating football clubs, instigating a transformation of Italian football.

## Italian football in the global market

Although Italian football club owners have been reluctant to integrate foreign capital into their clubs for fear of losing control, there are indications that this approach may be softening. After the death of her father, Rosella Sensi sold a majority of her shares in Roma to Thomas DiBenedetto in 2011. As an Italian-American, DiBenedetto is not only indicative of the 'transnational capitalist class' (Sklair 2001) of football club owners, but also reinforces Castells' (1996) and Millward's (2011) notion of international collaborative networks operating globally. DiBenedetto is also a partner in Fenway Sports Ltd, which is the parent company of the Boston Red Sox baseball team and the Liverpool football team, and he also owns shares in a Nascar racing team. Fenway Sports Ltd not only reinforces Castells' (and Millward's) observations of transnational global networks but also adheres to Maguire's (1999) concept of the 'sport-media complex'. Fenway own two high-profile sports teams in separate continents; they also own an 80 per cent share of a regional television network dedicated to sport, NESN. In addition, the company is also part-owned by The New York Times media company. Significantly, Roma has also signed an agreement with Disney that sees Roma visit Florida to take part in a tournament. Roma's CEO, Italo Zanzi, stated that 'Our partnership with Disney is an important part of our efforts to connect with young fans worldwide' (Corriere della Sera 2014). Once again global sport and global media are horizontally and vertically integrated.

Inter has also been subject to foreign investment. In October 2012, an Indonesian businessman, Erick Thohir, bought a 70 per cent share of Inter. Massimo Moratti remained at the club as honorary chairman. Thohir's business activities include print and television media. Significantly, he also owns DC United in the North American Major League Soccer as well as a football club in Indonesia called Persib Bandung. Like DiBenedetto at Roma, collaborative networks are expanding globally, and into Italy. Millward (2011) has highlighted how the profitability and potential scope for global expansion of the English Premier League attracted investment from global entrepreneurs. Although this chapter has highlighted how some 'new directors' began to purchase Italian football clubs in the 1980s, this has not automatically been driven by the profit motive and consequently this has not attracted investment from outside of Italy. DiBenedetto's and Thohir's purchase of Roma and Inter are potentially significant for the future of Italian football.

It should be noted, however, that foreign investment is not necessarily new in Italy. As elsewhere in Italian football, foreign investment has helped strengthen political and business networks outside of the sport. A politically significant connection was between the regime of Colonel Gaddafi in Libya and Italian football (Foot 2006). There are long-standing ties between Libya and Italy as the former was an Italian colony. This gave Italian companies a historical advantage when accessing Libya's oil reserves. As the driver of the Italian post-war 'Miracle', Fiat was indebted to Libyan oil and the company forged strong links with Gaddafi's regime. Football became a space where these links could be reinforced. Gaddafi purchased shares in Juventus, who were owned by the Agnelli family that owned Fiat. Furthermore, the state-owned oil company, Tamoil, was an official sponsor of Juventus from 2002 to 2007. Foreign investment can come in various guises. Global geopolitics also entered the Italian football field when Saad-Ali Gaddafi, Colonel Gaddafi's son, signed for Luciano Gaucci's Perugia. Although Gaddafi did not play many minutes of football in the Italian league, his appearances were politically significant, when Gaucci stated that 'Berlusconi called me up and encouraged me. He told me that having Qaddafi in the team is helping us build a relationship with Libya. If he plays badly, he plays badly. So be it.' (Foot 2011). The *quid pro quo* of Italian politics influenced Italian football once more. Another politically significant investment took place in October 2012 when the Al Thani family began negotiations with Silvio Berlusconi about the future of AC Milan. The Al Thani family from Qatar also owns the controlling interest in Paris Saint-Germain, to whom AC Milan sold Ibrahimovic and Thiago Motta for €80 million in the summer of 2012. The sale of these players, and no subsequent investment in new players by Berlusconi, prompted many to question Berlusconi's desire to maintain AC Milan. The crisis was exemplified when the club offered to refund the season tickets of angry fans who felt that the club had lost ambition after the sale of their two star players. This continued after the club's relatively poor start to the 2012-13 season and the club took the unprecedented step of pleading with fans to attend the Derby della Madonnina with Inter, one of Europe's biggest fixtures. The well-publicized financial problems of Finninvest, resulting from fines levied as a result of corruption, led many to speculate that Berlusconi did not have the resources to invest in Milan. The announcement of the discussion with the investors from Qatar at least highlighted the desire to bring in new investment.

Significantly, part of the proposed investment was to improve the stadium facilities of the club. Part of the debate of Milan's poor start to the 2012-13 season was due to the state of the pitch at the San Siro. Since the stadium was renovated for the Italia '90 World Cup and had a roof installed, the shadow from the new structure inhibited grass growth. Inter and Milan had to resurface the pitch up to five times a year at a cost of €200,000. In the summer of 2012 they installed a semi-artificial pitch to rectify this problem, but with the added result of impacting Inter and Milan's performances. By investing in a new stadium, or giving the San Siro a complete refurbishment, the club could address the problems of the pitch, as well as introduce a better matchday experience for fans. In contrast to the worst sales of season tickets since Berlusconi took over, Juventus had record season ticket sales. The Turin club had traditionally found it difficult to attract many fans as they come from across the peninsula. With the construction of their new stadium in 2011, however, they began to transform the matchday experience and attract more fans, which would bolster the matchday revenues for the club.

The Qatar deal reinforces Castells' and Millwards's notion of collaborative global networks. Much of Berlusconi's financial success has been derived from his establishment and ownership of the television organization Mediaset. Collaboration between Mediaset and Al Jazeera had been part of the negotiations with the Al Thani family. Al Jazeera is an apposite example of a global media organization that utilizes internet and satellite technology to access and broadcast its content. It also operates outside the Western hegemony and draws its influence from across the Middle East, Asia and Africa. Al Jazeera is also owned by members of the Al Thani family, who are also exhibiting the tendencies of the 'sport-media complex'. Not only do they own a global media company, but also they own the controlling interest in Paris Saint-Germain, and potentially own a stake in AC Milan. With family groups controlling significant interests in sport and media, they are able to draw on a variety of patrimonial networks to collaborate and exert influence. With Berlusconi and the Al Thanis, this collaboration will operate across football *and* media. Significantly for both parties, the personalized networks that operate also extend into politics. As a royal family in the Middle East, the Al Thanis are connected to governments across the geopolitically significant Middle East region, especially as a member of OPEC. Furthermore, Berlusconi is personally connected to other leading political figures across Europe, including Vladimir Putin in Russia. Business and football creates a space where these networks can be reinforced.

## Summary

Italian football has undergone a series of transformations throughout the twentieth century. From its English roots, various authorities, from the federation and fascist government tried to 'Italianize' the sport. English words were removed and Italian traditions implemented. Industrial leaders began investing in football clubs and the teams from the industrial heartlands of Turin and Milan started to dominate. This continued after the Second World War and the economic Miracle. Although Torino went into decline after Superga, the clubs from these cities established a hegemonic position that lasted until the 1970s and the social and economic problems of the time. The processes of globalization that had transformed sport elsewhere was starting to demonstrate their effect in Italy. Silvio Berlusconi introduced the media spectacle to football and a commercial approach to the sport. The forming of the Champions League helped establish a European group of elite clubs, and this contributed to the success and revenues of Juventus, Milan and Inter. With the complete deregulation of television contracts, the hegemonic position of the three elite clubs had been re-established by the 1990s.

Despite Italy broadly following wider global processes throughout the history of the game, certain specific features pervade. Replicating the wider crisis of legitimacy of the state, the Federation also struggled to impose itself upon the football clubs. The elite clubs have consistently challenged the authority of the FIGC. From Milan, Genoa and Torino boycotting the 1908 championship in retaliation to the ban on foreign players to the pushing the boundaries of acceptable doping, the Federation has consistently failed to establish its legitimacy. This has been undermined by its own actions. Revoking bans on players shows the Federation as toothless, especially in the case of Paolo Rossi, who was permitted to rejoin the Italian national team for the World Cup after *Totonero*. The dense power networks that exist across business, politics and the Federation help maintain the hegemonic position of the elite clubs. The initial success of the globalized commercial media practices briefly permitted Fiorentina, Roma, Parma and Lazio to join the elite group. Yet their success was built on unstable foundations. The following chapter illustrates how the Italian game went bankrupt at the beginning of the twenty-first century. Financial irregularities and match-fixing scandals blighted the Italian game and demonstrated the bankruptcy of the patrimonial system. The following chapter builds on this historical analysis to highlight how financial problems and scandal have intensified since the 1990s as power has concentrated around a few specific personalized networks.

# 4

# Scandal

Fabio Cannavaro, the handsome and tattooed captain of the Italian national football team, stood upon the podium and raised himself above his *azzurri* teammates. The captain, wearing the world-famous azure blue kit of Italy, received the World Cup and held it triumphantly above his head. Fireworks and confetti erupted from the back of the podium as Cannavaro and his Italian teammates celebrated their 2006 World Cup win, the fourth time the nation had won the competition. Only Brazil has won the competition on more occasions. The *azzurri* had just beaten France in a dramatic penalty shoot-out in the final in Germany. As the Italy team huddled around the cup and took turns in kissing the gold trophy, they became drenched in confetti and emotion. Over the public address system, the 'Triumphal March' from Verdi's Aida reinforced the Italianness of the victory. The World Cup triumph appeared to be a vindication of the players who had endured a turbulent two months after allegations of match-fixing surfaced in the Italian media. This scandal affected the futures of many of the players at the tournament, and the World Cup provided a suitable liberation from the travails at home.

There have been regular episodes of scandal and success throughout Italian football history. The confluence of political and economic resources has helped provide the elite clubs with the ability to compete on the national and world stage. However, the relative power of elite clubs has also brought them regularly into conflict with the governing bodies. The Federation, like the state, has struggled to impose its authority on its members. Italian football has followed broader globalization processes and undertook extensive deregulation in the 1990s, with the authorities finding it much more difficult to regulate the sport and bring continued success for Italian football. Despite their early success in the 1990s, Serie A has slipped behind German Bundesliga in the UEFA coefficient table. While the world's best players of the past went to Italy to make their name, contemporary stars are frequently choosing the Premier League, La Liga or the Bundesliga to ply their trade. This is partly the patrimonial because model has not had the sustained resources to compete globally. The model's failure was dramatically exposed through bankruptcy and corruption scandals in the twenty-first century. This chapter will begin by illustrating the patrimonial ownership model that emerged during the 1990s. It will then show how leading businessmen (and they are all men) incorporated football into their business empires. These individuals are also politically connected, which helped afford a certain degree of protection. Yet it has not prevented the financial collapse of Italian football (the details of which will follow in the subsequent section). The following section will provide details of the *calciopoli* scandal that reinforced the continued weakness of the authorities and the personalized power networks within the elite clubs. The chapter will conclude with an analysis of *calciopoli* and argue that previous lessons have not been learnt.

## The financial rise and fall of Italian football

The latter decades of the twentieth century saw an unprecedented quantity of money flow into Serie A. New owners, commercial practices and deregulated television deals helped transform Italian football into the world's best league. With the advent of the Champions League, Italian football looked well placed to continue its dominance globally into the new millennium. The popularity of the Italia '90 World Cup and the continued success of clubs like Milan were reflected in the global marketplace. Moreover, football's popularity ensured the economic support for clubs to purchase the best players in the world. Milan's success was underpinned by the Dutch trio of Marco van Basten, Ruud Gullit and Frank Rijkaard, while Napoli sought to break the Turin–Milan hegemony with the help of Maradonna. Later, Juventus signed players such as Roberto Baggio, Zinédine Zidane, and Edgar Davids. In 1992 alone, the Italian clubs had broken the world transfer record three times.[1] As Serie A attracted the best players in the world, it fuelled interest in the league and provided increased revenue from global television deals. It was this success and popularity that saw the television programme *Football Italia* broadcast on British television.

The economic transformation coincided with an increase in industrial patronage in Italian football. The political processes of deregulation that affected the media and business also occurred in football. Regulations governing the ownership of football teams were relaxed in the 1980s, and this allowed Silvio Berlusconi to purchase AC Milan (Porro and Russo 2000). The transformation of European football acted as a catalyst for other businesses to intensify their links with Italian football. As Tim Parks states, 'In Italy, you haven't really arrived until you own a football club' (cited in Arie 2004). In addition to the Agnelli family, who owned Fiat and Juventus, and Berlusconi, who combined his media operation and AC Milan, many other clubs became incorporated into this wider patrimonial network. Fiorentina was bought by the film producer Mario Cecchi Gori in 1990. Three years after his death, the club was inherited by Vittorio Cecchi Gori, who was also a film producer and the owner of Telemontecarlo. The 'sport-media complex' ensured that Fiorentina signed star players like Gabriel Batistuta and Rui Costa. Meanwhile, Sergio Cragnotti, the owner of the food conglomerate Cirio (which owned Del Monte), bought Lazio in 1992. He funded the transfers of a number of international stars, such as Pavel Nedvěd and Paul Gascoigne. Lazio became the first club to float on the Milan Borsa stock exchange in 1998 before winning its second *scudetto* in 2000. Roma followed Lazio's lead and floated two years later. The oil industry tycoon, Franco Sensi, purchased AS Roma in 1993 and funded the signing of players like Gabriel Batistuta from Fiorentina, as well as Cafu, Hidetoshi Nakata and Vincent Candela. The financial contribution from flotation led Roma to win the championship in 2001. Elsewhere, the dairy company Parmalat, which was controlled by the Tanzi family, bought Parma and other football clubs in South America. They chiefly used these clubs and their players to act as ambassadors and advertising agents for Parmalat. Many players were also exported to play for Parma in Serie A. The intensification of links between business and football has also seen the Vatican become involved after its Centro Sportivo Italiano purchased an 80 per cent share of Ancona in 2007.

The Italian model of family capitalism permits the direct involvement from owners and presidents. Many Italian club presidents remain in close control of their clubs, especially over the recruitment of players and managers. For example, the president of Livorno is Aldo Spinelli, the owner of a major Italian logistics company, Gruppo Spinelli.[2] Towards the end of the 2008-2009 season, as the team faltered while pushing for promotion, Spinelli took an active role in the management of the squad. Apart from sacking the manager with just two matches remaining in the season, he gave motivational speeches to the players at training and watched the final matches from the bench. This trend continued into the following season when Spinelli sacked the young manager Gennaro Ruotolo a mere two months into the new season and replaced him with the effervescent Serse Cosmi. However, Cosmi resigned his post in January 2010, citing constant presidential interference. He subsequently retracted his resignation after talks with Spinelli. Cosmi was eventually sacked three months later, which saw the return of Ruotolo. Local newspapers also dedicate regular space for Spinelli's opinions. Before every match, there is a comprehensive preview of the match, with sections dedicated to the journalists' preview and the comments of the manager. In addition, there is a section detailing the thoughts of the president, Spinelli. This is replicated in television broadcasts and the national newspapers, where the quotes of the president often take precedence to those of the manager or players.

Livorno and Spinelli are not unique within Italian football. Some owners revel in the autocratic image they portray. Maurizio Zamparini, the owner of Palermo, is a self-confessed *mangiallenatori* (manager-eater) who, between Venezia and Palermo, has sacked twenty-seven managers in fifteen years. Likewise, Aurelio De Laurentiis, the film producer and owner of Napoli, has also taken an active role in the running of the club. This includes him entering the changing rooms at half-time and interrupting the manager's team-talk to give his own motivational speeches. More recently, Massimo Cellino, the president of Cagliari, has given his new team of Leeds United a taste of his hands-on style. In June 2014, he released the goalkeeper Paddy Kenny because his birthday fell on the 17th, and Cellino had a superstition about the number seventeen.

Berlusconi's interest in AC Milan was also not restricted to the business aspects of the club. Berlusconi still maintained some direct involvement with Milan even after his Vice President Adriano Galliani assumed the presidency when Berlusconi entered politics. In the summer of 2009, Berlusconi is alleged to have made former World Player of the Year, Ronaldinho, stand on a table and declare that he would act more professionally. The following summer, Berlusconi unveiled the new manager of AC Milan, Massimiliano Allegri, at a press conference and fielded every question from journalists, as well as insisting that the new manager play two strikers. Berlusconi was even emphatic that had he been Milan's coach in the 2009-10 season, it would have won the *scudetto* rather than finish third. So it is no surprise that as soon as Berlusconi was ousted from his position as prime minister, he resumed the presidency of Milan.

The direct involvement of presidents ensures that interactions are personalized. As has been demonstrated elsewhere in Italian society, the networks of industrial patronage extend into politics. Many of these new post-industrialists operated in extensive political–industrial patrimonial networks. Silvio Berlusconi is the embodiment of this, as the former Italian prime minister is also Italy's richest man and owner of AC Milan. His counterpart at Inter was Massimo Moratti, the son of Angelo, who constructed the Grande Inter side of the 1960s. In addition to being a director in his late father's oil company, he is also a director of Telecom Italia and Pirelli. His sister-in-law is Letizia Moratti, who was the Mayor of Milan between 2006 and 2011, was a former education minister in Berlusconi's government and a former employee of RAI and Sky.[3] Elsewhere, Gianni Agnelli, the owner of Fiat and Juventus, was made a senator for life in Italy's parliament on account of his business success.

There is a long history of political involvement in Italian football. Bologna was successful during the 1920s and 1930s at the same time that Mussolini's friend, Leandro Arpinati, was mayor of Bologna, and president of CONI and the FIGC. The president of Napoli during the 1950s and 1960s was Achille Lauro, the billionaire shipbuilder, mayor of Naples and Member of Parliament for his own Monarchist National Party. Football club ownership provides a range of opportunities for political patronage. At Palermo in the 1970s and 1980s, the Vice President Salvatore Matta was the younger brother of the prominent local DC leader (Scalia 2009). The patrimonial connections worked in three ways:

> First, Matta delivered free tickets to matches to many bureaucrats of the regional, provincial and city administration, who often gave them to other friends or relatives. Second, people from lower classes were appointed stewards, which made it possible for them to let friends and acquaintances into the stadium for free. Third, *ultras* were also given free tickets, and some of their members were hired by the club as members of the security service staff. When electoral campaigns began, the *ultras*' headquarters worked as electoral committees, hosting conventions, feasts and talks from Christian Democracy candidates. The stand, finally, worked as a propaganda place where the electoral leaflets of candidates were delivered to supporters (Scalia 2009, p. 49).

Other club owners have been members of parliament, such as the DC supporting Franco Sensi of Roma and Luciano Gaucci of Perugia and Catania. Antonio Matarese, who was president of Bari from 1977 to 1984 (before transferring it to his brother), was also a member of parliament for the DC as well as being a president of the FICG and Serie A, and a vice president of UEFA and FIFA. These personalized, neo-patrimonial networks have allowed strategic actors to operate across boundaries to influence individual goals. For example, with Matarese's support, Bari successfully won government funding for the Stadio San Nicola to be built for Italia '90.

The neo-patrimonial network that exists between politics, business and football extends beyond the football clubs. The weakness of the central authorities has permitted the incorporation of the Federation into the patrimonial system of the elite clubs. The intertwined nature of Italian football sees powerful individuals in several positions in the FIGC. For example:

> On the one hand, we have Adriano Galliani, president of the Lega Calcio, champion of the unity of Italian professional football, and guarantor of equal treatment for small clubs with respect to the larger clubs. Moreover, he is also meant to protect the small clubs against the threat of secession of the larger, richer clubs. On the other hand, we have Adriano Galliani, a leading figure in the G-14 who participates in secessionist plans at the national and international levels. (Porro and Russo 2004, p. 226)

Galliani's position as head of Lega Calcio was fundamentally compromised by his position as vice president of Milan. The club was part of the G-14 group of elite European clubs that lobbied for increased individual control over national and European affairs.[4] Furthermore, Milan is also owned by Silvio Berlusconi who was in a unique position as prime minister to influence the laws regulating the finances of football. The interrelation between football, politics and business is not restricted to club presidents and owners. The former president of the FIGC, Franco Carraro, was a former Mayor of Rome, deputy for the PSI and Tourism Minister in the 1980s. He was also president of MCC, a merchant bank owned by Capitalia. This bank was the major investor in a number of Serie A clubs, in particular, Roma, Parma and Lazio. The financial underwriting of Capitalia permitted a number of clubs to operate despite accruing considerable debt. The president of the FIGC is also overseer of Covisoc, the financial regulator for the league. In this position the president has a duty to maintain the financial probity and integrity of the league. However, this was compromised through Carraro's involvement with an organization that underwrites certain clubs' debts. Consequently, patrimonial networks are entrenched in a small number of dense family and personal connections.

Although the neo-patrimonial networks permitted rapid success in the early years of the Champions League and expanding global television markets, they quickly proved unable to further capitalize on the globalized market. Incorporation into the business networks of leading families did not provide greater financial professionalism for Italian football. Stock market flotation for Roma did not bring financial transparency as the club was nearly bankrupt two years after winning the *scudetto* in 2001. Meanwhile, the links between Cirio and Lazio were so entwined that when Cirio encountered financial difficulties in 2002, the club was directly affected. Lazio continued to face widespread financial problems until they were bought by Claudio Lotito in 2004. In the same period,

Fiorentina entered bankruptcy in 2001 after the film producer Vittorio Cecchi Gori encountered financial difficulties. This saw the Florentine club relegated to the amateur leagues. A similar fate befell Napoli, who had €70 million of debts, in 2004.

The collapse of Italian industrial patrimony occurred spectacularly with Parma, the football club owned by Parmalat. When Parmalat went bankrupt in 2004, the football club was inextricably linked, which affected results on the pitch. The Parmalat bankruptcy highlighted the intricate nature of the patrimonial relationship between politics, business and football in Italy. The intensification of relationships within the network affords the owners of the businesses, and their businesses and clubs, a degree of support and legitimation. The owner of Parmalat, Calisto Tanzi, built extensive networks with many powerful politicians:

> In the almost 40 pages detailed by prosecuting magistrates [investigating the bankruptcy] there emerges a design created by 20 years of friendships, acquaintances and links, resembling a large and intricate spider-web that Calisto Tanzi spun with the political and institutional elite of the First and the Second Republic ... You could call it a work of lobbying. Tanzi did not corrupt politicians. He only wanted to establish strong links of friendship and collaboration, thus creating a layer of protection for his activities. He financed political initiatives, electoral campaigns, sponsored this or that event, provided advertisements, entered into business with those people nearest to this or that politician. Not much for the likes of him. From 4 to 6 billion old lira a year. In exchange he wanted attention paid to the fortunes of his businesses. From a certain moment onwards, however, Tanzi felt that he was being obliged to finance the initiatives of politicians, their electoral campaigns, newspapers or demonstrations. In some ways, to use a metaphor, from a spider that spun an intricate web to capture insects he became a prisoner of the same web he had constructed. (*La Repubblica* cited in Della Porta and Vannucci 2007)

Calisto Tanzi represents just one example of the extensive personalized neo-patrimonial networks that interlaced the worlds of football, politics and business.

The financial collapse of Italian football and companies like Parmalat and Cirio highlighted the full range of creative accounting that was taking place within the football clubs. The difficulty with football accounting is that it is very difficult to account for the skills and depreciation of a footballer. As a result, statements of accounts become 'visible illusions' (Morrow 1999). They only present an image of the financial situation of a club. This saw a range of illusionary measures being employed in Italy. The most serious example of this style of accounting was called *plus-valenze*. This is where the profit made on the sale of players could be spread over an accounting term, '*Sales* are immediately entered into the accounts, while *purchases* are spread over the entire period of the contract [original italics]' (Foot 2006, p. 491). Traditionally, the smaller clubs would benefit from this system through the sales of players to larger clubs, however the larger clubs realized that they could also benefit. By 2002, over 70 per cent of profits were comprised of *plus-valenze*. Complicated transactions took place where players transferred between clubs at inflated prices to balance the accounts. This permitted clubs to inflate their immediate accounts and provided a short-term solution to financial problems. A good example of such a practice was the swapped transfer of Fabio Cannavaro and Fabian Carini between Inter and Juventus in 2004. Cannavaro was the Italian captain (who subsequently lifted the World Cup in 2006) while Carini was a Uruguayan reserve goalkeeper at Juventus. They were exchanged for the same value. Effectively, Inter gave away their best player, suggesting that there were a number of reciprocal favours exchanged between clubs. Several players were exchanged in similar ways between both Milan clubs during the 1990s.

Although *plus-valenze* accounting was technically legal, other clubs adopted more controversial approaches. Roma was nearly bankrupt, despite winning only their third ever *scudetto* in 2001. By the start of the 2003 season, they had to declare to Covisoc, the financial regulator, that they could financially fulfil their obligations for the season. They produced signed *fideiussione*, financial guarantees, to assure the financial eligibility for the season. However, these *fideiussione* later turned out to be forged. Roma claimed that they were innocent and had been the victims of fraud themselves. Consequently, they were allowed to continue operating. Subsequently, in 2005, Torino were guilty of using similar methods. The result demonstrated that, as Porro and Russo (2004, p. 223) state, that:

> Covisoc has had its powers hollowed out over time to such an extent that it now operates on the opaque frontier between respect for accounting rules and a technical-financial free-for-all.

Covisoc was a façade, and Italian football was beginning to collapse. Wider economic problems of Parmalat and Cirio affected Parma and Lazio. Meanwhile, clubs such as Roma, Napoli and Fiorentina were in severe financial turmoil. The lack of political support for Fiorentina and Napoli saw them subsequently relegated for financial irregularities.

The collapse of the Italian neo-patrimonial system was highlighted in another documentation scandal. Illegal passports were used to circumvent controls over players. Prior to the Bosman ruling in 1995 that deregulated the transfer market for footballers, many national leagues imposed restrictions on the number of foreign players that were permitted to play in their league. The Italian Football Federation has experimented with a number of quota systems since its disastrous foray in 1908, which saw a number of clubs withdraw in protest. The situation was further complicated by the use of *oriundi*, foreign-born players of Italian descent. Quotas permitting *oriundi* as additional foreigners saw the opportunity for players and clubs to invent Italian ancestry in order to evade the restrictions. This led to a number of scandals involving false passports. Many emerged in the 1940s and 1950s, yet the most widespread passport scandal occurred in the 1990s. A large number of non-Europeans, specifically from South America, produced passports with invented Italian ancestry. Major players, such as the Lazio and Argentina midfielder, Juan Sebastian Veron, Inter winger Recoba and Milan goalkeeper Dida were implicated in the scandal. The FIGC once again demonstrated their inability to deal with the problem. As the problem was so widespread and the repercussions potentially explosive, they decided to remove the regulations of foreign players, at a stroke legalizing those who had infringed the rules. The FIGC reinforced its own crisis of legitimacy by legitimizing the actions of the clubs.

The crisis within the Italian football was severe and required political intervention. The interlaced neo-patrimonial networks operating in Italian society resulted in the strategic actors within football operating in politics. Berlusconi, in particular had a vested interest in finding a resolution to the financial crisis. Despite the deregulation rhetoric of the 1980s, Berlusconi's government attempted to reassert state control and reinforced the interrelated networks affecting football and politics. In January 2003, the Berlusconi government passed a special debtspreading decree. Dubbed *Salva Calcio* (Save Football) by the media, it allowed clubs to spread their debts over ten years. Clubs such as Milan and Inter saved over €200 million. Juventus meanwhile accused the government and the clubs of 'administrative doping'. Luca di Montezemolo, the manager of FIAT, the owners of Juventus, declared that this emergency decree was 'the exact opposite of that which should be done in a serious country' (Foot 2006, p. 493). Despite the political support in Italy, the decree was declared illegal under European law as it contravened competition laws and budgetary regulations. This led to the government amending the decree to conform to European law, while still retaining the original intentions. These decrees permitted clubs to minimize the amount of tax they paid to the state and effectively this turned Italian football into a state-subsidized industry

(Porro and Russo 2004). Thus, the state made it easier for clubs to obtain licenses from Covisoc. The neo-patrimony of Italian politics and football ensured that the individual interests of strategic actors in football were supported without addressing the fundamental issues which caused the crisis.

The financial crisis further demonstrated the weakness of the federation's regulation and the growing strength of the elite clubs. Political–institutional decline of the FIGC and Lega Calcio was undermined by clubs who took their grievances to local courts, rather than to the federation. Despite undermining the financial regulator Covisoc with the debtspreading decree, Silvio Berlusconi's government tried to restore the jurisdiction of the sporting bodies with a law dubbed 'TAR stopper'. The law aimed to bypass the local courts, the *Tribunale Amministrativo Regionale* (TAR), who always supported the local clubs whenever they took their cases to court. The federations that felt that justice was not being exercised by the local TAR, could go direct to the Lazio TAR. The inability of the federation to arbitrate its members was a central cause of the crises and reinforced its own crisis of legitimacy:

> When an institution is no longer capable of resolving its internal disputes based on its own rules and mechanism, forcing actors to look at other spheres of justice, then the crisis has reached a condition that is close to terminal. (Porro and Russo 2004, p. 228)

The deregulation of the football federation had a direct impact on its ability to regulate the elite clubs. Those that had powerful political patronage were able to circumvent the regulations. This was supported by the government who granted the clubs the right to evade the federation's arbitration courts. In addition, the government attempted to provide state subsidies through *salva-calcio*. The Italian patrimonial system was bankrupt.

The collapse of the regulatory bodies reinforced the neo-patrimonial system. Reciprocal favours became more significant in the absence of effective regulation. Inducements were not always financial. In 1992, the Sporting Director of Torino, Luciano Moggi, was alleged to have provided prostitutes for referees of Torino's UEFA Cup matches. Moggi claimed that they were interpreters, and that he wasn't culpable if they weren't used for interpretation (Foot 2006). In the circumstance, no one could prove who requested the three women, and no charges were found. There are also many instances of physical gifts being provided to referees. In 2000 Roma president, Franco Sensi, was accused of trying to corrupt referees when he gave two £8,000 Rolex watches to the head of the referee panel, as well as lesser priced Rolexes for the other thirty-seven referees in Serie A. Sensi claimed conspiracy and said that it was a normal practice to give gifts and that this had never been questioned in the past. Indeed, in 2004, Sensi gave six bottles of Krug champagne in a Christmas hamper to every Serie A referee. Similarly, the president of Perugia and owner of a racehorse stable, Luciano Gaucci, provided a referee with assistance in purchasing three racehorses. The referee, coincidentally, officiated in the same division as Perugia, and the Umbrian club subsequently went on to win promotion. Occasionally, the authorities punish infringements of the rules, and this simply helps to reinforce the crisis of legitimacy. In light of these events, the Roma president Sensi escaped censure. Gaucci's Perugia, however, was prevented from being promoted, while the referee was banned for life and Gaucci for three years.

Football provides significant symbolic capital in Italy. The media interest provides the president with public exposure; something that Berlusconi has exploited to his advantage when entering politics. As Agnew (2006, p. 114) highlights:

> By June 2003, the accountancy firm Practice Audit estimated AC Milan to be €142.8 million in debt, while the club returned a €51.5 million loss for the financial year 2003-4. Berlusconi, however, understood that, in terms of image, AC Milan was well worth the investment, and each year he came up with the cash to meet the club's debts. For someone with huge commercial and ultimately political ambitions in a country where football is encoded into the DNA, four [now five] European Cup/Champions League trophies and seven Serie A league titles over the next 19 seasons were worth more than money could buy.

As the interdependencies have intensified between politics, business and football the prestige and symbolic capital have grown. Clubs and presidents have pushed the boundaries of authority in order to maximize the benefits for themselves and their families. Yet owners are not the only actors within these power networks. Other strategic individuals operate within these networks and seek advantages for their clubs. The following section details the exposure of the biggest match-fixing scandal in Italian history and clearly illustrates how these networks operate.

## *Calciopoli*: Network football

The extent of the Italian neo-patrimonial system was spectacularly demonstrated in 2006. The *calciopoli* scandal demonstrated the extensive neo-patrimonial networks operating within Italian football and how personalized contacts and *quid pro quo* favours had become embedded in the system. Politics, football and the federation were so intertwined that the scandal could only emerge through the media and the judiciary. Despite the details being initially passed to the president of the FIGC, Franco Carraro, a full investigation was not undertaken. The details were subsequently leaked through the media. The scandal started after an initial investigation into the Neapolitan-organized crime network, the Camorra, revealed an illegal betting ring in Naples. Separate investigations also took place into further illegal betting rings in Parma and Udine. These were combined with earlier investigations into the use of drugs by Juventus and a separate investigation into the sports agency, GEA World, in Rome. As a result of these inquiries, the results of thirty-nine matches were investigated and over forty people were investigated for sporting fraud. Over 100,000 conversations were transcribed over eight months by six transcribers. The leaked transcriptions permitted the various strands of the scandal to be woven together by the media and named after the *tangentopoli* scandal. The subsequent investigation was even conducted by a *tangentopoli* magistrate, Saverio Borrelli. Finally, the parallel with the previous political scandal was reinforced with the investigation being dubbed *piedi puliti* or 'clean feet'.

Global deregulation and extensive media coverage has facilitated the emergence of charismatic individuals who could bypass regulations and use media to communicate directly to the public. This occurred in Italy with personalized politicians and football club presidents. *Calciopoli* demonstrated the emergence of a charismatic individual who operated out of the media spotlight. The main focus of the scandal was placed on Luciano Moggi, the director of football at Juventus, who was alleged to have fixed matches for the Turin club. Moggi began his career at Napoli under Italo Allodi, the manager of Juventus in the middle of Brian Glanville's 'Golden Fix' allegations of the 1970s (Glanville 1999a; Hawkey 2006). He then went to both Roman clubs before making a similar cross-city move from Torino to Juventus. It was while at Torino in 1992 that Moggi was implicated in the alleged procurement of prostitutes for referees before a UEFA Cup game. Through these various positions he built strong networks with the politicians in the capital as well among the games' administrators.

*Calciopoli* revealed an extensive patrimonial network of reciprocal favours. Moggi was nicknamed the 'lollipop man' (*la paletta*) because he controlled the traffic between the clubs, referees, players and their agents; he acted as a patron. He was at the nexus of a network of referees, players, politicians and agents and made over 400 telephone calls per day across the network to create *la sistema*

*Moggi* (The Moggi System) (Mensurati 2007). Within neo-patrimonial networks, reciprocal relationships are established where both parties seek to fulfil their obligations to each other. Anthropological accounts have long highlighted how these networks are embedded within Italian society (Banfield 1958; Boissevain 1966; Silverman 1965; Silverman 1975). The informal hierarchies established by patron–client relationships parallels the Church. Saints were seen as closer to God than the individual, and the clergy were closer to the saints. To gain access to God, one must negotiate through the intermediaries of the clergy and saints. Ultimately, the patron's success relies upon their ability to provide services to their clients and fulfil their obligations to their patrons. The greater range of favours a patron can call upon provides for greater power and influence within the network. This in turn enhances the position of the clients, who benefit from having a powerful patron. Legitimation comes from fulfilling the *quid pro quo*. As Mauss (1967) highlights, the exchange of gifts symbolizes future obligations. The gift exchange establishes solidarity and obligations of future reciprocity. Within neo-patrimonial networks, exchange does not have to be a physical gift, but can also be services. Once fulfilled the patron or client is obliged to reciprocate, although there is no immediate duty to return the favour. Moggi's patrimonial network rested on similar future obligations; effectively a 'favour bank' was established where these future obligations are held.

Moggi's system required a network of compliant referees. Distrust of central authority has resulted in match officials being viewed with suspicion. Fans felt that referees suffer from *sudditanza psicologica* (physiological subjection) and would naturally favour large clubs to ensure a successful career. The central authorities have successively tried but failed to address this. In the 1926 Viareggio Charter, a committee was created to select referees for matches. The details of these selections were kept secret in order to prevent corruption. This situation quickly became unworkable, however, as the information became valuable to fans and clubs. By the 1980s, allegations were made regarding two back-to-back championship wins for Juventus in 1981–2 that were categorized as 'thefts' (especially by the fans of Roma and Fiorentina who lost out) due to the refereeing decisions in favour of Juventus. As a result, the FIGC implemented a ballot to draw referee names at random and in the only year this was performed, a small provincial team, Hellas Verona, won their only *scudetto* in 1985. This has become an oft-quoted example used by fans to 'prove' the favouritism towards larger clubs. The FIGC reinforced its lack of authority by reverting to a selection committee in the following year. Under this system, in 1999, Paolo Bergamo and Pierluigi Pairetto had become the joint heads of the Italian referees' association with the power to designate referees for matches. Three years later, Pairetto became the vice chairman of UEFA's referees' commission. As a consequence, they became important figures in coordinating the network of referees.

Moggi incorporated Pairetto and Bergamo into his own network. Moggi was close friends with both referee designators and persuaded them to use their discretion to direct compliant referees to certain games. They recruited another referee to act as an intermediary. Massimo De Santis was a world-respected referee who had been selected to officiate at the 2006 World Cup in Germany; a position he subsequently lost after the scandal broke. De Santis took a certain amount of pride in the role he played. He had been accused by Livorno president, Aldo Spinelli, of being part of the 'Roman Gang' and as a consequence was 'punished' by De Santis. While refereeing a match between Livorno and Siena, De Santis sent off the Livorno player Fabio Galante after seventeen minutes. The referee was recorded speaking to Innocenzo Mazzini, the vice president of the FIGC. After Mazzini said 'poor Spinelli … you were, as always, splendid', De Santis replied, 'Did you see? Ready and go, one off' (*La Repubblica* 2006a). De Santis was utilizing his position to exact revenge on non-compliant individuals. Those who were not incorporated into the network were not afforded its protection. Meanwhile those within the network gained advantages. Compliant referees would assist Juventus by dismissing rival players like Fabio Galante at Livorno or by showing leniency to Juventus players. This system also applied in games that did not involve Juventus. The star players of Juventus' rivals would be booked or sent off so this would impact their ability to compete. They were also carefully timed so that their suspensions would coincide with the game against Juventus.

The patrimonial network required reciprocal favours. Moggi's position at Juventus granted him access to the resources of Fiat. As Juventus was owned by the car giant, Moggi could access staff discounts on Fiat cars. He could then provide these discounts, of between 23 and 50 per cent, to acquiescent referees. In one case, he called the Agnelli house to request a four-door Maserati as a gift for an important friend (*Corriere della Sera* 2006). Pairetto subsequently called the vice president of the FIGC, Innocenzo Mazzini, to state that he had the car. Gift exchange is an important feature of performing solidarity along the network. Franco Sensi, the president of Roma, stated that it was common practice when he was discovered to have given referees gifts of Rolex watches in 2000 and Krug champagne in 2004. Moggi was operating no differently; his gifts were simply worth more.

Gifts can establish a reciprocal relationship but the threat of physical violence can also intimidate individuals in the network. As Gramsci argued, hegemony is maintained through coercion *and* consent. In the absence of reciprocal favours, Moggi could resort to violence and intimidation to make his point. In doing so, he would ensure that that referee would be more favourable in future games. In one transcript, the referee observer Pietro Ingargiola was overheard speaking to Tullio Lanese, the president of the Italian Referees' Association:

> I've never seen anything like it in my life. Moggi and Giraudo [Juventus' Chairman] go in, and Moggi starts really threatening him [the referee, Paparesta], with his finger right up to the referee's eye. He was shouting at the linesman too, 'You're an absolute disgrace, not giving that penalty, how dare you?' I pretended not to see anything and went to the toilet. (Marcotti 2006)

Moggi himself confirmed this. In another transcript he states that, 'I locked the referee [Paparesta] and linesmen in the toilet and took the keys away with me to the airport' (Marcotti 2006). This shows that not only was Moggi making a symbolic gesture to ensure compliance in the future, but also he was making tacit approval from the club. The chairman of Juventus, Antonio Giraudo, was part of this meeting and although we cannot be sure what was communicated between him and Moggi afterwards, he would have been clear about Moggi's actions.

Moggi also exerted psychological pressure on Pairetto and Bergamo in order to make his intentions clear. And this was not restricted to matches in Serie A. The following exchange demonstrates the tone and exasperation of Moggi after Juventus drew 2-2 with the Swedish minnows in a Champions League qualifying match:

> Moggi: But what the fuck kind of referee did you send us?
> Pairetto: Fandel is one of the best ...
> Moggi: Miccoli's goal was valid.
> Pairetto: No it wasn't.
> Moggi: It was valid, it was valid.
> Pairetto: He was in front ...
> Moggi: What are you talking about in front? And anyway, all through the game he messed things up for us.
> Pairetto: But he's one of the top ...
> Moggi: He can go and fuck himself. And for Stockholm [the return leg] I'm counting on you. (*Corriere della Sera* 2006)

Moggi clearly expected a favour in return from Pairetto for the 'poor' performance of the German referee Herbert Fandel. He later discovered that the English referee, Graham Poll was to officiate the second leg. He subsequently rang Pairetto to find out why the Portuguese referee Lucilio Cardoso was not officiating. Pairetto expressed surprise and stated that 'something must have happened at the last moment, I have Cardoso, something must have happened ... he must have been sick or something like that' (*Corriere della Sera* 2006). Graham Poll was seen as conscientious and incorruptible. Moggi clearly did not feel that Juventus would gain any favours from the English referee. Despite having a key ally in Pairetto at UEFA, Moggi's influence was not as powerful across Europe. He had a more extensive and denser network within Italy.

The transformation of television has contributed to distrust of referees. As demonstrated in previous chapters, neo-television has contributed to an increasing television audience for football. The football talk show is a significant contributing factor of this audience share. These shows, like *Il Processo*, make extensive use of the *moviola* (slow motion replay) to analyse contentious decisions, especially disallowed goals, offside decisions and fouls. The *moviola* helps to increase the emotional and dramatic narrative of the game as it fuels debate throughout the week. The centrality of the technology has entered Italian language, with an *episodio da moviola* being a controversial incident within the game. Every Monday the most popular Italian national newspaper, *La Gazzetta dello Sport*, has a match-by-match round-up of these *episodi da moviola*.[5] Despite the fallibility of referees, the *moviola* 'proves' their incompetence. The hyperreal emotion of neo-television becomes heightened as the referees' decisions become scrutinized. This has led to the role of the *moviola* being pinpointed as a key factor in discontent and destabilization of the referee. It has been attributed as a causal factor of fan violence and the referee's association took Aldo Biscardi, the host of *Il Processo*, to court (Foot 2006). In the year before *calciopoli*, Pairetto and Bergamo admonished the media for their excessive use of the *moviola* by highlighting the fact that television had the benefit of the images of forty television cameras, and the time to replay and dissect decisions, whereas the referee had to make the decision in 'real time' (Monti 2005). More recently, the respected ex-referee, and the 2010 chief referee, Pierluigi Collina, stated that 'the problem in Italy [is that the referee] whistles every contact: the referees have fear of being judged in the evening by the *moviola* and in this way, in doubt, they whistle' (Palmeri 2010). In this way neo-television reinforces the *sudditanza psicologica* exerted on referees to benefit influential teams. The distinction between the neo-television of Mediaset and the regulation of RAI was confirmed in 2010 when the state broadcaster announced that it would be ceasing to use the *moviola* during its football talk shows (*La Gazzetta dello Sport* 2010b).

Moggi exploited the distrust fuelled by television and the *moviola* to exert more psychological pressure over the referees. He realized that more people watched football at home on the television than physically in the stadium. Consequently, if he could manipulate what people saw at home, then their opinions could be surreptitiously shaped. He was a close friend of Aldo Biscardi, the creator and presenter of the longest-running and most popular football show in Italy, *Il Processo*. Once again, Moggi's social capital lubricated the network. Moggi helped choose the guests and even fixed the results of phone polls. He asked Biscardi to minimize analysis of debatable decisions. For example after AC Milan striker Andriy Shevchenko was controversially denied a penalty, he called Biscardi and said, 'You need to lay off the referee in this one. You either say the referee was correct in his decision or you don't show the images at all and gloss over it' (Marcotti 2006). Referees that refused to cooperate would be disgraced on air. Moggi could request a debatable decision to be shown, and debated at length to discredit the referee. For example, the following conversation took place on 18 October 2005 between Moggi and Fabio Baldas, one of Italy's most famous football presenters and an ex-referee:

> Baldas: How are you? Well?
> Moggi: Good.
> Baldas: Listen Luciano, today we haven't got much … there is … [just] Rodomonti [the referee for a game between Cagliari-Milan over the weekend, later investigated but cleared by the tribunal]. Is it OK if we make him look bad? If you agree, of course …
> Moggi: Oh naturally.
> Baldas: And then? And then? There's always Siena-Fiorentina …
> Moggi: But was there a penalty?
> Baldas: Er … bloody hell, yes, there was a penalty! … And there Rosetti [a referee, also cleared by the inquiry]. You know the guy … But if we show him, what are we going to do?
> Moggi: No, no, leave him alone … just drop the Siena game.
> Baldas: OK … if I need a favour will you do me a favour?
> Moggi: No problem.
> Baldas: You'll call me back soon?
> Moggi: Yup, soon.
> Baldas: Fine, bye. (*La Repubblica* 2006b)

As with previous conversations, there is succinctness. Moggi did not request any particular action against the referee Rodomonti; he trusted Baldas to perform correctly. In return Baldas requested of Moggi, 'if I need a favour will you do me a favour?'. A 'favour bank' was created where Baldas now had a credit. As with those referees that complied, television presenters that acquiesced to Moggi's demands got favours in return. Although Moggi exerted power along the network, this was not a zero-sum game. He had to provide something in return. As general manager of Juventus, Moggi had access to the players of Italy's most popular club, and some of the best-known players in the world. Many of these players were Italian international stars, which increased their desirability to the media. In return for showing the highlights that Moggi requested, Juventus' general manager would provide exclusive access to these players for interviews and features. Moggi also had access to a wider network of players through the sports agency GEA World.

Globalized sport has seen the increase in third-party intermediaries. This has expanded the opportunity for familial patrimony. Deregulation of sporting contracts, accelerated by the Bosman case, has seen the introduction of a professional group of lawyers, agents and accountants to the network. Investigations by the Italian anti-trust commission during *calciopoli* highlighted that there were 233 agents working in Italy at the time (AGCM 2007). GEA World was the largest sports agency in Italy with nearly an 18 per cent share of the market. The agency was formed in 2001 when three agencies merged: General Athletic; Football Management; and Riccardo Calleri. These three agencies demonstrate the familial nature of Italian football and business (see Figure 4.1). Calleri is the son of a former Genoa and Lazio president, Gianmarco Calleri and General Athletic was comprised of Andrea Cragnotti, who is the son of former Lazio and Cirio president Sergio Cragnotti. Cirio went bankrupt at the same time as Parmalat, who was owned by the Tanzi family. Their daughter, Francesca Tanzi was also a shareholder of General Athletic. Alongside Francesca Tanzi was Chiara Geronzi, the daughter of a leading Italian banker, Cesare Geronzi, who was also investigated as part of the Parmalat collapse. Another major investor in the agency was the bank Capitalia through a trust called Romafides. Capitalia was also a major investor in Parma and Lazio, as well as underwriting Roma (owned by the Rolex-giving Franco Sensi) and Perugia (owned by racehorse-training Luciano Gaucci). In addition, Capitalia owned a merchant bank called MCC whose president was Franco Carraro, the president of the FIGC who suppressed the original details of the *calciopoli* scandal.

The third body within GEA World exemplified the familial networks operating in Italian football. Football Management employed one of Italy's leading agents, Franco Zavaglia as well as Giuseppe De Mita, a former Lazio

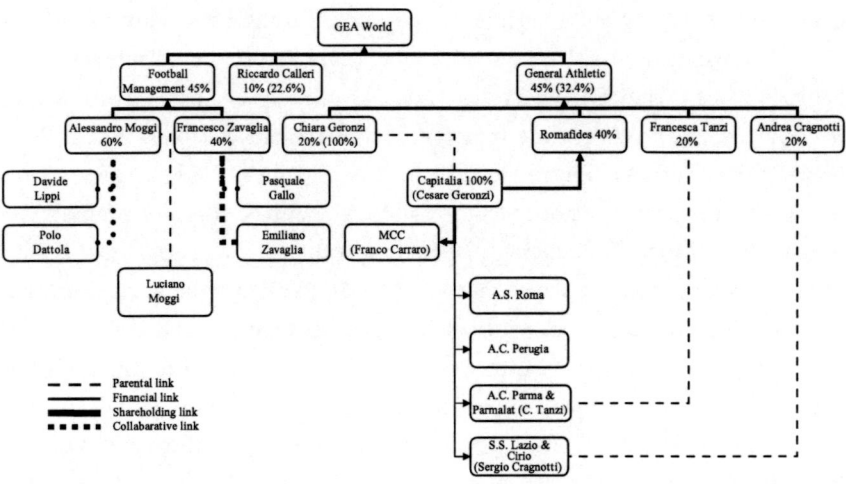

**Figure 4.1** (Hamil et al. 2010).

official and son of former Italian Prime Minister, Circiaco De Mita. Another key member was Davide Lippi, the son of the Italian head coach Marcello Lippi. Lippi senior had also managed Juventus on two separate occasions, from 1994–9 and from 2001 until he took the Italy head coach position in 2004. In his position as Juventus head coach he would have worked closely with Luciano Moggi, who began working at Juventus in the same year as Marcello Lippi started his first spell as Juventus manager. Most significantly, the agency also employed Luciano Moggi's son, Alessandro. This provided Moggi with access to a wider range of players, and through these he could dispense favours to television and the newspapers. In return, if players signed for GEA World, they would have access to the networks that could provide them with the potential opportunity to play for Italy's biggest and most successful club, Juventus, or for the Italian national team. Indeed, there were serious allegations of favouritism towards both Juventus and GEA players ahead of Italy's participation in the World Cup finals in Germany (Foot 2006).

As with other aspects of Moggi's patrimonial system, threats and undue influence were used. During the investigations, Roma's general manager, Franco Baldini, claimed that youth team players were placed under undue pressure to sign for GEA (Leroux 2008). In 2005, the former Siena midfielder, Stefano Argilli, was forced to leave the club because he refused to sign for GEA. He said that 'Our new manager was GEA, our general manager was GEA, half the team was GEA. It was clear to me that if I wanted to stay, I would have to sack my agent and join GEA as well' (Marcotti 2006). It didn't end with players leaving clubs for not signing with Moggi's son's agency. Through his connections and control of agents he could end the careers of those players that displeased him. Fabrizio Miccoli and Enzo Maresca ended up playing in Portugal and Spain, respectively, effectively ending their international chances (Jones 2007). Even major players such as Thierry Henry, Zinedine Zidane and Edgar Davids were sacrificed when they did not succumb to Moggi's wishes. This also suggests the possibility of Moggi influencing players and teams. A classic example is that of Siena. When Juventus played Siena in May 2006 (before the scandal broke), the press highlighted the close financial links between the two clubs. As the midfielder of Siena argued earlier, many players were signed to GEA. Of the fourteen players in the squad to play against Juventus, seven of them were GEA players, as was the coach Gigi De Canio and the director of football Giorgio Perinetti. After a losing streak of seven games, Juventus duly went up with 3-0 just inside seven minutes; this did nothing to dispel the rumours of Juventus' undue influence.

The interconnections between Italian football, business and politics were further exposed during *calciopoli*. Moggi had many friends within politics and would extend the same acts of patrimony to politicians (Sarzanini 2006; Jones 2007; Kiefer and Fisher 2006). The Interior Minister Giuseppe Pisanu was a close friend of Moggi. Pisanu consulted with Moggi when Pope John Paul II died to see if the league could be suspended. Moggi wanted the games to go ahead because the various suspensions of players were favourable to Juventus. Moggi's power, in this case, was less influential than the Catholic Church and games were suspended. The relationship between Pisanu and Moggi was extended when Pisanu requested assistance in support of his local side, Sassari Torres del Viminale, who were given a 'problem' referee. When the team won away for the first time in two years a few weeks later, Pisanu rang back to ask Moggi if they could be helped from relegation. The Finance Minister, Dominico Siniscalco, was also in contact with Moggi to ask for favours. Within Italy, *raccomandazione* (recommendations) for jobs are also important obligations of the patron–client relationship (Zinn 2001). Siniscalco asked Moggi if his sons could attend a Juventus training school. In return Moggi wanted help for a friend who wanted to transfer within the Guardia di Finanza (Italy's tax police). These reciprocal favours expand power and social capital throughout the network of politics, football and business.

Although Moggi and Juventus were central to the *calciopoli* investigations, they were not the only avenues of investigation. There had been long-term suspicion within the Italian game over the influence of Moggi and some openly tried to fight the system. As repeatedly demonstrated, Moggi would use the network to damage those who did not cooperate. Fiorentina went bankrupt in 2002 and was relegated to Serie C2. Diego Della Valle, their new president and owner of Tod's shoes, took over in 2004 and guided the club back into Serie A. Della Valle frequently spoke out against the imbalance within the Italian game, especially in light of Fiorentina's relegation due to bankruptcy when clubs like Lazio and Roma were permitted to remain in Serie A. He also campaigned against the individual television rights that favoured the larger teams. However, during the 2004-5 season, Fiorentina's first season back in Serie A, the Florentine club was facing relegation due to Moggi's influence; an influence so strong that Fiorentina had two players sent off in the first eight minutes of a game against Sampdoria. Delle Valle repented and asked for Moggi's assistance. As a consequence, Fiorentina avoided relegation that season but were deducted points following the scandal.

Lazio had faced similar financial problems at the same time as Fiorentina but were not relegated. After Cragnotti's arrest following Cirio's bankruptcy, the club was bought by Claudio Lotito, the owner of a cleaning services industry. Lotito made similar requests of Moggi to help Lazio avoid relegation. Lazio were also supported by Franco Carraro, the president of the FIGC. Carraro called the referee designator, Pairetto, to say 'Listen, we need to give Lazio a hand ...'. In a subsequent conversation with the vice president of the FIGC, Lazio president Lotitio says 'So you have spoken to Carraro ... that's good ... that means he is on my side' (Burke 2006). In the following game, Lazio beat Parma 2-0 thanks to a penalty that was controversially disallowed. A further club, Reggina Calabria, was also investigated in the scandal as it transpired that club president Lillo Foti had asked Moggi for assistance to avoid Reggina's relegation. The Tuscan club of Arezzo were also penalized during *calciopoli* for trying to fix matches in Serie B.

*Calciopoli* revealed that Moggi and Juventus were not the only club to be developing patrimonial networks. Silvio Berlusconi's Milan was also trying to minimize the influence of Moggi and Juventus by building a rival network. Milan's referees' liaison officer Leonardo Meani was trying to build a separate influential network of compliant referees. Referee's Liasion Officers are employed by the clubs to accompany the referees, collect them from train stations, and generally make their time comfortable. Clearly, this gives them a great deal of time with the referee. Meani was heard in phone-taps talking to the Italian Football Association's head of assistant referees, criticizing the appointment of an assistant after Milan had lost to Siena and saying, 'I don't want him. I never asked for him nor wanted him.' As a result he advised that 'On Wednesday, try to send two intelligent ones' (Williams 2007). For a game against Chievo Verona, Meani asked for two linesmen by name, including one, Claudio Puglisi, a noted Milan fan. Meani was granted his request from Gennaro Mazzei, the head of linesmen and Milan subsequently won the match against Chievo.

Through the scandal it transpired that Leonardo Meani was performing his task with the full approval of the vice president of Milan, Adriano Galliani. As the prosecutor Stefano Palazzi stated: 'Meani was in telephone contact with linesmen, who were asked, when in doubt, to favour Milan. Galliani approved' (Dunne 2006). Until the scandal, Galliani was president of *Lega Calcio*, the Italian Football League. As a consequence, Galliani was the guardian of the probity of the leagues. He already had a conflict of interests in relation to the arrangement and negotiation of television deals. Now that he was condoning the operation of a 'Milan system', the integrity of the league was undermined. Although he denied the existence of a 'Milan system', Galliani resigned from his position at *Lega Calcio* for his part in *calciopoli* (although he has since rejoined the board of Serie A). Milan was subsequently docked points and disqualified from the Champions League. However, on appeal, they were reinstated and went on to win the trophy in the following year.

The expansive investigation into *calciopoli* highlighted the extensive networks utilized by two of the three biggest clubs in Italy. Inter was the third club of that triumvirate and was not investigated, even though they had the most to gain from the penalization of their two main rivals. After the initial *calciopoli* investigation had been concluded, an alternative power base emerged across the city of Milan. In October 2006, it transpired that Inter took an active role in the evidence gathered two years before the scandal broke. They were undertaking their own investigations into Massimo De Santis, the leading referee in the scandal, whom they suspected of favouring Juventus. They did this through the utilization of phone-taps executed by Telecom Italia. The telecommunications company was also instrumental in authorizing and placing the phone-taps that caught the various protagonists in the *calciopoli* scandal, and which were subsequently leaked to the press. Once again, business networks help piece together the story. The newspaper that leaked the story was *La Gazzetta dello Sport* which was owned by Carlo Buora, a former vice president of Inter, and a former managing director of Pirelli, who became CEO of Telecom Italia after being purchased by Pirelli. The telecom company was also part-owner of Inter and Massimo Moratti, the president of the Milanese club, was also a non-executive director of Telecom Italia (and Pirelli). The connections are reiterated by the fact that the second largest shareholder of

Inter is Marco Tronchetti Provera who also owns Pirelli, the company that sponsors the jerseys of Inter. Once again, personalized networks explain the shifting power structure in Italian football. Inter was complicit in compiling the evidence that led to the downfall of their biggest rivals. This downfall led to Inter winning the subsequent four *scudetti* and the 2010 Champions League.

Further documentary evidence emerged between 2010 and 2011. The *calciopoli 2* investigation revealed that Moggi was utilizing a wider range of telephone communication. It transpired that he had given a number of foreign SIM cards to Pairetto and Bergamo. This meant that they could not be intercepted by Italian investigators or Telecom Italia. This suggested another level of subterfuge. The transcripts from *calciopoli 2* also revealed that in addition to the complex network of Pirelli, Telecom Italia, *La Gazzetta dello Sport* and Inter directors potentially assisting the investigation, the former president of Inter, Giacinto Facchetti (who died in 2006), had also been in regular contact with Bergamo and Pairetto. This suggests a reason for Franco Carraro's intransigence when proffered the original findings. The depth and extent of the corruption would have made it difficult to tackle. Ultimately, the criminal trials found that many of the participants had been guilty of 'sporting fraud'. In addition, Juventus were fined a further €300,000 for their part. Juventus' lawyer, Franzo Grande Stevens, suggested that it was 'not an admission of guilt, but an act of generosity' (*La Gazzetta dello Sport* 2008a). To the end, the exchange of resources was still seen as a gift, and a challenge to the authority of the authorities.

As well as illustrating the extensive networks operating across Italian football, *calciopoli* also reinforced the lack of legitimacy of the FIGC and Serie A. The authorities were consistently challenged over the outcome of the investigation. The Federation's prosecutor recommended that Juventus be stripped of their 2005 and 2006 *scudetti*, relegated to lower than Serie B and docked points. Meanwhile, Fiorentina, Lazio and Milan should be relegated to Serie B and be docked points and Reggina should have a fifteen-point sanction but remain in Serie A. All of the clubs challenged this pronouncement and the authorities compromised. Juventus were stripped of the *scudetti* of 2005 and 2006, relegated to Serie B for the first time in their history, and deducted nine points for the 2006-7 season. The remaining clubs were permitted to remain in Serie A, but with deductions in points. The guilty teams from the 2005-6 season were also removed points as part of punishment. This meant that Milan would have lost out on their Champions League place. They challenged this ruling and were permitted to enter the competition the following season, and duly won the title against Liverpool in Athens. The adjustment in league positions also created some winners. Messina remained in Serie A thanks to Juventus' relegation, and Livorno were elevated into the UEFA Cup spot. Inter were also awarded the 2006 *scudetto* (the 2005 title remains vacant, just as in 1927).

Juventus continued to challenge the punishment. They threatened to appeal through the civil courts until FIFA made it clear that they would ban any national league from competing in international tournaments if any legal cases were heard outside the sporting jurisdiction. Thus only a global governing body could impose legitimacy onto the Italian football authorities. In 2012, Juventus won their first *scudetto* since the scandal. This represented their twenty-eighth title. However, if they had not had the 2005 and 2006 titles rescinded, then the total would have been thirty *scudetti*. In 1958 Umberto Agnelli, the president of Juventus, suggested that winners of ten *scudetti* should receive a golden star to commemorate the event. With thirty titles, Juventus would have added a third star in 2012; and they publicly announced that their jersey for the 2012-13 season would sport a third star. After negotiations with the FIGC, they agreed to keep the two stars. However, they suggested that they would instead place a slogan, '30 won on the pitch'. Italy's most successful club were publicly challenging the authority of the Federation.

## *Calcioscommesse*: A case of déjà vu again

The consistent challenge to the authority of the Federation undermines its legitimacy. This is exacerbated by the structure of the constituents of the governing bodies. Powerful individuals act as the directors of the organizations. Club presidents and directors also act as directors of the FIGC and Serie A. As Adriano Galliani embodies, there is a conflict of interest between the president of a football club, who as an employee of that institution should be seeking the best deal for them, and a director of the league who should be focused on the best interests of *all* clubs. These conflicts of interest even resurfaced in the immediate aftermath of *calciopoli*. As a result of the scandal, Adriano Galliani resigned as president of the FIGC. Guido Rossi was the person who stepped into Galliani's role and oversaw the investigation into the scandal. Rossi was a shareholder and former director of Inter. After the *calciopoli* scandal had been administered, Rossi resigned, and promptly became president of Telecom Italia, the company that initiated the wiretaps that precipitated the scandal. These conflicts of interest do not reinforce the legitimacy of the Federation and complicates its ability to regulate effectively.

*Calciopoli* did not precipitate a new dawn of regulatory practice. Although many participants, including Moggi, were found guilty of sporting fraud, some of the leading figures have re-entered important roles. Adriano Galliani remains as vice president of Milan and was elected as a vice president of Serie A in 2013. Franco Carraro remained a vice president of UEFA for three years after the scandal, and still remains a member of the IOC. Lack of decisive action over a scandal in a domestic competition did not preclude Carraro from participating in international federations. Fiorentina president Diego Della Valle and Claudio Lotito of Lazio were both banned from holding a sporting office for eight and four months respectively. Both have since resumed their former roles, with Lotito subsequently being elected onto the board of Serie A. No root-and-branch overhaul of the Federation took place.

Further match-fixing scandals emerged in the years after *calciopoli*. In 2008, a match between Livorno and Atalanta was investigated for match-fixing. Livorno's captain, David Balleri, was banned for four matches, while another three players of Livorno and one of Atalanta were fined. Atalanta was again involved when another larger *Calcioscommesse* or match-fixing scandal emerged three years later. The club was deducted six points, along with Atalanta's star player and former Azzurri member, Cristiano Doni, who was banned for three years for his part. The retired Beppe Signori was another former international star who was investigated and banned (Ceniti 2011). The investigative journalist Declan Hill (2008) has highlighted how match-fixers recruit former players because they have the trust and respect of administrators and current players. Personalized networks operate outside of the corridors of power and facilitate other corrupt practices in football. Twenty players and sixteen different clubs were penalized for their involvement in the 2011. The scandal was more shocking because of how it came to light. A member of the Cremonese team crashed his car and was discovered to have traces of sleeping pills in his blood. Earlier that day several of his teammates had collapsed during a Serie B match with Paganese. It transpired that Ceremonese's goalkeeper, Marco Paolini, had drugged his teammates in order to fix a match and pay off some gambling debts. Hill (2008) has also highlighted how players facing personal problems are recruited by match-fixers in order to exert some form of control. From the transcripts of the investigation, it transpired that Paolini was boasting of connections to star players in the hope of getting a higher payout. Social capital throughout the network was facilitating corrupt practices.

From the seeds of the Paolini investigation a wider match-fixing scandal took root. Evoking images of the *calciopoli* scandal before the 2006 World Cup, police dramatically searched the room of Azzurri squad member, Domenico Criscito, shortly before the 2012 European Championships. The Zenit St Petersburg defender was being investigated in another match-fixing scandal involving other leading players, including Stefano Mauri, the captain of Lazio, Juventus' manager Antonio Conte, and the president of Siena, Massimo Mezzoroma. The scandal centred on an alleged betting ring called 'the Gypsies' who were based in Eastern Europe. The scandal was high profile because Criscito was in the Azzurri squad for the 2012 European Championships. The defender had been photographed in May 2011 dining with a known Bosnian criminal, a leading player of Genoa, Giuseppe Sculli, and two other members of Genoa's *ultras* group. Criscito argued that 'I have nothing to do with this. I was only out for dinner with some Genoa fans' (Kington 2012). Not only does this illustrate the close connections between players and leading members of *ultras* groups; it also suggests that they are connected to organized crime.

Another branch of the 2012 match-fixing scandal took place in Bari. A parallel investigation was taking place in the southern port after the captain of Bari, Andrea Masiello, dramatically admitted that he had deliberately scored an own goal. Even more extraordinarily, this goal was in a local derby and it saved their local rivals, Lecce, from relegation. Rather than the leading *ultras* being upset that the club had lost to their local rivals, the investigation revealed that they had actually intimidated players to deliberately lose games. Three leaning *ultras* were investigated after two players revealed that the fans had approached members of the team to try and persuade them to lose so that the *ultras* could win money on bets. Although later chapters will illustrate how the *ultras* are incorporated into the patrimonial network, the examples of Genoa and Bari are illustrative of the strong legitimation of leading *ultras* from clubs and players.

## Summary

Italy has a long history of scandal and crisis. The state's crisis of legitimacy is similarly reflected in the football federation. This situation has become manifest in the distrust of referees who have become symbolic of the crisis. Patrimonial networks in business and politics meet in football and these networks are utilized to circumvent existing regulations. These networks of interdependency have intensified since the deregulation of the 1980s and power has concentrated around a small number of family and personal contacts. Despite social capital being generated, it is not contributing to a wider public benefit. *Calciopoli* demonstrated the bankruptcy of this system. Serie A now has a tarnished image that is impacting its ability to compete in the global marketplace. This is reflected in reduced attendances and interest in the game. The failure of the neo-patrimonial system is restricting Italian football's ability to implement the necessary changes. The following chapters will detail the matchday experience to illustrate that despite the political–economic transformations that have taken place in Italy, other wider transformations have not been undertaken by the clubs and authorities. The bankruptcy of the neo-patrimonial system is impeding Italy's ability to adjust to the new global order. Consequently, stadiums and policing have not been radically transformed to adjust to the transformations in global football, and these will be covered in the following two chapters.

# 5

# Stadiums

The match was being televised on the Friday evening so we had to board the coach at lunchtime to ensure we got to Piacenza in time for kick-off. Fans of all ages and genders congregated outside of the club's headquarters or popped into the cafe next door to purchase drinks and snacks for the long journey. Ten minutes after the appointed departure time, we boarded the coach and set off. Five minutes later, we stopped at the entrance to the autostrada. Another coach joined us, followed by two police cars. One of these cars pulled off onto the autostrada. The two coaches followed and the other police car took the rear. The police escort continued until we approached the city limits of Piacenza. After passing through the tollbooth, the two coaches were met by six police cars from Piacenza and ten motorcycles. This phalanx of police vehicles escorted us to the Stadio Leonardo Garilli and into the car park adjacent to the stadium. At this point we were allowed to disembark. The route to the stadium entrance was clear as it was flanked by two rows of approximately one hundred riot police. After being searched and having our tickets checked, we were allowed to take our places in the temporary away stand overlooking the pitch. After the long trip, many fans wished to purchase refreshments and approached the service trolley positioned behind the bars of the temporary stand. The sales assistants dispatched their wares from a supermarket trolley through the bars to the famished fans. Welcome to the stadium experience of an away fan of a club in Serie B.

The matchday experience represents a significant aspect of Italian football. The organization and administration of the stadiums and police are major contributing factors to the crisis in Italian football. As elsewhere in Italian football, the political and administrative bodies have not adjusted to the transformations in the global political economy. The continuance of existing patrimonial networks inhibits the opportunities for the game to reinvent itself and halt the decline. There has been little change in the policing of football matches or in stadium development and design. Consequently, Italian football has not embraced the changes that have taken place elsewhere, and this is impeding their ability to rectify the situation. Through analysis of the fans' experience, it will be shown how the failure of the organizing bodies to correctly identify and implement coherent strategies is affecting the fans, and ultimately harming the sport. This chapter will focus on the role of the stadium in the matchday experience. It will begin with an overview of stadium development within the wider political economy of the sport before addressing its development in Italy. Interviews with fans will be incorporated to illustrate the problems that have been encountered. This will be followed with a section illustrating the response from the authorities. The following chapter will contain a similar overview and analysis into the development of policing within Italian football.

## The political economy of football stadiums

The development of the football stadium reflects the political economic expansion of football. Despite the prevalence of Roman amphitheatres 2000 years ago, the current incarnation of the sports stadium is a modern phenomenon. Stadiums have evolved from public unregulated spaces into multifunctional entities. These changes reflect the global business of the sport. As football has developed into a multimillion dollar business with global appeal, the physical spaces have had to develop in line with these transformations. As Paramio et al. state (2008, p. 117), 'Modern and postmodern stadium developments need to be linked to both the socio-economic conditions of the capitalist mode of production as well as relevant sporting factors of every historical period.' It has been shown in previous chapters that political economic transformations during the 1980s contributed to a realignment of Italian television and politics. These have impacted the economic aspects of football and provided increased interest and revenues to clubs. Globally, these transformations have been replicated within stadium development. Stadiums have expanded their range of services in order to maximize income rather than focus principally on sports (Giulianotti 1999; Bale 1993a; Paramio et al. 2008). Italy, however, has not managed this transition well, and this is affecting the ability of football clubs to compete within Europe.

The football stadium reflects the privatization and commercialization of space. Before the codification of football, folk games were played in unregulated public spaces. Games took place in fields, churchyards and public squares. They were often confined by the existing natural boundaries, such as walls, ditches and buildings. Games of *Calcio Fiorentino* were played in the piazza in front of the church of Santa Croce in Florence. A 1555 painting by Jan van der Straet depicts the edge of the pitch being delineated by the crowds of spectators. Spatial regulation of this historic game emerged by the late seventeenth century. Pietro di Lorenzo Bini's 1688 print depicts railings around the Piazza Santa Croce. This highlights the increased social regulation to maintain the square free of traffic, rather than the regulation of an annual football tournament. Nevertheless, these games were still played in public spaces, accessible to all. The development of industrial cities saw the increased subdivision and regulation of space. As modern codified football evolved, the physical space for playing the game became privatized, regulated and commodified which assisted in the creation of football stadiums. The link between the wider political economy and sport converged as grounds were built near large industrial areas with easy access to the emergent railway infrastructure to encourage an active support.

Modern stadiums were functional and focused on the core aspect of the club: football matches. The distinct architectural periods of modern football stadium have been identified: from the late nineteenth century until 1920; 1920–40; and 1940–90 (Bale 1993b; Paramio et al. 2008). New forms of postmodern stadium appear after 1990 and coincide with the globalization of sport. Functional modern football stadiums began to emerge during the early period of football. During the interwar period, modern construction materials, such as steel and concrete, were used to increase the matchday capacity and enhance the comfort for the increasing numbers of fans. After the Second World War, clubs began to incorporate architectural features to maximize comfort and enjoyment. Floodlights were introduced to allow for regular midweek games and thereby increase the revenue from the additional games. Covered terraces and additional tiers were constructed so that fans were protected from the elements and capacity was maximized. Most importantly, these maximized the revenue for individual clubs. Lately, corporate boxes were integrated into stadiums during the 1960s in a bid to increase matchday revenue. Modern stadiums also incorporated increased social control. Not only was the space delineated to clarify and commodify the space matches, but it also demarcated class lines and provided clear social divisions. Ticket prices were valued according to facilities and comfort while barriers and fencing were added to physically demarcate the divisions and prevent antisocial behaviour, such as pitch invasions and hooligan fighting.

The Hillsborough tragedy proved to be provided the nadir for modern stadiums in Britain. After the tragic deaths of ninety-six Liverpool fans, Lord Justice Taylor published a report in 1990 recommending a number of changes to the football stadiums. As Bale (1993a, p. 181) suggests:

In British football, 1990 might be flagged as the beginning of the postmodern stadium when the metal fences surrounding many grounds were taken down and scrapped.

The Hillsborough tragedy highlighted the antiquated and dangerous stadiums in Britain that were incoherently policed. Lord Justice Taylor reviewed the state of football in Britain and recommended opportunities for resolution. The report recommended that all grounds should be converted to all-seater to provide more control and safety:

> Put together with progress towards all-seating, improved accommodation, better facilities, improved arrangements for crowd control, and better training of police and stewards, I believe these measures would give the best chance of eliminating or minimising football hooliganism. (Taylor 1990, p. 75)

A number of these recommendations combined to transform the British stadiums. All-seater stadiums have led to numbered seating for all ticket holders allowing cameras, police and stewards to identify and remove troublemakers. Aside from increased restrictions on fans (as detailed later), stadiums became increasingly comfortable spaces that could be enjoyed by all the family. This contributed to increased attendances and opportunities for market exploitation.

Stadium redevelopments no longer rely on the product of football to generate revenue. In keeping with the growing commercialization of the sport, superstores and outlets in the concourses have been incorporated into the stadiums, allowing the club to sell a variety of merchandise. The stores are open throughout the week and are not limited to fans' matchday consumption. Food and drink facilities are also incorporated into the new stadiums. Rather than buying these commodities outside of the ground, fans consume these within the ground, therefore providing a source of revenue for the club. Many stadiums have incorporated restaurants and hotels into their facilities that operate throughout the week. Clubs and stadium owners also rent out the corporate spaces within the stadium for meetings, exhibitions and conferences. All of these generate income and positive emotions towards a football club as the club markets established themselves both as a corporate venue for engagements and as a space for matchday hospitality. As a consequence, the postmodern stadium is synonymous with corporate commodification.

Stadiums have become tourist spaces where 'post-tourists' consume a range of experiences (Urry 1990; Urry 2002). Some clubs have added a museum to symbolize their status within world football. Barcelona and Manchester United are notable in this case and have also added stadium tours to their portfolio of facilities and services. Restaurants have also been incorporated so that unique experiences can be sold to fans for occasions like landmark birthdays and include tours, tickets and meals. Postmodern stadiums also use their facilities for other unique experiences that are not restricted to that of the football club. Often international matches or local tournaments are hosted. As the stadium is a facility that can host large numbers of visitors, this permits the stadium to host alternative large-scale events. For example, Wembley stadium has hosted Rugby Union, Rugby League and American football matches in addition to hosting England's national tournaments and international football matches. It also allows for various spectacular events to take place, such as car racing at the 'Race of Champions'. The 2015 Rugby World Cup, hosted by England, scheduled many matches to be played in football stadiums so that they could attract larger attendances. Similarly, Fiorentina's Stadio Artemo Franchi and the Stadio Olimpico in Rome have hosted Italian rugby matches as the sport has grown in popularity. Music events have also become popular features of new stadiums. International music stars invariably incorporate large stadium events into their touring schedule. As a result, stadiums have become self-contained service economies where consumers and fans purchase an increasing range of commodities and experiences. In the case of the Amsterdam ArenA, they have even generated their own currency for use within the stadium outlets.

Innovative design and architectural elegance in postmodern stadiums mark a distinct difference from the modern stadium with their functional approach. In addition to the incorporation of architectural features, such as shops, museums and corporate boxes, postmodern features are becoming architectural events. These redevelopments and renovations initially challenged fans' emotional attachments. Modern stadiums generated positive emotions or *topophilia*, among fans who ascribed a symbolic value to the stadium (Bale 1990). The personal attachment and the atmosphere generated by the collective solidarity of the crowd fuelled the construction of emotional ties to their physical environment. New symbols are being created as stadiums become markers of high architecture. As stadiums become designed by eminent architects, such as Wembley, designed by Sir Norman Foster, and the Michel Macary-designed Stade de France, stadiums are attracting renewed interests from fans (Horne 2011). These transformations now symbolize a club's standing among its peers; these stadiums become physical manifestations of the club's status. As King (2003, p. 130) argues 'The international standing of clubs like Real Madrid and Barcelona are physically demonstrated by the Bernabeu and Nou Camp stadiums.'

Working-class fans who resented the commercialization of Manchester United still took pride in the fact that Manchester United was one of the best run clubs, and that Old Trafford was the best stadium in England, especially in comparison to their rivals, Manchester City. New architectural status, allied with the shops, museums and tour facilities, is contributing to stadiums becoming symbolic spaces for fans and tourists alike.

Stadium redevelopment in Britain was facilitated by government support driven by the emotional tragedy of Hillsborough. As Piore and Sabel (1984) demonstrated, local government assistance facilitated the growth and expansion of small, family-owned businesses in the Emilian Model. Similar support from the British government assisted stadium redevelopment. Despite the free-market ethic of the Thatcherite government who implemented the Taylor Report, the stadium renovations could not be achieved through the free market alone. Most grounds in Britain were owned by the club and would not be able to afford the costs of renovation. As a result money from central government was provided through the Football Trust, the Football Grounds Improvement Trust and the use of money from the Football Pools. Taylor also recommended that cooperation could come from local councils or from private finance initiatives, such as supermarkets. Similar cooperation exists when countries, such as the Netherlands and Germany, host international tournaments and generate similarly powerful emotional foci for change. English football also benefitted from the initial injection of revenue generated by the formation of the Premier League. Clubs like Manchester United realized that they could incorporate the stadium into the overall package of football provided to fans.

## Italian stadiums: Mussolini, Italia '90 and beyond

Ironically, Italy provided an additional impetus for stadium redevelopment in England. The popularity and success of Italia '90 acted as a catalyst for the nascent Premier League as interest in football increased. It also demonstrated the inadequate and antiquated stadiums that were in use within Britain. As King notes (1998, pp. 103–4), Italia '90 not only 'demonstrated the inadequacy of English football grounds but also the potential market for football if it was properly organised'. Consequently, the newly renovated Italian stadiums were used as a benchmark against which English stadiums were measured. It is ironic that English stadiums were considered inferior to their Italian counterparts at that time, but now those same Italian stadiums are being criticized for their anachronism. However, it was the renovation for Italia '90 that meant that many Italian stadiums missed the reforms that arose out of the troubles of the previous decade. Giulianotti (1999, p. 77) held that Italian stadiums had 'all the architectural qualities of high modernism, in facilities, scale and shiny newness, but succumbed to the Fordist vices of soullessness and instrumentality'. For example, many of the stadiums constructed for Italia '90 failed to incorporate executive boxes into their structures.

Early success inhibited the opportunities for Italian football to capitalize on the economic transformation that was taking place in football. This has been compounded by the ownership structure of Italian stadiums. Most football stadiums in Italy are municipally owned and are located in multipurpose complexes that house a variety of sports, many of which date to the fascist period. The area around the Stadio Armando Picchi in Livorno houses a horse-racing track, basketball courts, football pitches and athletics tracks. Similarly, the Stadio Olimpico in Rome is housed in the Foro Italico complex built by Mussolini to host the Olympics. This complex also includes an international swimming pool and a tennis stadium that hosts the Rome Masters international tennis tournament.

As they are communally owned, stadiums are designed for the benefit of the wider community rather than the football club itself. The Stadio San Nicola in Bari is an apposite example of a stadium that is encumbered by its communal status. It was constructed for Italia '90 and the spectators' viewpoint is poor, despite its architectural aesthetics.[1] Many communal stadiums, like the Stadio San Nicola, have running tracks encircling the pitch which places the fans some distance from the pitch. Furthermore, as these stadiums are communal, the clubs take little interest in enhancements or security issues. This can create conflict between clubs and presidents. In April 2012, the owner of Cagliari, Massimo Cellino, decided to play the Sardinian club's home match in Trieste, 300 miles away on the Slovenian border. Cellino was in dispute over the upkeep of the Sant'Elia stadium that had two sides closed for safety reasons. Although Cellino funded his own redevelopment, he circumvented safety laws by allegedly bribing council officials (Masu 2013). Personal contacts and corruption undermined any health and safety requirements.

Club owners do not welcome investing in facilities that they do not own, especially when many of the clubs are in dire financial shape. The vice president of Juventus, Roberto Bettega, highlighted the difficulty Italian clubs are placed in because they do not own the ground:

> If we want to invest, to put money in to the stadium, to make it better, to make it nicer, make it a meeting point for the supporters, you have to do it in a place you know is yours or is yours for the next thirty or forty years. Why invest money in a stadium now when you don't know whether you will be playing in it next year? (King 2003, p. 130)

Since this statement, Juventus has been the only club to tackle this issue. The financial pressure of *calciopoli* combined with the reduction in television revenue since 2010 has resulted in them being the only club to purchase land from the council and build their own stadium. The Juventus Stadium was opened in September 2011 and represents the first transition to a new postmodern stadium in Italy (Doidge 2011).

Wider resistance to stadium redevelopment is also apparent within the media. After Inter defeated Chelsea in a Champions League match in March 2010, *Il Giornale's* Tony Damascelli (2010) wrote:

> Some people will be happy for the UEFA ranking points, I prefer to be happy for the fact of having seen one of our teams win in London. However, what matters isn't owning your own stadium and having a multimillion turnover, what matters is not blowing a big match in the key moment.

For this journalist, winning games was more important than any of the off-field aspects of football. Despite this resistance, clubs in Italy are slowly beginning to see the wider business benefits from stadium investment. Alongside Juventus' new stadium, Roma, Fiorentina, Palermo and Atalanta have all commissioned plans for new postmodern stadiums incorporating new commercial features.

The transition to consumerism that has grown in wider society has not been utilized by Italian football clubs. The lack of investment in the stadium not only impinges on spectator comfort but also affects the ability of the clubs to maximize revenue. Although the San Siro has a shop for Milan and Inter, other clubs do not have stores at their 'homes'. Some clubs, like Roma, have stores within the city centre, but not at the stadium. Smaller clubs, like Livorno, sell official merchandise in designated outlets like the local shopping mall. During the 2008-9 season, the club signed a deal with a local sports shop to sell official Livorno products. However, they are constrained by regulated business practices that prevent them from selling non-clothing items, such as pens and key rings, as this would infringe on the market of stationers and newsagents in the city. This limits the range available, minimizes opportunities to increase revenue and reiterates that deregulated market practices are not uniform across the globe.

Stadium facilities in Serie B are indicative of the poor quality of the Italian infrastructure. Many are still playing in stadiums that were built by Mussolini. Of the clubs that have been promoted in recent years, stadium facilities have not substantially improved. Of the clubs competing in Serie B during 2008–9, the three clubs that were promoted had the better stadiums. As previously stated, the stadium of Bari was constructed for Italia '90 yet failed to incorporate new facilities.[2] Parma was one of the 'Seven Sisters', the seven biggest clubs in Italy during the 1990s. Despite this, the Stadio Ennio Tardini highlights the incomplete development of Italian football stadiums. Constructed in 1923, it has undergone a series of modernizations.[3] The main stand has now incorporated fourteen executive boxes, a shop and disabled facilities, but the terraces at the ends of the ground still have uncovered 'temporary' stands that are in need of extensive redevelopment. While Livorno's Stadio Armando Picchi does not have any temporary stands, the only modernization that has been undertaken occurred in 2005 when the club returned to Serie A and this coincided with the visit of the president of the republic, Carlo Azeglio Ciampi, who was born in Livorno. This led to the renovation of the main stand, including the dining room, VIP area and seating – not to the rest of the stadium that houses the majority of the fans.

The stadium infrastructure of other recently promoted clubs is similarly poor. The stadiums of Atalanta, Siena, Bologna, Palermo, and Empoli were all built in the 1920s and have had little renovation since. Torino's Stadio Olimpico was built under fascism to host the 1934 World Cup. It underwent a €30 million reconstruction for the 2006 Winter Olympics. Although this has improved some of the fan experience, it does not directly impact the operation of the club. The second phase of Italian stadium building occurred in the 1960s. The stadiums of Sampdoria, Genoa, Brescia, Lecce and Novara all fall into this category. And as has occurred with the fascist-built stadiums, they have not seen significant renovation since. Verona's Stadio Marcantonio Bentagodi is indicative of the second wave of Italian stadiums that were built after the war. The Bentagodi was built in 1963 and was considered a state-of-the-art stadium fifty years ago. Despite both Hellas Verona and Chievo Verona playing there, significant modernization has not occurred since Italia '90. It is indicative of the poverty of Italian stadiums that of these stadiums, the ones of Verona, Bologna, Sampdoria and Genoa were refurbished for Italia '90, a quarter of a century ago.

In contrast to these larger clubs, many stadiums in Italy are comprised of poor-quality communal stadiums. As mentioned in the opening paragraph of this chapter, Piacenza's Stadio Leonardo Garilli is a typical Serie B stadium. The away support was housed in 'temporary' stands made of scaffolding. These were distant from the action on the pitch and the visibility was poor. There was no seating, only the metal steps of the temporary stand. The need for economic improvements was exemplified at half-time. Like many stadiums, the facilities are housed under the stands. These stands are subdivided into sections partitioned by steel fences with each section being able to be opened up dependent upon the away support. The refreshments were housed in a shopping trolley on the other side of the steel partition. The two vendors sold their items through the bars of the fence. Similar redevelopment was required for the toilets, which were unisex and in need of complete renovation. Piacenza was not unique. A similar structure existed in Grosseto at the Stadio Olimpico Carlo Zecchini. The temporary metal stands comprising of metal steps were ill-prepared for 3,000 Livorno fans attending for a Tuscan derby in February 2009. The catering facilities were more civilized than at Piacenza, where an attendant served snacks from a small kiosk. However, fans were unable to locate the toilets, and this made a large number of male fans utilize the back of the stands. The two unisex toilets were, in fact, housed in a section close to the home support, but which were ill-equipped to cope the huge number of away support. Ultimately this does not create an inclusive atmosphere for *all* fans; young and old, female and male. These facilities are not restricted to the stadiums of provincial clubs in Serie B. Similar problems of poor visibility and shade, and inadequate toilet and catering facilities, also exist at the stadiums of larger Serie A clubs; notably at Fiorentina's Stadio Artemi Franchi, Napoli's San Paolo and the Stadio Olimpico in Rome, home of Lazio and Roma.

The communal nature of Italian stadiums is clearly reductive. At the current time, no one is considering the experience of fans (with the exception of Juventus). By permitting the clubs to own their own ground, they will be inclined to consider the experiences of their fans. If the clubs can invest in the facilities then they can begin to capitalize on these investments and begin to compete with other leagues. They can also attract a wider range of fans, rather than the predominantly masculine fans that frequent the stadium nowadays. However, this has to come with clear regulation and safeguards. In certain situations in Britain, such as Plymouth Argyle, football grounds have been used as collateral to place significant debt onto football clubs, thereby threatening their survival. Similarly, the Goldstone Ground of Brighton and Hove Albion was sold to a development company, forcing the team to play in Gillingham, over seventy miles away. This situation has occurred with Cagliari. The club's owner, Massimo Cellino forced the team to play in Trieste after he did not get his way over a stadium redevelopment (that he was subsequently indicted for).

Juventus could lead the way for stadium redevelopment. In 2003, the club purchased the Stadio Delle Alpi from the council. Despite the fact that this stadium had been renovated for Italia '90, Juventus understood that it was not suitable for the club to compete in the twenty-first century. Even though 'old lady' of Juventus is the most successful club in Italy, their average attendance was under 20,000, one-third of the capacity of the Delle Alpi. The Juventus Stadium was built at a cost of €100 million and officially opened in September 2011 with an exhibition match against Notts County, the oldest professional football club in the world, and the club that Juventus took its club colours from. Not only was much of building resources of the Juventus Stadium reclaimed from the Delle Alpi but also the construction sought to make it one of the most environment-friendly stadiums in the world. Significantly, the architectural design built the stands closer to the pitch to provide better visibility for fans and improve the atmosphere. It has also copied other European clubs by incorporating a club museum, commercial space and hospitality suites (Doidge 2011).

Unfortunately, most clubs in Italy do not have the financial and political might of Juventus. Potential investment for new stadiums could come from local government. As the Italian state is significantly decentralized, local authorities could support clubs. This, however, leads to the impact on the local taxpayers. In an American context, Schimmel (2006) has argued that public investment in stadiums for sports' franchises and mega events operate as a form of irrational gambling and do not always provide value-for-money for the public. Elsewhere, Schimmel (2001) has highlighted how urban elites use sport to promote their own interests in the name of regeneration. In the contemporary Italian context, neither the football clubs nor the municipal authorities are compelled to invest in the stadiums. Italian cities have not yet become what Harvey (1989) terms 'entrepreneurial cities'. Elsewhere, Boycoff (2013) has argued that global mega events like the Olympics reflect 'celebration capitalism' where public money bears all the risk, while private corporations enjoy the profits. As shown in previous chapters, the development of deregulated neo-liberalism has taken a distinctive approach in Italy. Local and national elites are not utilizing public money to promote wider regeneration projects by utilizing football stadiums, as they are in the United States. Curiously, power and patronage have not incorporated architecture into the patrimonial network of football. Unlike the patrons of the past who commissioned churches or public buildings, contemporary patrons are not seeking redemption through football stadiums.

The Taylor Report in England reiterated the need for public financial support for stadium redevelopment. More importantly, without statutory regulation enforcing clubs to provide adequate facilities, club presidents seek to remain successful on the pitch. Club presidents will focus their attention on the playing staff until required by the state or federation to upgrade stadiums. There is an immediacy to contemporary football patronage. Presidents are not investing in the long-term viability of the clubs, nor seeking immortality through physical architecture. Short-term success on the pitch is the prime focus as presidents seek approval from fans. Failure to invest in the playing staff, and its effect on the performance of the football team, would see a president face extreme pressure from vocal fan groups, such as the *ultras*. Consequently, investment in a stadium is not seen as imperative.

Until stadiums are systematically redeveloped, the matchday experience for fans is poor. Even basic protection from the elements does not exist for many fans. Northern Italy especially, encounters the full spectrum of weather, from freezing temperatures and snow in the winter to dry, hot summers. This can make for an extremely unpleasant experience, as the following comment illustrates:

> For the stadiums, in my opinion, they should make the stadiums a little more covered, like in England. In Italy they make it disgusting for us. If it rains, we get soaked, if it is windy, we get blown by the wind. This is the minimum. (Paolo, official Livorno supporters' club director, personal interview, June 2009)

The location of Livorno's Stadio Armando Picchi near the sea means that it feels the full effect of extreme weather, as Paolo states. This makes for an extremely unpleasant matchday experience for fans. The opposite also occurs in the extreme heat in the interior of the country. The lack of roofs at the Artemo Franchi in Florence, for example, exposes fans to extreme sunshine. Stadiums have not adapted to their environments and only four Italian stadiums are fully covered. With poor toilet facilities and inadequate catering facilities, the matchday experience for fans is not always pleasant.

It is illustrative of the Italian stadiums, that only four of them are fully covered. In addition to the new Juventus Stadium in Turin, the San Siro in Milan and the Stadio Olimpico in Rome, the Stadio Comunale Luigi Ferraris in Genoa is fully contained. Along with the Juventus Stadium, it is one of the few Italian stadiums which could be classed as postmodern in Italy. It is the home of Sampdoria and the oldest club in Italy, Genoa. After redevelopment for Italia '90, it incorporates an architectural style with user-friendly facilities. Although many redevelopments of postmodern stadiums in North America and Northern Europe have seen stadiums constructed outside the city, the Marassi, as it is known locally, is located in the heart of the city. In a clear indication of a post-Fordist approach, the city council decided to sell the stadium. However, the council did not sell it to either of the clubs. Instead it sold the Marassi to a third-party business consortium who will seek to capitalize on their investment. Although the introduction of new business practices are seeing the council release their interest in the facilities, none of the clubs are likely to be able to increase their own revenues, as the additional events that could be located at the stadium, such as conferences and music events will profit the individual business owners, rather than the clubs themselves. Similar problems occur with communal stadiums, especially at Roma and Lazio, Hellas and Chievo Verona, and Inter and Milan. The problem for shared ownership is that no club benefits financially.

Revenue from television has contributed to the lack of stadium development in Italy. In contrast to the economic stimulus provided to the English Premier League from Sky, which was utilized for stadium redevelopment, television money is underpinning the Italian clubs' finances. This is impinging on their ability to capitalize on their matchday revenues. One respondent highlights how the clubs are completely over-reliant on television revenues:

> The clubs are totally dependent on television. They do not have commercial aspects. They do not own the stadium and there are no merchandising outlets. They do not invest in the stadium and depend exclusively on television. The system is for television royalties only. Therefore the system is very weak ... [We need] less money from television and young people to return to the stadium. [We need] stadiums in an English style ... to be a fan is more comfortable, more customer focused, and above all, the type of police are more civil. It is a civil country. (Levriero, official Livorno supporters' club member, personal interview, June 2009)

The patrimonial nature of Italian business and politics permitted the complete deregulation of television rules. Football clubs became over-reliant on television money. This precluded the development of other revenue streams and help shield clubs from other structural problems in the game. As already stated, the club presidents do not feel the need to invest in their stadiums when they do not own them. They also do not have to invest in them when they are competing in the national league as television money allows them to compete with their peers. Television also necessitates the requirements for fans at the stadium. The choreographies in the stadium generate an additional atmosphere for the fans watching football on television at home. In keeping with this notion, Silvio Berlusconi has suggested that in the future, football spectators will be allowed free access in order to generate the collective atmosphere required to enhance the television audience at home. Despite the improvement in the social capital, the Italian patrimonial system is not generating the collective will required to transform the stadium experience for fans and that could enhance the television event for viewers at home.

In light of the prestige accorded to football, the governmental approach to stadium safety is unplanned and haphazard. There seems to be no overriding principal driving change within the Italian context. Part of the drive for change in England came through the Taylor Report. This formed the legislative framework to facilitate improvements. More importantly, the government was willing to enforce the rules. Money for safety improvements came from the Football Pools and government incentives. Allied to this, commercial pressures in England led clubs to invest in their own stadiums as they sought to maximize revenue from all avenues. As King notes:

> the Taylor report, despite its own intentions, did little more than provide judicial legitimacy to the free-market arguments which proposed the easiest line of reform for football in the light of the organic development of the sport, on the one hand, and the transformations of British society, on the other. (King 1998, p. 106)

The post-Fordist approach from government, allied with the desire to impose the rule of law saw the legal and economic support to these transformations.

In recognition of the necessity for new stadiums in Italy, the president of Livorno, Aldo Spinelli, has suggested one proposal. Few clubs have the resources or access to private capital that Juventus had. He proposes that the state should provide tax relief to the clubs to allow the reconstruction of new stadiums:

> The Italian State received 100% of the taxes that we pay, I believe it is right that for 2 or 3 years they reduce the levy in a way that the club, together with the councils and the government, can make new stadiums. (Liguori 2010)

Clearly, Spinelli is openly absolving club presidents from the responsibility for stadium improvement. He also does not take into account the *salva calcio* debtspreading laws that were implemented in 2003 which effectively acted as state aid to the clubs (as discussed in the previous chapter). Yet, Spinelli is also highlighting the need for state involvement and sees the development of stadiums as a cooperation between the central state, the council and the club. Stadium renovations in England could not have been achieved through the free market alone. Similarly, Spinelli is proposing an opportunity to inject public funds into the stadiums and launch the transformations within Italy. However, without clear management of the funding, it is unclear how stadium renovations would be managed in compliance with safety regulations. Assurances would have to be made that the funds are used only for stadium development and not to be appropriated for players or for other functions of the clubs. Furthermore, there needs to be a clear and unequivocal legal document with the appropriate sanctions to drive through this change. The Football Trust and Football Licensing Authority implemented new regulations governing safety in England (Hamil et al. 2010). These were supported by the government enforcing the Taylor Report. The problem in Italy, as Francesio (2008, p. 88) states, is 'money and will'. Many of the rules are in place, but no one enforces them. New regulatory frameworks are required and need to be supported politically.

There is an acknowledgement from the football authorities that Italy's stadiums need to be renovated or rebuilt. The FIGC submitted bids to host the 2012 and 2016 European Championships for this reason. Both of these bids failed, however, due to the ongoing economic, corruption and hooliganism problems in Italy. Like Italia '90, these tournaments were predicted to act as a catalyst for stadium rejuvenation. However, the patrimonial nature of Italian politics has accumulated the power within a small number of elite clubs. Therefore stadium regeneration would only benefit certain clubs who hosted the tournament, and these would be the elite clubs. This is illustrated by the two exceptions to the communally owned stadium in Italy. As its names suggests, the Stadio Olimpico in Rome is owned by the Italian Olympic Committee, CONI. Two of the biggest clubs in Italy (Roma and Lazio) have a better stadium because the Italian public pays for their facilities. As a publicly funded body, CONI's support for the Stadio Olimpico ensures that the taxpayer is subsidizing some of the biggest clubs in Italy. The equivalent does not occur for clubs like Siena, Brescia or Livorno whose grounds are paid for by the communes only. The patrimonial connections within Italian politics, business and sport permit the state subsidence of elite clubs to the detriment of smaller provincial clubs like Livorno.

The lack of stadium development is also contributing to the economic crisis in Italian football. Stadiums are not generating the additional revenue required to allow Italian clubs to compete financially in Europe. Reliance on patrimonial networks circumvents the need to make profound changes to the infrastructure and allow Italian football to move forward. This point was clearly made by Marco Mazzocchi, a former football analyst on *Il Processo*:

> The stadiums are old, the tickets cost a lot and so the fans arrive and they are already angry. The fans feel that the soccer world doesn't respect them and we are hearing these days the same phrases from officials that we have heard in the past. If they don't do something now, Italian soccer will die. (Kiefer 2007a)

Unsafe stadiums and poor facilities are contributing to fan apathy and declining attendances. This has been exacerbated by the government that has attempted to impose increased regulations, called the Pisanu Law, on those attending matches, rather than focus on stadium redevelopment and safety. The following section will describe the impact of the Pisanu Law that was implemented after the death of Filippo Raciti in Catania and its impact on Italian football.

## The Pisanu Law: An Italian Taylor Report or criminalization of fans?

The deregulation of the nation state and the football authorities has magnified the financial crises within Italian football. It permitted the increased control and manipulation of the situation by the elite clubs. Despite the carnivalesque image of Italian football fans, there have been increased controls over individual fans as extensive regulations have been introduced to control disorder at football matches. Mirroring other aspects of neo-liberal society, as the state decreases regulation of corporations, it has increased regulation on the individual. Foucault (1991b) has argued that 'the art of government' has slowly changed since the eighteenth century. Rather than sovereigns exercising power over specific subjects within a territory, 'government has at its purpose not the act of government itself, but the welfare of the population, the improvement of its condition, the increase in its wealth, longevity, health etc.' (Foucault 1991b, p. 100). Foucault's theory of governmentality observes how the state, through legal, bureaucratic, and economic means, exerts power over the individual and forces them to change their behaviour. The centralization of power helped create 'docile bodies' (Foucault 1991a) as individuals would be aware that they could be being watched at times, and thus moderate their behaviour accordingly. Despite this centralization of power, however, it also dispersed power across the network as it created 'a multiplicity of points of resistance' (Foucault 1990, pp. 95–6). This aspect will be dealt with in the following chapter on the police.

Aligned to the approach of the police, the government have passed a number of measures to try and combat the problem of violence at football matches.

An early attempt at controlling fan behaviour occurred in 1989 when police authorities were given the authority to serve a Daspo[4] (*Diffida ad Assistere alle Manifestazioni Sportive* or prohibition to attend sport events) on fans causing trouble. Those holding a Daspo have to sign a register at the time of the game at the local police station, thus ensuring that they are not in attendance at the stadium. Legislation related to Daspos have been amended regularly since. There are two fundamental criticisms of Daspos: the type of legislation and the power of the police. Testa (2013) highlights that Daspos have been introduced by *Decreto Legge* (Decree Laws). These are emergency decrees permitted under the Italian Constitution for acts of urgency. Consequently, they are not fully debated in parliament. It was a Decree Law that Bettino Craxi used to deregulate television and permit Berlusconi to cement his media empire. Testa (2013) highlights how these Decree Laws have become the norm during Berlusconi's tenure as prime minister. The consequence is that laws require constant moderation. As the lawyer Lorenzo Contucci highlights, these laws need to be debated and thought through:

> In Italy when there is *confusione* you know, when there is an accident in the stadium, after two or three days you have a new law. It is an emotional law and sometimes it is not fair and it is not correct. In Italy the Daspo it is done directly by the police and there is no control over it. While in England there is a proposal I think, by the police, and then there is the judge that gives the banning order. (Lorenzo Contucci, AS Roma and lawyer, personal interview, January 2014)

Contucci's comments also highlight the other issue with Daspos; the police implement them. Unlike England, where the judiciary uphold or dismiss football banning orders, Italian magistrates do not have the same power. Problems have arisen when these measures appear to be misused or badly enforced. Daspos have been issued for having keys, flagpoles and mobile telephones as these could constitute weapons (Marchi 2005). Five Pisa fans received Daspos for taking toilet rolls to a match. The reason given for issuing Daspos to them was that they were holding 'inflammable' materials (Lo Bianco and Messina 2008). The notoriously slow judicial process in Italy also has the effect of penalizing fans. As it takes so long to appeal against police's decision, fans having to comply with a Daspo are restricted from attending matches (Testa 2013). As Contucci suggests, the police should recommend the imposition of a Daspo to the court before they are enforced.

The death of Filippo Raciti, a policeman, during fan violence securely focused the attention of fans, the media and the government. The Pisanu Law was an attempt to rectify the violence in Italian football through increased regulation. Unsurprisingly, it was also a Decree Law, and was not adequately debated in parliament. The law was named after Giuseppe Pisanu, the Interior Minister from 2002 to 2006 who drafted the original legislation. Pisanu was also implicated in the *calciopoli* scandal, as the minister who wanted assistance for his local team, Sassari Torres del Viminale, as well as consulting with Luciano Moggi when Pope John Paul II died. The Pisanu Law illustrates the lack of enforcement within Italian football. The law was enacted in 2005 but was only enforced in 2007 after the death of Filippo Raciti in Catania. In addition, due to the heightened interest after the riots in Catania, a full-scale review of all stadiums was undertaken. This highlighted that only four stadiums were safe to hold matches (Roma, Palermo, Siena and Turin). Few questions were raised about this lack of safety and no provisions were made to fund the necessary improvements. There were rumours that that the Finanziaria (Italian Budget) in 2009 would provide special credit for clubs to renovate their stadiums. However, this was not implemented after the worldwide recession and increased austerity measures placed on Italy. Once again, global factors impacted on Italy's ability to change.

The Pisanu Law orders that if authorities deem there to be a potential problem with a fixture they can authorize the match to be played 'behind closed doors' or with certain restrictions. Every month the central authority, the *Osservatorio Nazionale sulle Manifestazioni Sportive*,[5] review the forthcoming list of fixtures. Those that they deem to cause a substantial risk to fans and the public are placed under additional restrictions. These measures intensified six months after the death of Raciti after thousands of ticketless Napoli fans descended on Rome for the opening game of the season in August 2007. Police permitted the fans to board the train at Napoli, even though they knew that many did not have tickets. En route, some fans released firecrackers and smoke bombs, as well as vandalizing the trains and injuring four members of the train's staff.[6] Problems continued on their way to the stadium, as transport buses were vandalized, as well as incidents taking place during the match. Napoli fans were banned from attending all away matches for the remainder of the season as the authorities began to clamp down.

The restrictions placed on fans provide a clear avenue of protest for fans. As Foucault (1990) argued, the centralization of power also provided more 'points of resistance'. For example, the *Ossevatorio* deemed that both games between Pisa and Livorno during the 2008-9 season were to be subjected to restrictions. The police blockaded every road and rail entry between the two cities to prevent movement of fans. This had the desired effect on disorder, but led to fan protests and banners being attached to prominent buildings in Livorno stating that 'without fans and colour, this is a derby of repression'. As the Daspos have demonstrated, inconsistent prognosis reinforces an anti-authority narrative of fans. In May 2010, the match between Livorno and Lazio was permitted to go ahead with fans.[7] This was in spite of the fact that there is a history of conflict between Lazio and Livorno due to their political identities. Livorno has a strong left-wing identity, whereas Lazio fans are noted for their right-wing politics. In contrast to this declaration was a decree from 17 March 2010 related to Livorno's local rivals, Pisa.[8] The Serie D (amateur league) game between Pisa and Chioggia Sottomarina had a ban imposed on away fans from Chioggia, a small fishing port south of Venice with 50,000 inhabitants. For some reason this match was deemed by the *Osservatorio* to be a greater risk than the match between Livorno and Lazio. Away fans from Chioggia were banned from travelling even though there is no history of disorder between the fans and only a small number of fans would have attended. Despite some of the more forceful attempts to prevent away fans from travelling, lack of enforcement means that fans still circumvent the restrictions. A decree by the *Osservatorio* was passed for the Livorno game against Napoli in January 2010.[9] Restrictions were placed on ticket sales to Napoli fans and away fans were banned. Despite these restrictions, approximately one thousand Napoli fans attended the game. They obtained tickets from friends and family members in Livorno and congregated towards one section of the ground. Despite these restrictions, fans still circumvented them.

The most striking feature of this monthly review is the composition of the *Osservatorio* panel. It contains representatives from each of the police authorities (police, road police, train police, Carabinieri, specials, Guarda di Finanza), the football federation, CONI (the Italian Olympic Association), the League as well as interested businesses, such as Autogrills and the train company, Trenitalia. However, it does not contain any representatives from the provincial councils or any fan groups, such as FISSC. Not only does this illustrate the lack of political involvement of the fan groups but also it reinforces the patrimonial nature of Italian decision-making. A select network of interested parties dominates decision-making. Powerful groups can actively exclude others to maintain their hegemonic position. Furthermore, the reasons for the decisions taken are not explained and alternative assistance is not always put in place to deal with any potential breaches. For example, the game between Juventus against Inter in April 2009 was considered 'a risk' and that the committee 'is invited to value the opportunity of suggesting measures to make the contest with the participation of both the fans, but with restrictions on the sale of tickets'.[10] The suggested measures were not published and if any were implemented, they were unsuccessful. Mario Balotelli was still subjected to racist abuse by Juventus fans, while the Inter team bus was pelted with eggs and bottles. The result was that Juventus had to play their next home game without fans. This effectively criminalizes *all* fans regardless of their involvement. Similarly, in 2009, Livorno fans were banned from attending Frosinone because Frosinone fans had performed the fascist salute. This effectively penalized Livorno fans for the actions of Frosinone supporters. Unsurprisingly, this has not addressed some of the main issues and has further contributed to the narrative against central authority.

The Pisanu Law passed a further draconian measure that banned all articles that make the choreographies at matches. All items that are deemed to be offensive or could constitute a weapon could be banned from stadiums if the chief of police deemed it necessary. These items could include megaphones, banners and flags (except flags in the team colours). At a stroke, the government banned the one element that differentiated Italian football from other leagues. What will be seen in the subsequent chapters is that this has become a dominant narrative among a significant number of fans. As Francesio (2008, p. 197) observes, the rationale for this was that 'we [the Italians] must do the English model, and since in England they do not have banners, megaphones and drums, we ban banners, megaphones and drums and we have done the English model'. This syllogism does not solve the problem, especially as Filippo Raciti was not killed by any of the items, nor was he killed in the stadium. The weakness of the central authorities contributes to fan resentment. This is reinforced by regionalism; Italian regions and cities are granted autonomy over the designation of items. Certain banners and items can be allowed with the prior agreement of the club, police and relevant authorities. This can create a wide range of difference in the designation and implementation of these items as the following demonstrates:

> In Italy, for example we make an example of Livorno, it is prohibited to enter with microphones. It is prohibited to enter with drums. The things that make noise. In this case musical instruments are prohibited. It is prohibited because the *Osservatorio* have said. Last Saturday we were in Salerno. There at Salerno there were trumpets, loudhailers and also drums. (Max, official Livorno supporters' club director, personal interview, June 2009)

Livorno's *questore* have designated that flares and certain flags constitute a breach of the law. The southern Italian city of Salerno has a different outlook as they deem that trumpets, loudhailers and drums are within the law and can be taken to games. Elsewhere, in March 2013, a head steward at Verona ordered Livorno fans to remove a banner detailing the supporters' club, Club Luca Rondina. The head steward said that the banner was not on the authorized list, so should be removed, even though the banner was making no offensive or political statement and was taken to many different stadiums. The diverse approach to the designation of dangerous items causes resentment and delegitimizes the law.

Similar confusion occurs over the designation of political symbols. For Livorno fans, political symbols constitute a significant aspect of their identity. Under the Pisanu Law, these come under the jurisdiction of the *questore*, the local chief of police:

> The *questore* of Livorno says that 'this and that' cannot enter. According to him Che Guevara is a political symbol. Perhaps, I don't know. At Florence, it is not the same ... At Florence the *questore* decides that Che Guevara is not a political symbol and can enter. Because the laws in Italy make it this way. (Stefano, Livorno *ultras* member, personal interview, June 2009)

The autonomy of the regions creates opportunities to dispute the legitimacy of the central state. Only fascist political symbols are illegal in Italy, therefore it is not forbidden to display images of Che Guevara. However, within the jurisdiction of the Pisanu Law, the *questore* is permitted to prohibit these images if they feel that these constitute a breach of the regulations. Consequently these markers of Livornese identity are banned at certain away games and contributes to the overall incredulity of the fans.

The Pisanu Law does not take into account local football culture. This automatically brings them into conflict with fans and contributes to resistance from fans. Although the actions of the *questore* represent a significant infringement of local identity, the fans will continue to inflect other symbols with cultural meaning. In the case of the fans of Livorno, green military-style jackets and caps become inflected with greater significance and symbolizes left-wing politics. In the case of the fans with right-wing identities, the cultural inflection becomes more problematic, as one fan observed,

> Some fans in Italy, Lazio, Roma, Verona and many others, the tricolour is not shown for nationalistic pride, but is shown to signify that this is a *curva* of the right ... the origins are not political, however now it becomes associated as a political symbol. In Italy, a political symbol cannot go into the stadium. The hammer and sickle, the Celtic cross. So what happens, a right wing fan shows the tricolour, it is as if they were showing the Celtic cross. (Stefano, Livorno *ultras* member, personal interview, June 2009)

Fans with a right-wing identity have inflected the national flag as a symbol of the Right. The fans of Roma, Lazio and Verona have reframed the national flag as a marker of xenophobia and right-wing politics and this becomes difficult to legislate against. Yet this also contributes to fan resentment and apathy. During the match between Livorno and Lazio in May 2010, Lazio fans displayed several tricolour flags, including one prominent national flag, which stood over twice the height of the carrier, and was waved throughout the match. The pole required for this flag would undoubtedly fall within the remit of the Pisanu Law and could constitute a weapon. In spite of the contravention of the law, and the reputation of the Lazio fans, the flag was permitted in the stadium. The hypocrisy of this situation was not lost on the fans of Livorno. Many pointed to examples of fans being prohibited from taking large flags with poles and political flags into away grounds. For example, at Parma in December 2008, Livorno fans tried to enter with a range of flags. The longer flagpoles were deemed to be weapons and had to be returned to the coach. This led to a number of confused interactions between fans and stewards that eventually saw a senior fan instruct one fan to return the flag to the coach. The contrasting implementations at Livorno and Parma undermine fan confidence in the lawmaking authorities and amplify fan antipathy.

The operation of the *Osservatorio* reinforces the creation of more regulation on fans, despite the trend for deregulation elsewhere. In an attempt to regulate the display of banners, the *Osservatorio* created the *Albo nazionale degli striscioni* (National Register of banners). This highly bureaucratic approach attempts to legislate every type of banner that is allowed to enter the stadium. Contucci and Francesio (2013, p. 59) are highly critical of this approach:

> Instead of proposing effective solutions for the improvement of the situation of Italian stadiums, the *Osservatorio* has found its raison d' être is the high mission of imposing bureaucracy on one of the few places left 'free' in Italian society, with ridiculous initiatives such as *Albo nazionale degli striscioni* which is nothing more than an absurd and preposterous attempt to curb the spontaneity and the irreverence of the stadium. (Contucci and Francesio 2013, p. 59)

Not only is the *Albo* highly bureaucratic; it is seen as an attempt at control of fans. Once again, all football fans are regulated, except those who display offensive *striscioni*. Such a regulation is seen as an attack on the culture of fans.

The Pisanu Law also implemented regulation over the sales of tickets. These controls insist that fans must purchase a ticket from an official source, either an official supporters' club or an official ticket vendor. To obtain the ticket, identity must be provided. The ticket vendor enters the fan's details into a ticket database that verifies that the fan is entitled to attend the ground. Any fan with a Daspo is prohibited from attending the match. However, this does not preclude people without tickets causing trouble before or after the game, as had occurred when ticketless Napoli fans visited Rome in August 2007. In addition to taking identification to ticket vendors, fans must also take their identification to the ground. Overall, the process is laborious which makes it difficult for casual fans to attend the match. As all matches are televised, fans are incentivized to stay at home, as Matteo confirms:

> It's hard work to get tickets and more expensive than watching it on television. I can sit at home in comfort, with a beer, and not have to worry about travelling.
> (Matteo, Livorno fan, personal interview, March 2009)

Matteo reinforces the impact that full deregulation of television contracts has had on attendances. Furthermore he takes a holistic approach to match attendance. He identifies the time involved. It takes time to purchase a ticket and to travel to and from the stadium. He could spend more time with his family by remaining at home and watching the match on television.

As with the Daspos, the ticket controls are not effectively controlled. Two months after the death of Raciti, presenters on the satirical television programme *Le Iene* (The Hyenas) purchased tickets in the names of Benjamin Franklin, Karl Marx and Alessandro Volta.[11] The same programme highlighted that the presenter was able to enter the San Siro Stadium in Milan, to watch Inter, without documentation. These factors contribute to fan apathy and yet still inhibit the casual fans from attending matches. Criminalization of all fans is compounded through lack of enforcement that undermines and delegitimates the central authorities.

The regulations over ticket purchases necessitated additional security at the stadium. The Pisanu Law instructed all clubs to install fencing around the stadium with a series of checkpoints. Upon approaching the stadium, tickets are checked by stewards before entering the stadium confines. Thereafter, one enters the turnstiles and places the ticket into a barcode reader. Both processes together can slow down entry to the stadium, causing confusion and resentment. Such an incident occurred at Parma in December 2008 when the supporters' coach arrived late after being held up in the *settore ospiti*. With two minutes before kick-off, the queue awaiting ticket inspection by the two stewards was leading to a crush. There was increased anxiety and emotion among the fans who felt that they would miss the start of the game. Fortunately, the stewards sensed the changing mood and made cursory glances at the identification to facilitate a rapid entrance into the ground. Thus the stringent checks required were abandoned due to insufficient processes being in place to deal with the large numbers of football fans arriving at the same time. The rules were circumvented in the interests of expediency and undermined the rule of law.

A more insightful incident occurred prior to a game with Lazio at Livorno's Armando Picchi Stadium in May 2010. A group of over hundred Livorno *ultras* marched towards the gates of the Livorno *curva*, waving flags, chanting anti-fascist and anti-Lazio songs and performing in an image of unity and strength. As they approached the gates at the end, riot police mobilized and marched forward. The gates were opened to allow the *ultras* to enter so a public order incident did not occur. They marched directly into the stadium, continuing to chant and wave their flags. No tickets were displayed, so there were no identity checks performed. If *ultras* were a public order problem, the police and stewards at the ground permitted them entry without legal checks. Moreover, these situations could lead to significant health and safety issues as a number of fans get crushed. The lessons of Hillsborough have not been learnt. The fact that there has not been a tragedy like Hillsborough in Italy can be attributed to sheer luck and the decline in attendance, rather than to a systematic focus on the safety of fans.

The tragic death of Livorno's midfielder Piermario Morosini in 2012 highlighted the piecemeal approach to stadium regulation and safety. In the thirty-first minute of a Serie B match between Livorno and Pescara at the Stadio Adriatico in Pescara, Morosini collapsed and died on the pitch. Subsequent autopsies would confirm that he had suffered a heart attack from a pre-existing and undiagnosed condition. At the time, however, players and medical staff of both teams worked quickly to try and resuscitate Morosini. However, the ambulance was delayed access into the stadium because a car of the traffic police, the *vigili urbani*, was blocking the vehicular entrance to the stadium. Police had to break into the car in order to move it out of the way and allow the ambulance access. Without a coherent approach to regulations around the stadium, fans are still permitted access without checks and members of the state's authorities block access for medical vehicles. All of this threatens the safety of fans and players and does not enhance the matchday experience.

These security measures, just like the regulations over ticket purchases, also make it increasingly difficult for casual fans to attend matches at home. The ticket office, by law, has to be separate from the stadium; one cannot buy a ticket at the turnstile. An illustrative example of the difficulty in obtaining tickets occurred in January 2014. I wanted to purchase a ticket for the match between Roma and Genoa before I arrived in Rome. Unfortunately the AS Roma online ticket sales did not recognize British postcodes for credit card purchases, so the payment could not be authorized. I arrived at the stadium one hour before kick-off and asked some city police the directions to the ticket office. They replied that one could not buy tickets on a matchday. At this point, one of the officers interrupted his phone conversation and said that one could, but only for the *tribune* (sides of the stadium). He pointed me in the direction of the ticket office, about a mile away from the stadium. There were no signposts, and no indication that the building was a ticket office. As stated by the police officer, the only tickets available were in the *tribune* at a cost of €60. This entire process took an hour. The distance to the ticket office, the restrictions and the cost do not encourage more fans to attend.

At Livorno, there is a similar situation. The ticket booth is part of the sports complex adjacent to the Armando Picchi Stadium, about 200 metres from the stadium. Livorno's stadium, however, is located in a residential area with access from a number of residential streets. The erection of the steel fences prevents fans from accessing different areas around the ground without a ticket. Many of these steel fences block the various streets. Therefore, to go to the designated ticket office, one has to go around the residential streets, onto the main road and back around the other residential streets, as one fan states,

> There are the regulations at the stadium. At Livorno, perhaps there is the most classic example one can make. If you decide on Sunday or Saturday to go to the match and do not have a ticket you must then go practically five long kilometres: first to the only open ticket office and then you must return to the other side to the sector of the stadium for that ticket. Therefore [removing these] would be the simplest thing [to correct]. (Paolo, Livorno official supporters' club director, personal interview, June 2009)

With the imposition of barriers around the ground, someone who decides to go to the game on the day must walk further to buy a ticket before going to the stadium. As Matteo mentioned earlier, watching the match on television saves travelling time. This is in addition to the long journey required to buy a ticket. As the state struggles to impose its authority, it treats all fans as potential hooligans. This situation acts as a serious disincentive to casual fans. The result is that only the hard-core fans attends the stadium; consequently, the *ultras* see themselves as the authentic voice of the fans as they are still jumping through these bureaucratic hoops.

In an attempt to streamline ticket purchases, the *Osservatorio* has also implemented an identity card for fans, *la tessera del tifoso*. The card is supposed to make the purchase of tickets easier as the card will be the only form of identification required. In theory this should prevent away fans from purchasing home tickets, as was witnessed with Napoli fans in Livorno. Initially this card was going to be mandatory, but has since been made voluntary. There was widespread resistance from *ultras* and other fans to the introduction of the *tessera*. It provided an opportunity for *ultras* to unite in opposition against the state regardless of pre-existing rivalries (Guschwan 2013a). If the *tessera* were mandatory, it would further affect the casual fan, who may not have the *tessera*. It would also make it difficult for non-Italian citizens to purchase tickets to away matches, thus reducing potential revenue to clubs. The card also presupposes that consumers of football only watch one team, and will not watch another.

The ill-considered nature of the regulations ensures that there are continued problems. In some cases, when the *Osservatorio* deems some games to be 'at risk', they restrict ticket sales to fans in the region of the club, or ban ticket sales to fans from the region of the other club. This presumes that all fans live in geographical proximity to the football club. For example, the match between Bologna and Lecce on 6 November 2010 was deemed a risk and tickets were restricted to fans of the region Emilia-Romagna, where Bologna is located (Contucci and Francesio 2013). Clearly fans of Bologna only live in the immediate environs of the city. The following week, ticket sales for Juventus against Roma were restricted to people from the Lazio region, where Roma is located. Again, the authorities think that Roma fans only live around the city and not elsewhere. Even holders of the *tessera* are restricted. One Inter fan who lived in Rome, and held a *tessera* for Inter, was forbidden from buying a ticket for the Inter-Roma match because it was forbidden to sell tickets to residents of Lazio (Contucci and Francesio 2013). Even possessing a *tessera*, which, in theory, affirms that a fan has no prior criminal convictions or history of hooliganism, prevented this Inter fan from travelling to see their team. More bizarrely, this fan rang the Inter helpline where this restriction was not only confirmed but also suggested that as the fan lives in the Lazio region they should buy a ticket for the away end! Clearly these restrictions are not helping control potential violence.

The card does, however, provide marketing opportunities to access the loyal fan base. Once again, AC Milan has seized the initiative. They instigated the *Cuore Rossonero* card, which also operates as a Maestro card, and a loyalty card. It allows users to accumulate loyalty points. These can be redeemed against cheaper tickets, gifts or events with players, such as training or a meal.[12] Likewise, Livorno have implemented the *Triglia Card* (Mullet card, named after the fish mascot of the club, and one of the symbols of the city). Like AC Milan's card, the *Triglia Card* accumulates points that can be redeemed against gifts, and also acts as a MasterCard. Although these initiatives demonstrate an attempt to deal with the problems in Italian football, the lack of stadium renovation is a major discrepancy. Furthermore, the 'Q&As' related to the *Triglia Card* at Livorno are instructive of the wider distrust of authority which undermines effective regulation.[13] Alongside general questions related to its purchases and Daspos, there are two following questions:

1. Is it true that the card has a microchip that emits a radio signal indicating the physical location of the card owner?
2. Who stores the data of the Triglia Card?

The response states that the details are for the football club only, and that any details sent to the *questura* are only temporarily held to allow them to check for Daspos and 'crimes at the stadium'. Both of these questions reflect a distrust of the police and central authorities. Ultimately, the card has done very little to reverse this attitude. In fact, it has become counter-productive as fans are uniting against the authorities.

## Summary

Mussolini built many of Italy's stadiums. The second phase occurred in the 1960s. When some of these facilities were upgraded for Italia '90 they predated the transformation of stadiums that took place across Europe. Consequently, many stadiums are in a bad state and with even worse facilities. The matchday experience is poor. The Pisanu Law exacerbates this. The piecemeal and chaotic implementation of the Pisanu Law and the lack of full-scale investigation and implementation of adequate safety regulation contribute to fan malaise. The poor stadium infrastructure affects the clubs' ability to compete financially, from restricted revenue streams, but also because of poor comfort for fans. This is exacerbated by national regulation that does not address safety and actually inhibits matchday attendance.

The catalyst for the transformation of English stadiums was the Hillsborough tragedy where ninety-six fans were crushed to death. The lessons have not been learnt from this and the fact that a similar tragedy has not arisen in Italy is a miracle. The draconian response to football fans is actively working against the authorities. This is not helped by the suspicion of the police. Therefore the role of the forces of order is central in understanding the matchday experience and in accounting for the decline in participation in football. The following chapter will outline the development of the Italian police forces and highlight how this contributes to the poor matchday experience for fans. Ultimately, these factors also reinforce fan identity and do not minimize violence and antisocial behaviour in stadiums.

# 6

# Policing

The early summer sun ensured a relaxing morning on the beach. At the cafes on the seafront, hundreds of fans were enjoying a pre-match drink or lunch. Opposite the landmark bar called the Barrachina Rossa, the police were anticipating the arrival of Lazio fans to Livorno. Riot police stretched across the road that led to the entrance of the *settore ospiti* where the coaches of the away fans would be directed. Meanwhile, further along the road, young local male fans amassed behind the trees and bushes that divide the seafront from the road, in similar anticipation of the Lazio coaches. The buzz of excitement filled the air as a police motorcycle drove down the boulevard, quickly followed by four Lazio coaches flanked by police patrol cars. A flurry of activity ensued as bottles and objects were thrown at the coaches as they sped through to the away end. The youths melted back into the bushes and the patrons of the cafes continued with their drinks. The occasion marked a strange contrast to the exclusive villas that line the esplanade. The Stadio Armando Picchi is located in the fashionable Ardenza district in close proximity to the sea. Every matchday the residential roads are closed by police cordons to control access to the stadium. We walked the two miles around the cordons to the home end to guarantee good vantage points for the match. Approaching the turnstiles, a chant erupted and a group of *ultras* began marching towards the entrance, singing and waving a variety of flags. Anticipating a queue at the turnstiles, we quickly showed our tickets and identification and walked through to be confronted by a wall of riot police with their shields ready and batons wielded. They rushed towards the gates at the same time as the *ultras* descended on the entrance. The police stopped and the gates were opened. All of the *ultras* were admitted into the stadium. Stewards quickly beckoned us through the second turnstile as a similar situation occurred with the *ultras*. The gates were opened and they marched towards the home end, continuing to wave their flags and sing their songs.

None of them showed identification or a ticket. Matches are not just conflicts between groups of fans; the police also have a central role to play.

This book has addressed several key groups within Italian football. Initially it illustrated how the worlds of politics, business and football operate within dense patrimonial networks that are emptying out public involvement and facilitating the emergence of charismatic individuals. Subsequent chapters will show how the *ultras* and official supporters' club members operate within these patrimonial networks yet reflect the lack of involvement in political life. Significantly, there is another group operating within the Italian football network. The Italian forces of order are key factors in the execution of state policy and represent an important aspect of the patrimonial network. The police forces simultaneously reflect the Italian transition to deregulated business practices and illustrate the problems and contradictions of this approach. This chapter will highlight the historical development of the Italian police force to illustrate how they have reflected the unplanned organic growth of the nation and the failure of the central state to impose control. As key actors within the Italian patrimonial system, the police play an important role in the presentation and control of football fans, and this can affect the chances of violence. Changes to European policing will be also presented to illustrate the continuance of certain patterns of policing and their effect on the continuing crisis in Italian football.

## The Italian forces of order: Development and continuity

There are various divisions of the Italian police that combine under the term 'forces of order'. These divisions reflect the contested nature of the Italian state and lead to confusion and lack of cooperation. As we have seen, the Italian state comprises semi-autonomous regions, with enduring local histories and memories; these help to undermine the central state. Likewise, conflict between the FIGC, Lega Calcio, CONI and Covisoc has undermined the ability of the federations to regulate efficiently the finances and operations of Italian football clubs. These patterns are reflected in the development of the Italian police. Before unification, the House of Savoy instigated a two-tier approach to local security. The Corpo Arma dei Carabinieri Reali (Royal Carabinieri Corps) was based on the French Gendarmerie and was introduced to Savoy by King Vittore Emmanuelle I in 1814. With unification, the corps was institutionalized as the

'First Force' of the new nation and represented an armed corps for the state.[1] In 1852, the Corpo delle Guardie di Pubblica Sicurezza (Guardians of Public Safety Corps) were also introduced to Savoy. This created a dual model of Carabinieri and State Police that has continued from unification to the present day. Although there are further police divisions within Italy; these do not have direct jurisdiction over the policing of social order and have less impact on football.[2] In addition to the other forces of order, there is a section of the State Police with special responsibility for undercover surveillance. The Divisione Investigazioni Generali e Operazioni Speciali (Division of General Investigations and Special Operations), known by their acronym Digos, are charged with investigating serious offences such as terrorism and organized crime. Under this remit, the Digos also have to investigate football hooligans. They operate as non-uniformed police who infiltrate fan groups and record their patterns of behaviour in order to obtain positive identifications of known activists. As a result, this sees football hooligans being placed under the same umbrella as terrorists and the Mafia. This constitutes one area where the Italian police are following similar, pan-European, patterns of surveillance (Tsoukala 2009).

The dual nature of the Italian police reflects the failure of the state to gain control over individual interests. There are two conceptions in academic literature of the police: the state's police imposed from above; or the citizens' police from below (Della Porta 1998). In Italy, since the inception of the police, the forces of order have been seen as a function of governmental interests imposed from above. This has been amplified through the police having the absolute right to stop any Italian citizen for identification. As Barbagli and Sartori (2004, p. 167) state:

> The forces of order in fact have the power and duty of identification, which no citizen can avoid. They can stop any person and request an identifying document, and, in some cases, when some irregularity is noted or if there is something suspicious, they may escort the person to the commissariat or to the carabinieri station.

Despite the attempt by the state to impose control over its citizens through identification, the dual nature of the Italian police reflects its weakness. After unification, the two forces were granted distinct remits. The Carabinieri were granted control of the countryside while the State Police monitored the cities. This was semi-clarified in a law of 1919 which stated that the State Police would be responsible for:

police functions that [are] preventative, repressive, and related to maintaining public order in the larger population centres, leaving the supervision to maintaining public order of the remaining territory of the State to the Royal Carabinieri. (Barbagli and Sartori 2004, p. 163)

The irregular development of industrialization and urbanization, exacerbated by chaotic patterns of migration, contributed to the inconsistent growth and development of the two corps. Both ultimately depended heavily upon local factors and political involvement to grow and sustain their units. By the 1960s however, parity in numbers was achieved between the two corps.

The dual model prevented the creation of an independent, strong and centralized force. As a consequence the divided forces could be incorporated into the patrimonial system. Maintaining two parallel forces with similar responsibilities over public order has been inefficient and has led to confusion and lack of cooperation. It has contributed to Italy having the largest police force in Europe (Tavares and Thomas 2008). The two forces have frequently refused to cooperate. This occurred during the 'years of lead' in the 1970s, and ultimately failed to prevent the assassination of the Christian Democrat leader, Aldo Moro (Collin 1999). Attempts have been made to rectify this situation and develop cooperation between the two forces, principally with Law 121 of 1 April 1981. This law required that Provincial Committees for Security and Public Order be set up which contain the chiefs of the three main forces of order, as well as the mayor of the provincial capital and the president of the province. Orders made in these meetings, however, 'are at times "reinterpreted", if not actually ignored, by the carabinieri' (Barbagli and Sartori 2004, p. 177). The lack of enforcement of the forces of order ultimately leads to the lack of enforcement of order further along the network of crimes. Law 121 also proposed a joint operations centre; the first of which was opened in Milan in 2000, nineteen years after the law was passed. As of 2004, 74 of the 119 provinces did not have these joint operations rooms implemented, and none were functioning correctly.

The political nature of the Italian forces of order has seen them develop a significant position within the patrimonial networks of Italian politics. The forces of order help shape public opinion as they seek to protect their institutions and generate public goodwill:

Police have a notable discretionary power, not only to the complex level, but also that of the single politician. The forces of the police can be considered as policy makers, in the sense that they 'make' the politics. (Della Porta and Reiter 2003, cited in Ferreri 2008, p. 100)

The forces of order are conscious of public opinion and their public image. Consequently, they choose appropriate action that will give them the most public support and in turn this constructs an image of a force that operates appropriately. The 1960s saw a sharp increase in certain distinct forms of crime, specifically, public protest and crimes against property. This provided the police with an apposite opportunity to manage their public image. For example, the police would not use force against a group of pensioners protesting about the cost of living. Therefore, the selective use of violence presents an image to the media and general public that this particular group required violent action. As Juvenal prosaically stated 2,000 years ago, 'Quis custodiet ipsos custodies [who guards the guards]?'

## Football violence: Forward panic and Folk Devils

The problems associated with political unrest subsided after the 1970s. As will be demonstrated in the following chapter, incidents surrounding football matches increased. This has resulted in the policing of football matches being one of the largest exercises performed by the Italian police. Building on Cohen's seminal work, Marchi (2005) suggests that through selective use of force, the police help create 'Folk Devils' as well as the media. This becomes self-fulfilling. As the football fans are constructed as 'Folk Devils', the police feel increasingly justified in using force against them. Their discrimination in other fields reinforces this construction and magnifies the events surrounding football. Ferreri develops this argument by stating that the use of the Digos, the anti-Mafia and anti-terrorist force, to infiltrate the *ultras* transformed these fans into viable targets. 'With the Digos', Ferreri (2008, pp. 100–1) argues, 'the *ultras* ceased to be simply hooligans from the stadium and were transformed into a subversive phenomenon, that needed repression with force'. The Pisanu Law legitimated this political role of the police. In the previous chapter, it was highlighted that the *Osservatorio* designated certain matches 'at risk'. The forces of order are key members of this group and become clearly situated within the patrimonial network. Consequently, through a variety of measures, specific groups, and particularly football fans, have been targeted, and this helps account for a number of incidents related to football.

Violence at football is not inevitable, despite the political influence exerted by the forces of order. In his theory of violence, Collins (2008) suggests that violence is led by a small number of key proponents who are supported by the crowd. Violence is often ignited over flashpoints, which in turn, are caused by 'forward panic'. When parties are engaged in the emotional cauldron of physical confrontation, they have to maintain 'face' and preserve the advantage. This can erupt into violence as one party's emotions rise and they seek to capitalize on a perceived weakness of the opponent. The propensity for violence increases as the duration of the tension increases before a confrontation. This allows the emotion to build, and lengthens the period for this emotion to abate. Utilizing a Durkheimian perspective, Collins advocates that an increase in the crowd will build the emotional energy of the situation and fuel the emotional tension in the parties. A flashpoint will instigate violence as one of the parties utilizes this emotion to gain advantage. Collins (2008, p. 464) recommends that participants in these events need 'to reduce their confrontational tension'. This is especially true as the numbers of police increase: 'the more officers called to the scene, the greater the chance of a forward panic or other kinds of police violence, quite apart from what the suspect does' (Collins 2008, p. 464).

Rumours can spread in this emotional atmosphere and this can fuel the opportunity of miscommunication and violence. This occurred spectacularly during the 'Derby of the Dead Child' in 2003 (Marchi 2005). Rumours circulated that the police had killed a child. Police use of tear gas and batons led many to believe that this rumour could be true and ultimately increased the tension in the stadium. The build-up and stand-offs in these circumstances increase the opportunity for forward panic to occur and for one side to provide the flashpoint. The perception of the police is crucial to the initiation of violence (Della Porta 1998; Stott and Reicher 1998). If parties enter into a situation expecting violence then this increases the possibility of forward panic occurring and violence ensuing.

The active role of the police in manipulating political and public opinion has combined with the weakness of the central state. There is a history of aggressive policing in Italy which has facilitated the construction of narratives that reinforce the lack of legitimacy of the state. The G8 summit of 2001 became the zenith for aggressive Italian policing. The summit was held in Genoa and attracted a number of anti-globalization, anarchist and leftist demonstrators from around the world. Riots ensued, resulting in one protestor being shot dead, over 500 people injured and an estimated £30 million damage caused to property (Johnston 2001; Vidal 2001). Of the 200,000 demonstrators, many claim they were there to protest peacefully. However, chaos descended as the police took a hard-line with the demonstrators. The manner in which the protestor was killed highlighted the confusion of the police approach. *The Guardian* reported that 'Witness accounts of the fatality were conflicting, but it appeared last night that the young man had been shot and then run over by a police armoured vehicle' (MacAskill and Elliot 2001). This account was by no means unique as *The Telegraph* reported that armoured vehicles were used to plough into the dustbins that protestors hid behind. Thomas Harding, the reporter of *The Telegraph*, was attacked by the Carabinieri, as were other officially accredited reporters. Harding (2001) states: 'Anyone, lawbreaker or not, was fair game in the eye of the carabinieri, which showed itself to be as badly led and ill-disciplined as it was thuggish.' Indeed, the police action in Genoa was used as an example by the Scottish police, of what can go wrong when the police act aggressively (Macleod 2005).

The Italian police had demonstrated a clear sign of forward panic by attacking first to gain the advantage. This forward panic culminated in the raid on the headquarters of the protestors at the Diaz school. Accounts suggested that the police had employed right-wing activists to attack the protestors (Carroll 2007; Davies 2008; Carroll 2001; Ginsborg 2004; Jones 2007). Indeed, it was reported that the police sang fascist songs as they acted. These infiltrators and the police raided the school at night, while the protestors slept. Accounts suggest that people were kicked and beaten with batons while they slept. The police methodically went through the school beating all protestors in their way, regardless of their physical position. Fire extinguishers were fired in peoples' faces, while others were spat upon or had their heads thrust down toilets. Several women were threatened with rape and all ninety-three occupants of the school suffered serious injuries, some life threatening. Such tactics caused international outrage and strained relations with the Italian government.

## Football violence: Policing the *ultras*

The heavy police presence at football matches, like the G8, provides several potential flashpoints that could generate forward panic. As described in the introduction above, a potential flashpoint occurred before the match between Livorno and Lazio at the Stadium Armando Picchi in May 2010. A group of over hundred Livorno *ultras* marched towards the gates of their *curva*. As they approached the gates, armed riot police approached the gates from inside the ground in anticipation of an attempt to attack the gates. The *ultras* were marching, waving flags and chanting anti-fascist and anti-Lazio songs. They were not armed, throwing objects or performing any form of ritualized violence. In spite of this the riot police prepared themselves for violence and marched forward. No violence ensued, as the *ultras* were allowed into the stadium without having their tickets checked. This was an apposite example of how forward panic could escalate; the police were responding not to any specific acts of violence but to the (incorrect) perceived threat of the *ultras*. In this case the Livorno *ultras* were more focused on their hatred of Lazio and fascism than confronting the police. In other contexts it would be clear that the police could ignite the emotional tinderbox.

A further example of aggressive Italian policing surfaced in the media in May 2010. The Gugliotta affair highlighted the aggressive approach taken by certain sections of the Italian police (*Corriere della Sera* 2010; *La Repubblica* 2010a). Stefano Gugliotta lived in the vicinity of Rome's Stadio Olimpico. On the night of the Italian Cup final between Roma and Inter, Gugliotta was riding his scooter with his cousin in order to go to a party. He had not attended the match but was stopped by a policeman. The incident was filmed from the window of one of the neighbouring apartments. This video appears to show that the policeman held his arm outstretched onto Gugliotta's chest to prevent him riding off.[3] Gugliotta pushed the police officer's arm away and was subsequently punched in the face. Gugliotta's cousin was confronted by the same policeman and ran off, before a number of Italian police descended on Gugliotta. Gugliotta had a broken tooth and evidence of head injuries. The young Roman was arrested and alleged that 'When I was brought in jail I was asked to sign a sheet with an X already deleted, which states that I refused additional medical visits, but I opposed. Only after I was able to sign a sheet with boxes still empty.' (*La Repubblica* 2010a). The case demonstrates the forward panic of Italian police as they seek to use violence early, rather than as a last resort. They subsequently attempted to fabricate evidence to suggest that he had refused to seek medical advice. As they act as an independent, politically orientated body, some police attempt to manipulate their position.

Aggressive policing in Italy has not been restricted to Italian football fans. Fans of English clubs and the England national team have faced considerable difficulties from the Italian forces of order (Stott and Reicher 1998; Stott and Pearson 2007). The police's perception of England fans ensured that fans entering Sardinia for the 1990 World Cup were treated as hooligans as soon as they arrived; as many as a third of Italy's police force were there to meet them. Similarly, recent games involving English clubs in Rome have highlighted the continued perceived threat against English fans. Against Liverpool and Manchester United in 2001 and 2007, respectively, similar patterns emerged. Roma fans attacked both sets of fans as they approached the stadium; the police did not intervene. Inside the stadium riot police were stationed in the away end. There were no police in the home *curve*, only stewards. The Roma fans threw missiles over the barrier into the English fans, who subsequently threw them back. In the case of the Liverpool fans, they were attacked by the police for throwing these missiles back. The incident involving the Manchester United fans occurred after United scored and Roma fans surged towards the barrier. The United fans responded, whereupon the riot police charged down and began to baton charge indiscriminately into the United fans. It is clear from the actions of the Italian police in relation to English fans that they police the situations based on perception of the fan group. A video clip from Danish television highlights the treatment of young Danish Manchester United fans.[4] Although English fans had a reputation for trouble and disorder that has subsequently subsided (although not disappeared). The globalization of football, and English football in particular, now sees many clubs having an international fan base. Indiscriminately treating all fans as nationally homogenous is fundamentally flawed.

## Police and the Government: The role of politicians

The intricate political networks operating in Italian society legitimizes these actions. Politicians and the media want to be seen taking a firm line and support the police in their conduct. The prime minister, Berlusconi, defended the tactics of the police at the G8 in Genoa by saying in parliament that 'We found ourselves faced with protests that grew in intensity and numbers that grew beyond all expectations. As a result it was necessary to intervene in such a way as to guarantee the maximum security for all the delegations' (Johnston 2001). Similarly, Achille Serra, the Prefect in Rome who was in charge of the police during Manchester United's incident, argued that 'The stewards were overrun by drunk fans, the police had to intervene. I was there and from what I saw they followed the established protocol. If you're going to try and establish order over a drunk, angry mob, you're not going to do it carrying a bunch of flowers' (Marcotti 2007). This reinforces the prominence of police perception in their handling of these situations. If the authorities and police perceive a group to be violent, then they are more likely to adopt an aggressive stance. This increases the likelihood of forward panic and resulting violence. Training needs to be undertaken by the police to understand the culture of the fans before a match (Stott and Adang 2003; Stott and Pearson 2007; Foot 2007a). Although public drunkenness is rare in Italy, it is relatively common around travelling British (and north European) football fans. Making the correct perceptions allows the police to operate more effectively and prevents the opportunity for forward panic to occur.

At the highest level, the Italian police and politicians have not adopted a flexible approach to policing football fans. Fans are treated as one homogenous group, rather than dealt with as diverse individuals or groups. Most of the focus is on the away fans in the *settore ospiti*, the area designated for away fans to park before being escorted to the ground. There are extensive regulations governing the *settore ospiti*:

> In Italy, I speak of our experience of Livorno, when we organise an away trip, a major part of the club organised trips is by coach. Therefore depending on the number of people going, the *Osservatorio*, or its better to say, the responsibility of the forces of order in Livorno, require a list of the number of people going. They order an escort of one or two patrols to go with us in police cars and therefore they escort us from the motorway toll booth and escort us to the stadium ... When we make an away trip the *questura* calls every club to find out what time the coach is leaving and to know what route we are taking. (Max, official Livorno supporters' club director, personal interview, June 2009)

Official supporters' clubs are called by the *questura*, the chief of police, to detail the number of people going, the route and expected departure and arrival times. This allows for coaches to convene at the motorway tollbooths and await the police escort. Usually two police cars will escort the away coaches – one at the front, one at the rear. On arrival at the outskirts of the destination city, the away coaches are collected by a police escort from that municipality and escorted to the *settore ospiti*. This will comprise of a number of police patrol cars and motorbikes. In addition to the escorting patrol cars and motorbikes, the route will be well-marshalled by other police patrol cars and motorbikes that stop and direct traffic to facilitate a clear route for the escorted coaches. When away fans arrive in Livorno, as stated in the opening paragraph to this chapter, the road along the seafront approaching the stadium is blocked of traffic. In most cases, the *settore ospiti* is directly alongside, or inside the stadium. In the case of a trip to Brescia in March 2009, the *settore ospiti* was on the outskirts of the city. The coaches parked in the designated zone and were escorted onto modified city buses to be taken to the stadium. The buses were fitted with a Perspex barrier separating the fans from the driver and front door of the bus. Alongside the driver, behind this Perspex barrier, stood two policemen clearly armed with semi-automatic rifles. Fans of all ages and genders are treated as potential hooligans.

The political imposition of the Pisanu Laws reinforces how the authorities treat fans as one homogenous group. On arrival at the away end of the Italian stadiums, a wall of riot police, standing behind full-length riot shields, greets the visiting fans. They act as a funnel towards the turnstiles where State Police, Carabinieri and stewards meet the away fans. At this point, the stewards will check any baggage for prohibited items and ascertain the details of flags and banners. Any banned items can be confiscated for being too political, or for constituting a weapon. Prior to a match against Parma in December 2008, two Livorno fans were prevented from taking a large flag sporting the image of Che Guevara. The pole accompanying this flag was about four foot tall. They were refused because the pole was too long and they had a political symbol on it. However, a smaller flag with the words 'Livorno' on it was permitted.

Security checks are also performed on the fans. This consists of the usual 'patting down' and is consistent with many sporting events and airports. This replicates Foucault's (1991a) observations of state power being exerted on individuals to create 'docile bodies'. After the security checks, the stewards check tickets against the fans' form of identity. In compliance with the Pisanu Law, they have to ensure that the name on the ticket matches the identity of the person holding the form of identification. Once this check has been performed satisfactorily, the fans approach the turnstiles where they insert the barcode on the ticket into the barcode reader of the turnstile and proceed into the stadium. Stewards and police remain in the sections underneath the stadium but do not make their presence felt within the *curva*.

The entire operation creates an overwhelming image of force and control and increases the tension and emotion of the situation. In a country where the state has faced a long-standing crisis of legitimacy, the presentation of force at away games is potent. Not only does it criminalize all fans; it can present an altogether different image. Armoured police and carabinieri confront fans, while helicopters circle overhead. It feels like a war zone. This analogy reinforces the notion of a lack of legitimacy. It suggests that the authorities are an occupying force which has not won the 'hearts and minds' of the people they are supposed to be protecting. It also strengthens the suggestion that the police and fans are enemies. The police are acting not as intermediaries but as adversaries, and this provides ample opportunity for forward panic and potential violence. It is for this reason that a number of Italian authors utilize the analogy of war in their research. This is particularly apposite in Dal Lago's (1990) seminal *Descrizione di una Battaglia* (Description of a Battle). Despite this, however, no violence was witnessed at any of these games during the ethnographic fieldwork in 2009, and none was reported subsequently in the media. As Collins (2008) highlights, it is rare when fights start as most people avoid them. However, when the ingredients are right, and the tension and emotion on both sides increases, it can lead to the flashpoints and forward panics that precipitate violence.

By treating all fans as one homogenous group, politicians and the police do not take account of the range of fans within the *curva*. Not all fans are hooligans or looking for violence. This is compounded by the *Osservatorio*, which designates a particular game as 'at risk' and places certain restrictions on fans. This effectively criminalizes all fans that may have attended that game and restricts them from watching their team. The police response to away fans is to treat them all as potential hooligans. The construction of this homogenous 'outsider' group contributes to the creation of a unified identity within the group (Stott and Reicher 1998; Stott and Pearson 2007). Consequently, when violent incidents occur, many fans sympathize with group members and understand why violence took place. This further delegitimizes the police.

Despite the treatment of fans as one homogenous group by politicians and the police authorities, the officers on the front line operate with extreme flexibility. In specific situations, police officers circumvent the rules depending on circumstances. This is often done in coordination with the police hierarchy. One example related to an incident encountered by the author at Brescia's *settore opsiti*. The area was directly outside the Stadio Mario Rigamonti and entry was under police authority, although I was allowed entry without being questioned while waiting for my contact, who had my ticket. There was a delay in the arrival of the buses from the parking area that saw the buses immediately directed into the away end. This led to a series of negotiations inside and outside the ground to allow my admission into the ground. On admission it became apparent that no bags or other objects would be allowed on the terrace. As the fans had transferred to the specially modified city buses there was nowhere to store my rucksack. A negotiation took place with the Digos, who refused to take it and suggested to the officer in authority that it should be allowed to be taken into the ground. This was permitted, without being searched. This example, as well as the examples described above of English fans having bottles thrown at them in Rome, illustrates the way that some Italian police make an exception in certain situations. However, this can increase the opportunity for violence.

Group identities and potential incidents are magnified through the police's 'all or nothing' approach to policing football. By not proactively responding to minor incidents, the police allow the tension and emotion to build. This increases the chance of flashpoints occurring and violence ensuing. Francesio (2008) argues that the British police take a more active role than Italian police at prevention and control. Stott and Adang (2003) suggest a more flexible attitude to policing football crowds that centres on a more interactive and less intimidatory approach. They argue that a good police model is to not wear riot gear and maintain a low profile with high levels of positive interactions with fans. This can help prevent major incidents before they start, as well as preventing the construction of symbolic events that reinforce existing narratives. By treating all fans as one homogenous group, the collective identity and memory of the group becomes shaped by events that reinforce the collective narrative. When the police used tear gas and riot equipment on fans at the 'derby of the dead child' in Rome in 2003, the wider groups of fans could understand and believe that a child had been killed. Likewise, English fans who were subjected to a baton charge from riot police in Rome could have been spared this ignominy had the original missile throwers been identified and arrested.

The poverty of the stadiums inhibits control within the stadium. This encourages the extensive policing and restrictions outside the stadium. The lack of stadium development has meant that they have not taken advantage of the transformations in surveillance and stewarding that have been adopted elsewhere in Europe. This allows the *curve* to remain liminal spaces for the creation of the *ultras* identity and legitimized their activities. Consequently, stadium redevelopment should coincide with changes to the operation of the police:

> [We need] stadiums in an English style ... to be a fan there is more comfortable, more customer focused, and above all, the type of police are more civil. It is a civil country [Interviewer: the police are not civil here?] No. The police do what they want. Unfortunately the police arrest all the time and also, when the police are culpable, they always have the cover of personal liberties and are not punished. [There are] many cases, for example, the case of the G8 at Genoa in 2001. (Levriero, official supporters' club member, personal interview, June 2009)

Not only are the episodes of the G8 at Genoa used to reinforce the image of police brutality; there is a strong feeling that the Italian police are unaccountable. This image of accountability contributed to the transition to postmodern policing in Britain, especially after several high-profile miscarriages of justice (Reiner 1992).

Deregulation of the state also impacted the position of the police. As occurred in other areas of the British political economy, policing was also deregulated and privatized. In particular, as Bayley and Shearing (1996, p. 586) argue:

> The state's monopoly on policing has been broken by the creation of a host of private and community-based agencies that prevent crime, deter criminality, catch lawbreakers, investigate offences, and stop conflict.

The emergence of private security firms has seen the commodification of policing and the restructuring of police and policing. This has not occurred in Italy as in Britain. As ruling hegemonic groups seek to maintain control, they have not undertaken any systematic privatization. Likewise, there have been no new regulations introduced, by the Pisanu Law or other legislation, to force clubs to be more accountable. In England, the Taylor Report introduced the use of third-party security at stadiums, forcing the clubs to take responsibility for the safety of fans.

## Stewards

Privatization of police and security has seen the increased responsibility of stewards at football matches in Europe. The transition from privatization of security was made explicit in the Taylor Report that facilitated the redevelopment of stadiums in Britain. Taylor (1990, p. 33) stated that:

> The safety of the public inside the ground is the responsibility of those who stage the event and administer the ground in which it is held, *ie* the 'management'. This responsibility applies in both normal and emergency situations.

Not only did Taylor place the responsibility for the hosts to manage their safety and policing; he also introduced the commercial element into the equation:

> In my view a more consistent and businesslike approach should be made to such charges. If clubs were to find it more economical to recruit efficient stewards than to delegate duties to the police, there could be a significant reduction in the number of police deployed at football grounds to the benefit of the community at large ... Some clubs presently have efficient stewards whom they recruit individually and train fully with the assistance of the police. Others hire security firms to bring in a well-trained team of stewards. (Taylor 1990, p. 37)

The outcome of this approach was that the police should charge the clubs for the use of their services within the football stadium. Outside of the private space of the stadium, the police had the duty to maintain public spaces as part of their legal duty. Should the costs involved be too high, the club could have recruited their own stewards or employed a third-party security firm.

This approach has spread across Europe. Reflecting the free-market approach of the European Union, UEFA have reiterated the importance of stewards to fan safety. Şenes Erzik, the Chairman of the Stadium and Security Committee stated that:

> If stewards are well-trained and well-placed, they are the best people to help the police and allow the game to go smoothly and safely, hopefully, there will be more work for the stewards in the future, and less for the police. (Jackson 2008)

In England and the Netherlands, for example, stewards have become a professional organization that acts as the clubs' arbiters between the police and the fans.

As with other aspects of stadium safety, stewards have not been fully implemented in Italy. Although proscribed by law, the stewards in Italy do not fulfil the same function with the same vigour as in England or the Netherlands. The *Osservatorio* provides guidelines for stewards and has published a manual to assist stewards with their functions.[5] However, they are not provided with sufficient support from the state, the police or the authorities. Many stewards are voluntary and this permits their incorporation into the patrimonial network. Stewards are provided with free entrance to the matches and do not have the skills or support to manage disorder. The continuing presence of the police places the legitimacy of the steward into question. They are reluctant to place themselves in difficult situations and therefore do not seem to enforce any rules. Bottles and other objects are frequently thrown at Italian football matches with impunity. Rather than adequate stewarding, architectural features such as netting and Perspex barriers are added to preserve the safety. The opportunities for an incident like Hillsborough are manifest.

The lack of stewards' authority reinforces the legitimacy of the *ultras*. As demonstrated above in relation to the police, the lack of enforcement over minor infringements amplifies the opportunities for tension and emotion to increase. Some stewards have been complicit with transgressors and this reinforces the group identity of the fans. The incidents with Liverpool and Manchester United fans in Rome saw stewards cooperating with the fans with 'some even allowing Italian fans through the segregation line to collect missiles that they then throw over the barriers' (Stott and Pearson 2007, p. 4). In many stadiums, including Fiorentina, Roma and Livorno, there are no stewards in the stands and this reinforces the liminal space of the *curve*. An incident during the match between Livorno and Mantova in September 2008 occurred when an assistant referee gave a 'debatable' corner decision. This resulted in the assistant referee and the player taking the corner being the focus of a barrage of bottles and other assorted objects. No fans were reprimanded or ejected and the sanctity of the *curva* remained. The club was subsequently fined €5,000 for this infringement. This acts as a calculable cost. The costs of employing dedicated, trained stewards can run into several thousands of euros.[6] The costs of €5,000 for occasional infringements are minimal compared to the costs the club would have to pay if they were charged by the police and stewards.

There are signs that certain areas are adopting an alternative approach to policing and stewarding at matches. Two Tuscan clubs have experimented with extensive stewarding. Empoli and Fiorentina have played a number of matches with minimal police. In addition, Fiorentina is planning a new stadium, which includes removing the perimeter fencing and incorporating increased stewarding. As Giudici (2010, p. 199) states, 'The project has the objective of "demilitarising" the stadium, improving excessively the commercial appeal of the event.' The Florentine club will provide an apposite example for the future of Italian football. This point is affirmed by the chief of police of Florence, Franceso Tagliente who stated that:

> At Florence it is not like this, because in this city a project was taken forward. Launched by the *Osservatorio* and strongly backed by the head of police, it has taken away the nets from the away end and to make it that the forces are order are always moved away towards the centre of the city. The fans, initially sceptical, have started a constructive dialogue with the chief of police and the authorities. Florence is a reality seen as a model in international football. I speak for Florence; there are other problems of security for others. (Cellini 2009)

By taking away the nets that cover the away stands, the police and Fiorentina football club are beginning to treat the fans in a different manner to other clubs. Furthermore, by removing police from the stadium, they are acknowledging that the police are not passive in relation to fan violence. This approach was taken in the Champions League match between Fiorentina and Liverpool in October 2009. Fan choreographies from both sets of fans helped create a carnivalesque atmosphere and Liverpool fans freely went around the city (Giudici 2010). This situation contrasts with the response of Manchester United and Liverpool fans in Rome. It will take time to see if the 'Florence model' works, but it suggests a move towards a more progressive approach when dealing with fans.

## Summary

The bankruptcy of the Italian patrimonial system has impeded its ability to undertake the wider transformations necessary to compete globally. Over-reliance on the revenue from television has permitted clubs to remain in communal stadiums with poor facilities. The lack of stadium redevelopment is contributing to the reinforcement of existing corrupt practices, as witnessed during *calciopoli* and the financial scandals. Lack of redevelopment is also impacting safety. *Curve* are surrounded by Perspex fences and netting that prevent easy exit in the event of an emergency. Without important stadium safety regulations being introduced, the potential for a Hillsborough-type tragedy is a time bomb waiting to explode. The poverty of the stadiums is also necessitating increased security outside as the police struggle to maintain order. Excessive legislation and police actions are effectively criminalizing all fans and contributing to the articulation of localized identities. This is heightening the already emotional situation that takes place at a stadium and amplifies the possibility of violence. The political role of the two police forces legitimates this violence as they seek to maintain their own profile and create the *ultras* as a 'folk devil'.

Despite these factors, there is acknowledgement that Italy needs to change. The FIGC submitted bids to host the 2012 and 2016 European Championships to act as a catalyst for stadium redevelopment. At the moment, only Juventus has constructed a purpose-built football stadium. Meanwhile, Fiorentina has started the planning process to build a new stadium and has trialled matches without police. Roma, Atalanta and Palermo are also planning new stadiums. Despite these plans, the widespread failure of the neo-patrimonial system to adjust to the global political economic transformations have impacted the matchday experience of fans and contributed to a decline in attendance at football. Ultimately, the role of the *ultras* is central to this.

# 7

# The *Ultras*

Boom! As the players marched onto the pitch the bangers were detonated. The loud bang coincided with the chants emanating from the *curva*. These bangers and chants combined to create a cacophony of noise that was both powerful and intimidating. Among the chants, the fans were engaged with rhythmic clapping that added to the wall of noise. Alongside the bangers and the chanting, a series of smoke bombs were ignited. These filled the end with smoke and fuelled the sense of disorientation and chaos emanating from the *curva*. As the smoke dissipated, every individual in the *curva* held aloft a piece of coloured card. The terrace was subdivided into three. The fans in the outer thirds were holding aloft pieces of card in the deep-red colour of Livorno football club. The middle third was coloured white, and the centrepiece was the number '99' in gold. Not only was the number '99' the squad number of the captain of Livorno, Cristiano Lucarelli; it was also the suffix of the Livorno *ultras*, BAL 99, denoting the year of their formation. Elsewhere in the crowd, other fans waved a variety of flags. Among these were flags with Livorno's badge, as well as the flags of Jamaica, Palestine, Cuba and the Soviet Union. The visual and aural effects combined to create a powerful spectacle that demonstrated the powerful organization of the fans, as well as the approaches used to perform the group's identity and intimidate opponents. These spectacles are carefully planned and choreographed by the *ultras*, and they constitute a significant element of football fandom in Italy. These ritualistic spectacles are performed with varying intensity depending on the opposition. The more important the opposing team is seen by the fans, the greater the participation and intensity of the spectacle.

The recurring themes of this book re-emerge in relation to the fans and fan groups. These groups operate within their own familial and patrimonial networks, which are incorporated into the wider networks of the football clubs and their owners. In some cases, however, it provides a site of resistance and a way of reinforcing the group's sense of identity. Global political economic transformations have directly impacted the identification of fans with their local clubs. The intense politicization of Italian society has led to an amalgamation of regional and political identities. Furthermore, these identities are impacted by the prevailing regionalism and distrust of the central government that exists in Italy. With the rolling back of the state and changes to the global political economy, mass participation in football and associated fan groups has fragmented into smaller groups with a diverse range of outlooks including extreme politics and violence. In the face of the state and police action against the activities, however, the *ultras* have started to unify against this 'repression'. In parallel to the fragmenting group identities within club support, a collective national *ultras* mentality is also forming. This chapter will present an overview of the key elements of the *ultras* style of support. It will then trace the historical development of the *ultras* in relation to the political economy of Italian football. Through this, the ritualistic element will be elucidated to highlight how local *ultra* groups grow, fragment yet remain united to an overarching social movement.

## '*Ultras stile di vita*': Performing the *ultras* identity

Italian fan culture is a central image of Italian football. Passionate fans help create a carnival atmosphere full of flags, fireworks and songs. It can also result in violence, as the death of Filipo Raciti demonstrates. This focus on violence, argues Cere (2002), has rendered female *ultras* invisible as academics and the media continually ignore them to focus on the masculine forms of fandom. This is unusual as the countercultural origins of the *ultras* meant that groups were always open to different genders. Although there are relatively more young women in *ultras* groups, the leaders and core *ultras* tend to be male. The term itself derives from French politics; during the French restoration period (1815–30), an *ultrá-royaliste* was a partisan supporter of Absolute Monarchy (Testa 2009). The term has been adapted to refer to all hard-core football fans that demonstrate an unwavering support of their team. The terms *ultrá* and *ultras* are used interchangeably, and without reference to singular or plural (Cere 2002). This support is highly ritualistic and is characterized by the extensive displays of flags and banners, igniting of flares, and chanting of songs. Arranging these choreographies takes a lot of coordination and *ultras* are highly organized with a *direttivo*. This organizing committee has members responsible for fundraising or design of the choreographies. They are presided over by the *capi-ultrá*, the head of the *ultras* who leads the direction of the group, the chants and the choreographies.

The central aspect of the *ultras* style of fandom is the impressive matchday choreographies generated by the *ultras*. These spectacles are an important way of presenting the identity of the group and distinguish the *ultras* style of support:

> Italians refer to the staging of a match as a spettacolo [spectacle]. No English word adequately conveys the spettacolo, but it involves creation of a special atmosphere characterised by a combination of colour, vibrance and noise. (De Biasi 1996, p. 116)

These spectacles are highly organized and incorporate a variety of key elements. *Ultras* utilize a variety of local and political symbols in their spectacles. These reflect the dominance of politics and locality in everyday Italian life. Matchdays are characterized by extensive displays of flags and banners that create a riot of colour. The flags depict the colours of the team and of the city and are waved at the start of matches, and at various points throughout the game. Banners or *striscione* are unfurled across the *curve*. These depict membership of the group, political messages or taunts to rivals. In addition to the visual display, the fans produce an aural performance through orchestrated choruses and combined with drums and trumpets, in some cases. Many of the songs reinforce the aesthetics through expressing support of the team, city or political views. The choreography is often supplemented with flares and smoke bombs that add to the aural and visual spectacle.

These ritualistic displays help to create the collective *ultras* identity. Durkheim (1915) has demonstrated that the rituals of the group create a collective effervescence that connects participants to a collective. This emotional energy stands in contrast to the mundanity of everyday life and helps create a bond that exists beyond the congregation. This is symbolized by a totem that embodies the group. Likewise, Turner (1969) saw rituals as a way of creating a focus and location for group identity, or *communitas*, to exist. The community is created in the liminal space of the ritual. It does not exist in the mundane everyday world. This sense of liminality was also important to Bakhtin (1984) and his concept of the carnivalesque. As Bakhtin (1984, p. 7) states:

> Carnival is not a spectacle seen by the people; they live in it, and everyone participates because its very idea embraces all the people. While carnival lasts, there is no life outside it. During carnival time life is subject only to its laws, that is, the laws of its own freedom.

The traditional rules and borders of everyday life became subverted as degradation of the sacred becomes permitted. Just as Turner argued that a *communitas* formed out of the liminal space of the ritual, Bakhtin suggested that a folk consciousness emerged from the rituals of carnivalesque festivities. Individual identity is about being part of the wider collective of *ultras* as well as supporting the team.

The stadium becomes the central location for the articulation and expression of this imagined community of *ultras*. As Dal Lago (1990, p. 37) argues:

> In a stadium, according to the sectors or groups that occupy it, behaviours become accepted that in other situations of daily life tend to be hidden, or however protected from the gaze of the forces of order. In this way, in a 'curva' one can smoke marijuana with relative impunity, one can throw objects onto the field, simulate brawls, tear up the symbols of rival teams and above all express in various ways transgressive behaviours.

The atmosphere generated by the collective solidarity of the crowd fuels the construction of emotional ties to their physical environment. This contributes to a feeling of *topophilia* to the stadium (Bale 1990) and turns the stadium into a temporary sacred space that subverts the normal everyday practices. The *curve* are decorated with the signs and symbols of the various groups, and these operate as sacred markers that depict temporary ownership.

The various elements of the spectacle are produced by the *ultras*. They are active producers and consumers of their own performance. In this way they are undertaking what Hills (2002) calls 'performative consumption'. Through the production and consumption of the *ultras* choreography, the group are actively performing their group identity. The performative aspect of the carnivalesque atmosphere is reinforced through the adoption of certain clothing. This highlights the sense of group identity through wearing club colours, political symbols or clothing related to the *ultras* movement. Flags and scarves are also incorporated to blend the individual into the group. This is performed in interaction with other *ultras*, the authorities and the media. Goffman (1959) reiterated that social interaction permits these performances to take place. Through reflexive interaction, *ultras* maintain their group identity. This is a team effort and all participants seek to present a unique identity. Giulianotti (1991) has highlighted how members of Scotland's 'Tartan Army' reflexively maintained the boundaries of their image so that they would not be confused with the hooligan image of England fans. To reinforce their carnivalesque identity, the boundaries between the group and their rivals need to be carefully policed and negotiated.

## *Campanilismo* and the creation of the spectacle

Fans and *ultras* see themselves as embedded in local culture and football provides a space for the articulation of this identity. Local rituals and governmental autonomy have helped create a strong local identity in Italy. Termed *campanilismo*, this is literally the love of one's bell tower and represents the love of one's hometown. While Putnam (1993) ascribes local identity to civic traditions, many of these practices were shaped through historical narratives and Catholic rituals. Friendships and rivalries were affirmed through politics and regionalism and this helped shape intra-group dynamics. *Campanilismo* also facilitated the emergence of inter-city rivalries. The more passionate derbies operate between close neighbours, such as Vicenza and Verona, or Ascoli and Ancona. There has been long-running conflict between Pisa and Livorno in spite of their common political affiliations. These rivalries are performed through the spectacle of the *ultras*.

Some of the most spectacular choreographies take place in Genoa. The derby between Genoa and Sampdoria is called the *Derby della Lanterna* after the medieval lighthouse that symbolizes the city of Genova. Significantly, as with Milan, a local symbol is used to signify the football match between the city's clubs. The choreography of the Genoa *ultras* group, Figgi do Zena ('Children of Genoa' in the local dialect), for the 2011 derby provides an apposite example of the scale and intensity of the spectacle. There is an excellent visual depiction of the process involved in organizing the choreography on YouTube.[1] As with many choreographies, preparation is undertaken weeks in advance of the match. This highlights that the rituals associated with the game are confined not just to the ninety minutes of the match but also throughout the week, or weeks, beforehand. The communal gathering of the participants builds in intensity as the choreography is discussed, fabricated and implemented. Ideas for the choreography are discussed in bars and supporters' clubs to determine what visual effect is desired. Once finalized by the *direttivo*, a team of *ultras* begin production of the various effects that will be utilized in the display. This requires weeks of hard work and dedication, and no small amount of talent. For the 2011 derby, the choreography virtually covered one side of the football pitch (approximately 100 metres). In order to accommodate this, the organizers needed to fabricate sheets of cloth that were large enough to cover the area. For this choreography, three sheets were required. The creative and artistic members began by sketching the outline onto the sheets. This was all performed outside due to the size of the cloth. Once the sketch was confirmed, the outline was emboldened while other members began the process of painting the details onto the cloth. Despite the active participation of both male and female members, the division of labour was still gendered. The men took care of the design and production, while the women undertook the stitching of the cloth. For the Genoa choreography, there were a variety of elements that needed to be made. A *striscione* taunting the Sampdoria fans was made in the colours of the Genoa team, so this also had to be painted. In addition, an eighty-metre flag of St George, the flag of the city, was made so that it could be incorporated into the choreography. Once completed, the various elements were taken to the stadium on the morning of the match. The club provides access so the *ultras* can assemble the various components.

*Campanilismo* is central to the choreography.[2] There is a dual process in operation that seeks to valorize the group of Genoa fans, while simultaneously denigrating their Sampdoria rivals. The choreography for the 2011 *Derby della Lanterna* was spectacular. The various elements that were put in place helped build the intensity of the choreography and build the atmosphere and collective effervescence of the fans. While the teams were being announced over the public address system before the match kicked off, the large *striscione* in the colours of Genoa was unfurled and stated (in Italian), 'The city does not want you … go from Genova Samp.' The semiotics of this *striscione* are important. The colours of the banner were in the red and blue colours of the football club. Genoa Football Club deliberately use the English spelling of Genova to denote its English origins. Yet the *striscione* clearly used the Italian spelling of Genova to denote that the city itself, not the football club, did not want their rivals there. By incorporating the colours of the football club the *ultras* are clearly stating that the club and the city are one. Sampdoria have no place with either.

Other elements of the spectacle were released after the teams had been announced. The eighty-metre flag of St George, the patron saint of the city, was unfurled directly above the *striscione* calling for Sampdoria to leave the city. Once again, key markers of local identity were incorporated. Using the flag of the city to denote the fans of Genoa, the *ultras* were clearly linking their club with the city and reinforcing their sense of place. This was emphasized with the *pièce de résistance* of the spectacle that had taken weeks of preparation and planning. As the players entered the pitch, the three large sheets were unfurled beneath the flag of St George. In keeping with the first *striscione*, the scene depicts the city of Genoa. The *Lanterna* is clearly visible on the left-hand section. Central to the scene is a large griffon, the heraldic symbol immortalized on the club's badge.

This griffon is firing a large cannon towards a small boat on the third sheet. Piloting this boat is a caricature of an old seadog sporting the colours of Sampdoria. This old sailor, called *Baciccia* in Genova, is the symbol for Sampdoria and is depicted in silhouette on their badge. The choreography is symbolically forcing Sampdoria from the city using a cannon. As the cannonball approaches his small boat, he exclaims '*minghia*'. This is a vernacular form of '*minchia*', a term from Southern Italy for '*cazzo*' and translates as 'fuck', 'shit', or 'dick' depending on the context. By using a piece of southern vernacular, the Genoa fans are drawing on local history. Many people from Southern Italy migrated to Genova after the Second World War. Firecrackers enhance the image and reflect the blast from the cannon. The successive performance of the rituals over time increases the intensity of the spectacle while reinforcing the key aspects of the images. Once again the symbols of Sampdoria were denigrated, while the symbols of Genoa Football Club are seen as synonymous with the city of Genova.

Meanwhile, another spectacle was being performed in the *curva* behind the goal. Another St George's flag was covering one stand. Emblazoned within this flag were the words 'FC Genoa 1893'. Once again the football club is placed centrally within the flag of the city to reiterate that they are one and the same. The date is also important as Genoa is the oldest in Italy, giving the club an air of majesty. As English migrants founded the club, the flag of St George has a double meaning. It ties the club to both the city and its English founders. Underneath this flag, the lowest section of the stand is divided into different sections. Each section holds alternate cards of red or blue, the colours of the team. Consequently, the stand is transformed into a blue and red striped block. Set square in the middle of this sea of cards is another large banner. Once again this banner is subdivided into red and blue. Adorning this banner was the badge of the club, a griffon on a shield of red and blue. The colours, symbols and words all signify important local narratives that communicate to participants. They denote membership of the group, even if this membership is only for the ninety minutes of the match. Yet the very act of performing these rituals creates and recreates the symbols of inclusion for the group.

## The political origins of the *ultras*

To understand the *ultras* phenomenon, it must be analysed in relation to the political economic transformations that have occurred across Italy. Widespread internal migration fuelled by the 'Miracle' contributed to an upsurge in interest in football in the larger industrial cities. In the 1950s, fans established supporters clubs like *I Moschettieri* (the Musketeers) at Inter and *Viola Club Viesseuax* in Florence (Guerra et al. 2010). The earliest *ultras* groups originated in the late 1960s with AC Milan's *Fossa dei Leoni* and Fiorentina's *Settebello*. The phenomenon developed throughout the following decade and has seen various transformations. In this way we can identify four distinct phases of the *ultras* (Roversi 1994; Roversi and Balestri 2000; Cere 2002; Ferreri 2008; Testa and Armstrong 2008; Scalia 2009). From its development and growth in the early 1970s, the homogeneity of the groups began to fragment during the 1980s. This decade was characterized by smaller groups focusing on violence, neo-localism and racism. Despite this fragmentation, a new form of umbrella *ultras* identity emerged in the mid-1990s.

The *ultras* phenomenon developed in the politically fertile period of the 1970s. The political turmoil during the decade saw the emergence of political terrorism, termed the 'years of lead', and also witnessed the emergence of many political movements like the *Brigate Rosse*. The intense politicization of public life was extended to the football stadiums where the *ultras* adopted similar political language in the naming of their groups. Group names such as 'Red and Blue Commandos' at Bologna and 'Tupamaros'[3] and 'Vigilantes' at Sampdoria identify the militant tendencies of the groups (Podaliri and Balestri 1998). One Milan group were called *Brigate Rossonere*, to reflect not only the clubs' red-and-black jersey but also its explicit political statement. The *ultras* actively incorporated the political symbols of the piazza into the stadium. *Ultras* groups were broadly homogenous and started to reflect the wider political allegiances of the city or wider region. Bologna, in the Communist stronghold of Emilia, had left-wing supporters while the more conservative Veneto was reflected by the right-wing *ultras* of Hellas Verona. Political banners and flags, of the type paraded on marches and demonstrations, were displayed prominently in the *curve*, and political songs were sung throughout the match. These features were incorporated into the choreographies to create the conspicuous spectacle. Likewise, the military style of the street was also reflected in the clothes adopted by the groups. The 'urban guerrilla' style of combat jackets or camouflage outfits, with balaclavas and scarves obscuring the face, were taken directly from the political turmoil on the streets. This represented a marked contrast to certain styles of hooliganism, such as the English and Dutch, who developed a casual style of dress to evade police detection (Redhead and McLaughlin 1985; Giulianotti 1993; Spaaij 2006). As a consequence, the *ultras* became an extension of the politics of the city.

Specific local dimensions emerged within these political identities. Within the major cities, teams polarized around traditions and political affiliation. In Milan, Internazionale was seen as the team of the bourgeoisie and more conservative. Meanwhile, AC Milan was the traditional team of the railway workers and represented the working class. Similar patterns occurred in Turin where Juventus exemplified the owners and managers of Fiat whereas Torino represented the workers in the factories. In the capital, Roma denoted the inhabitants of the city, whereas Lazio characterized the more conservative region of the same name. Consequently, cities hosting two clubs developed distinctive political identities. Within smaller cities, fans reflected the politics of their region. The middle belt of Emilia-Romagna and Tuscany has traditionally voted for the PCI. This was replicated in the left-wing identity of *ultras* at Fiorentina, Bologna, Pisa, and Livorno (Doidge 2013a). Meanwhile, Verona and Padova mirrored the more conservative politics of the north. Since the very beginnings of the *ultras* movement, there has been no coherent political approach and it is not valid to suggest that *all ultras* are either left-wing or right-wing.

Throughout the world, football has been traditionally linked to geographical locations. As a result it has come to symbolize local, predominantly masculine, identity. Italy is no exception. The names of most clubs refer to a specific geographical location, such as a city or region as with Roma and Lazio. In rare cases, an area of the city provides the geographical marker, such as Sampdoria, which has its roots in the Sampierdarena area of Genoa. In rare cases, the club has no obvious tie to a specific area, such as Atalanta, Juventus or Internazionale. With many clubs, the link to the city is reinforced through their badges and colours. Both Hellas Verona and Chievo Verona wear yellow and blue kits that are derived from the colours of the city. Catania wears the red and blue stripes of the municipal flag, whereas Livorno sport the Amaranto colours of the port city. The club colours of Roma are red jerseys with yellow trim, which replicate the flag of Rome. The link to the geographical and historical space is reinforced with the she-wolf suckling Romulus and Remus from the founding myth of the city of Rome. Meanwhile, AC Milan, Bologna and Genoa all have the St George's Cross incorporated into their club badges which mirrors the municipal flags of their respective cities. Elsewhere, Fiorentina's badge contains the red fleur-de-lis, the official emblem of Florence.

The narratives that surround football also help tie the club and its fans to a specific location. More importantly, as Archetti (2001, p. 154) argues, 'no identity can ever exist by itself and without an array of opposites, negatives and contradictions'. Rivalries help reinforce local identities. For example, the Milan derby is called the *Derby della Madonnina* (The Derby of the little Madonna) and is named after the statue of the Madonna that sits atop Milan's cathedral. Elsewhere, the Genoa derby is named after the symbol of the Ligurian port, the *Lanterna* lighthouse. Football and local identity become intimately entwined and the rituals surrounding football help enhance both. Conversely, the derby between Juventus and Inter is called the *Derby d'Italia* (The Derby of Italy). This illustrates the fact that rivalries are not restricted specifically to the local. Anderson (1981) argued that nations were 'Imagined Communities' that were united through common cultural rituals, such as reading newspapers, historical memories and language. Once again, the rituals of football unite fans on a national level as teams compete in a league that encompasses all of Italy.

Despite the shared national rituals, the regular interaction still encourages local identification. If local identities were formed in the early years of football competition due to lack of alternative competitors, they were sharpened due to national competition. As Guttman (1978) has demonstrated, sport provides uniform measures with which individuals and clubs can measure their progress. With national competition, fans have an officially sanctioned measure to determine their superiority. Competition provides regular opportunities to play each other and demonstrate superiority on the pitch. If the teams are in different divisions then this becomes a clearer marker of distinction for fans. All of this helps to reinforce what De Biasi and Lanfranchi (1997) have argued on the 'importance of difference' to the *ultras* identity.

The complicated constructions of *campanilismo* reinforce this status competition between groups of fans. Dal Lago and De Biasi (1994) describe Italian football culture as 'a form of extended municipalism'. The battle lines of the football *ultras* are those of the ancient *campanilistic* rivalries between regions and towns. This conforms to what Dunning (1986) has termed the 'Bedouin Syndrome', where 'the friend of a friend is a friend; the friend of an enemy is an enemy'. As a result, the rivalries are negotiated through *gemmellaggio* or 'twinning' (Dal Lago 1990; Bruno 1992; Dal Lago and De Biasi 1994; Marchi 2005; Stefanini 2009; Testa 2009).[4] Historical traces became reinvented with the *ultras*. During the religious wars of the Middle Ages, those cities that supported the Pope (Guelphs) became enemies with those that supported the Holy Roman Emperor (Ghibellines). Pisa that feared the rise of the Papacy, supported the Emperor, whereas Genoa supported the Pope due to their proximity to the Emperor. As Pisa and Siena were political and trading rivals with Florence, Siena also became a Guelph. Similar patterns emerged centuries later with political and city rivalries. Although it is difficult to cast all fan groups as homogenous, these broad historic rivalries continue. Many fans of Florence's Fiorentina are still rivals with Pisa and Siena. Furthermore, supporters of teams that represented different political views became rivals while friendships were forged with groups of similar beliefs. In this way, *ultras* of Bologna became friends with AC Milan in the 1970s because of their left-wing politics, yet Hellas Verona became enemies because of their right-wing politics. Livorno, a team with *ultras* affiliated to the Left, has rivalries with Lazio and Hellas Verona, in addition to being rivals with friends of Pisa. Consequently, civic traditions become bound in with historical and political narratives and rivalries.

These local rivalries are so deeply embedded that many fans will actively support the opponents of their rivals. The second part of 'Bedouin syndrome' – the enemies – is equally important in Italy. The Italian language reinforces this. The verb *gufare* literally means to bring bad luck on someone or something. Practically this means to support against someone. This tradition of 'againstism' has a long history in Italy. Fans will actively support against their rivals and revel in their defeats. For example, when the AC Milan striker Luther Blissett scored the goal that caused Pisa to be relegated, Livorno fans held parties and subsequently unveiled a banner thanking him at their next game. (Foot 2006). In the same season as Livorno was promoted back into Serie A, Pisa was relegated to Serie C1. Livorno *ultras* displayed a *striscione* that taunted their local rivals with 'Livorno in A with Kaká [the Brazilian midfielder], Pisa in C in kaka'. By utilizing the homonym of 'kaka', the Livorno fans derided their rivals' status. Pisa were reduced to the level of excrement, while Livorno was playing with international star players.

## Fragmentation of the *ultras*: Violence, neo-localism and racism

Despite the high level of organization and planning involved with choreographies, the *ultras* have not been unaffected by changes to the global political economy and to the wider Italian society and have begun to fragment. During this period it was not possible to say that the *ultras* of a particular team were a homogeneous group. Following the highly organized groups at the movement's origins, the uniform political blocs began to fragment in the late 1970s. By the 1980s the movement adapted to new forms of display as younger groups began to focus on neo-localism and violence. These *cani randagi* (stray dogs) renounced the leadership of the previous groups, ignored official 'twinnings' and engaged in more violence. Alongside the choreographies, violence had always been a small part of the overall *ultras* identity as it was seen as a means to a political end. By the end of the 1970s the number of violent instances began steadily increasing and were becoming an end in itself. It is difficult to isolate the timing of this transition. There is some consensus that the patterns began emerging in the 1970s and crystallized in the early 1980s (Roversi 1994; Lanfranchi and De Biasi 1997; Podaliri and Balestri 1998; Roversi and Balestri 2000; Ferreri 2008). A clear demarcation of the transition can be assigned through identification of a significant event. During the Rome derby between Lazio and Roma on 28 October 1979, a nautical flare was launched from the Roma *curva*. It flew across the stadium and lodged in the skull of a Lazio fan who was using his brother's season ticket for the match. The fan, Vincenzo Paparelli, died on the way to the hospital and represented the first death attributable to *ultras*.

This transition phase ended in 1983–4 when there was a sharp increase in the number of occurrences of violence. Throughout the 1980s violence was a central feature of the younger *ultras* identity as they drew on the hooligan image that had emerged in England. In contrast to the earlier political names of *ultra* groups in the 1970s, the emerging groups' names highlighted the change of focus to violence (Roversi 1994; Roversi and Balestri 2000; Foot 2006; Stefanini 2009; Testa 2009). These smaller groups used names such as the Sconvolts ('Upsetters') or Kaos. Indeed, Juventus' group the *Drughi* were inspired by the ultra-violence of the Droogs in Stanley Kubrik's film, *The Clockwork Orange*.

As these new *ultras* groups focused on violence, they became more organized and militarized. The *ultras* had already become militarized through the political conflict of the *anni di piombi*. The military uniforms of the 1970s had been adopted; yet more organized tactics emerged during the 1980s. Alongside these tactics, groups started using weapons. Rather than using bare fists, as they did in the 1970s, the new groups started using knives, bombs, iron bars and rockets (such as the one that killed Paparelli). This has continued among some groups into the twenty-first century. Pictures released by Rome's police after the Coppa Italia final between Lazio and Roma in May 2013 highlighted the range of weapons used (Yorke 2013). A selection of kitchen knives, garden tools, and axes were taped to long sections of wood to have the maximum stabbing range. These weapons also reveal the planning involved.

This militarization has led to a number of Italian commentators using the metaphor of war when discussing *ultras*. Dal Lago and De Biasi (1994, p. 86) suggest that 'In order to defeat the enemies on the field, *ultrà* groups try to adopt urban guerrilla tactics (particularly setting ambushes near to stations and involving the police).' The parallels with urban guerrillas are used to illustrate the mode of operation of the groups. The creation of the *curva* and the city as sacred spaces has seen the groups attempting to defend their territory from outsiders by ambushing opponents and defending their honour. In line with this militarization, the police responded with an increased military presence. Just as had occurred with hooligans in England, the *ultras* that focused on violence adapted their tactics to evade the police, as well as incorporating them into the attacks on rival fans.

Localism became more entrenched during the 1980s. The liminal space of the *curva* became an apposite location to perform the new forms of politics emerging in Italy. The anti-south rhetoric of the *Lega Nord* was reflected with stronger regional rivalries in the stadiums. *Striscione* in particular, demonstrated the increasing anti-Southern sentiment. Verona is a city at the heart of the *Lega*'s imagined nation of 'Padania'. The city's historic football team, Hellas Verona, epitomizes the Northern anti-Southern bias that is utilized by the *Lega Nord*. In 1985 Hellas Verona *ultras* displayed a banner to rival Napoli fans stating, 'Welcome to Italy'. The inference was that the south was Africa and not part of the Italian nation. When Mount Etna started to smoke, Verona fans held up a banner against Catania declaring '*Forza Etna!*' meaning 'Go Etna!'. At the same time graffiti appeared in the north expressing the same sentiment. Similarly, Verona fans unveiled a banner at Napoli saying '*Vesuvio facci sognare*' – 'Help us dream, Vesuvius'. The fans of other football clubs also suggested that they wanted volcanoes to destroy Naples, just as had occurred with Pompeii and Herculaneum 2000 years ago. Highlighting the increasing fragmentation of the Italian state, AC Milan fans unveiled a similar banner at Napoli declaring, 'Give us a present Vesuvius'.

This invective between groups of fans is not confined to geography. The carnivalesque atmosphere of the *curva* also permits the desecration of sacred symbolic associations. Famously, Napoli fans retaliated against Verona fans with a *striscione* that drew on the city of Verona's literary connection with Shakespeare's Romeo and Juliet. The banner stated that *Giulietta è 'na Zoccola e Romeo Cornuto* – 'Juliet is a Slag and Romeo is a cuckold'. The sentiment has resulted in a series of books under that title, which have published the various humorous and offensive *striscione* displayed on the *curva* (see Militello 2004a; Militello 2004b; Militello 2005). Verona fans finally retaliated in 2013 with a banner declaring 'Neapolitans sons of Juliet'. Gendered norms are incorporated into the insults to reassert masculine localized identity. More importantly, it entrenches a culture of abuse that is incorporated into the *ultras* choreographies.

Italia '90 provided another apposite example of the increased regionalism within Italy. The World Cup provided a space where the culture of 'againstism' could be performed. During the group stages of the competition, fans in Milan supported Cameroon in their match against Argentina. Similarly, when Argentina played Brazil in Turin, the local fans supported Brazil. In both cases the fans were focusing their support on the opponents of Maradona. The Argentine star was the totemic player of Napoli who had transformed the fortunes of the southern club. On account of their footballing power and the renewed regionalism within Italy, Maradona became the focus for the animosity of the fans in Milan and Turin. Inter-club rivalry was a powerful factor in fuelling the abuse of players as fans sought to desecrate their rivals' sacred symbols (Back et al. 2001; Doidge 2013b). The clubs of these cities, Inter, AC Milan and Juventus, were fierce rivals with Napoli and consequently their fans supported Maradona's rivals in the World Cup. Fatefully, Argentina drew Italy in the quarterfinals of the competition; a match that was to be played in Naples. The situation prompted Maradona to declare to Napoli fans that 'For 364 days a year you are treated like dirt, and then they ask you to support them' (Foot 2006, p. 478). The statement divided Neapolitan opinion and revealed the contested nature of national identity in Italy. One banner stated, 'Diego, we love you but at the end of the day we are Italians' (Foot 2006, p. 478). Argentina defeated Italy to reach the final in Rome. Italian regional and footballing rivalries also entered the international arena of the World Cup final when the Roman crowd jeered throughout the Argentina national anthem.

The localism and anti-Southern abuse highlights a fragmentation of ideological political identity among the *ultras*. As the movement's origins were in the politically fertile period of the 1970s, the groups originally reflected the politics of left and right in their locale. During the 1980s, however, as the older groups lost control and new, smaller factions emerged, many of the *ultras* became politically neutral. For example, groups like Fedayn at Roma originated as a left-wing group, but became ideologically apolitical in the 1980s. Many moved towards political neutrality. Despite this some groups kept ideological politics at their core. Significant *ultras* groups at Livorno (BAL) and Ternana (Freak Brothers) have remained resolutely left-wing. Groups at clubs like Pisa (Ultras), Atalanta (Brigate Neroazzure) and Sampdoria (Rude Boys and Girls) also have had openly political agendas.

In parallel to this political fragmentation, there was also a growth in *ultras* groups who had an extreme right-wing agenda. This aligned with the growth of neo-localism that was occurring at the same time. 'This link to the small "mother country"', as Podaliri and Balestri (1998, p. 95) argue, 'is very close to extreme right-wing values, facilitate racist and xenophobic behavioural patterns inside the stadia.' Effectively, the city was becoming a 'small mother country' and it became openly acceptable to abuse outsiders. During the 1980s there was a growth in *ultras* groups who expressed far-right political views, not just among clubs that traditionally were considered right-wing, like Lazio or Hellas Verona. This occurred spectacularly with AS Roma. Testa and Armstrong (2010) highlight how 'The Boys' began to engage in extreme-right politics. Traditionally, Roma was associated with the working-class area of Testaccio and had a strong affiliation to the local Jewish community. Fans of Lazio drew on inter-club rivalry to present a *striscione* to the Roma fans of the *Curva Sud* stating, '*Curva Sud* full, Synagogues empty'. The racism became more acute when Lazio fans presented *striscioni* stating, 'Your home is Auschwitz' and 'Team of blacks, *curva* of Jews'. In recent years 'The Boys' of Roma have utilized the same anti-Semitic references against Livorno, another club with a strong Jewish connections. In 2006 Roma fans unfurled a banner declaring, *Lazio-Livorno, stessa iniziale, stesso forno* (Lazio-Livorno, same initials, same oven). The Roma fans utilized Livorno's strong Jewish history through the analogy to the Auschwitz ovens, just as Lazio fans had used against them. They also identify their move from the left-wing identity characterized by Livorno. By placing them in the same category as their fierce local rivals, Lazio, they were declaring that Livorno fans were now enemies. These sentiments were strengthened through word play with the poetic rhyme of 'Livorno' and 'forno' that reinforced the statement.

Alongside the growth in far-right extremism, there was also an increase in racism. Increased global migration saw many immigrants move to Italy to work in the northern factories or in low-paid work, such as fruit picking. As was witnessed in the 1970s, the politics of the *piazza* were transferred to the *curve*. Racist chants and banners became more widespread across the stadiums. This does not mark the *ultras* as right-wing, but identifies a shift in politics elsewhere. It is also important not to suggest that all *ultras* are racist. Back et al. (1999) argued that in Britain the antisocial behaviour of racism and hooliganism had been conflated. This 'racist hooligan couplet' over-simplified racism and did not take into account those individuals who were racist, but did not consider themselves hooligans. Likewise, there were hooligans who were not racist. The same is true of Italy; there should not be a 'racist *ultras* couplet'. Not all *ultras* are racist. In fact, it is mainly *ultras* (at groups like Rude Boys and Girls of Sampdoria and Livorno's BAL) that are among the small number of fans trying to combat racism in Italy. Similarly, not all of the people engaging in racism at football matches are *ultras* (Doidge 2014).

Despite the parallel growth in far-right extremism and racism, it is not automatic that the former causes the latter. Back et al. (2001) have highlighted how there are two types of racism that manifest itself within the stadium. 'Instrumental' racism is ideologically motivated and where far-right groups use the stadium to promote their beliefs. In contrast, 'organic' racism occurs when fans respond to events on the pitch or chant abuse that is considered racist, but without the wider political intent. Both forms of racism occurred in 1980s and 1990s in Italy, as Carlo Balestri argues,

> There was racism from teams who politically identified with the right, or who had been infiltrated by those from Fascist groups. This occurred more in the 1990s. This was very structured in Padova, Verona, Lazio and also groups in the *curve* of Roma. It was very instrumental and groups wanted to recruit fans to display the symbols of the right. In the 2000s there have been groups affiliated to the right at Inter, Juventus, Milan but the racism is more organic because of the behaviour of a player on the pitch. In this cauldron, it is not just racism, but abuse at any type of player. It was a purpose to attack the opposing player. Not political. (Carlo Balestri, UISP and founder of Progetto Ultrà, personal interview, January 2014)

Instrumental, politically motivated racism was more prevalent twenty years ago as many of the groups associated with the far-right were actively engaged in political action. There are now fewer politically motivated groups and this has seen a continuance of organic racism in the *curve*.

The growth of far-right extremism among some *ultras* groups reflects a similar trend in wider Italian society. Despite the lack of overarching Italian identity and strength of *campanilismo*, the change in Italy's demographic in the 1980s profoundly challenged what it meant to be Italian. As Ginsbourg (2003) highlights, 'the Italian population had been extraordinarily homogeneous – in colour of skin, religion, even increasingly in language. It was, in racial terms, deeply conservative, and was quite unprepared for, and hostile to, the idea of a multi-ethnic Italy' (p. 64). Immigration became a key political factor during this period, and this is when the *Lega Nord* emerged and started campaigning on an anti-Southern and anti-immigration agenda. As Lorenzo Contucci, a lawyer and webmaster for asromaultras.org argues, the stadium reflects wider society:

> You have to know that we had, until a couple of years ago, the Internal Minister [Roberto Maroni] was a very big exponent of *Lega Nord*, which is a xenophobic

party. So it is very stupid to think that in *curva* you can't do what your government does. (Lorenzo Contucci, AS Roma and lawyer, personal interview, January 2014)

Politicians often express racism and xenophobia and this accounts for many of the problems associated with football. Italy's first black member of the cabinet, the Minister for Integration Cecile Kyenge, has been likened to an orang-utan and called a prostitute by politicians from *Lega Nord* (Withnall 2013). Many of the sentiments expressed in banners and chants are also replicated by the media or by politicians that campaign on nationalist issues.

Racism is not simply an expression of the fans, but a reflection of the boardrooms and corridors of power. Based on his Romanian heritage, the former Juventus and Fiorentina player Adriano Mutu, has been the subject of 'gypsy' taunts from the *curve* and was even labelled a 'crafty little gypsy' by Maurizio Zamparini, the president of Palermo. Shortly after Mario Balotelli moved to AC Milan in January 2013, the editor of *Il Giornale* and brother of Silvio, Paolo Berlusconi was addressing a political rally for *Il Popolo della Libertà* and invited delegates back to a party to meet the president [Silvio] and 'the nigger of the family' [Balotelli] (*La Repubblica* 2013). The depth of racism within the game was highlighted in July 2014 when the favourite to take over as head of the FIGC, Carlo Tavecchio, stated his case by criticizing Italy's approach to foreign players. In doing so, he referred to a fictional player, Opti Poba 'who was previously eating bananas and now is a first team player for Lazio' (Monti and Valenti 2014). The inference was that foreign (specifically African) players are banana-eaters. These expressions of racism also reveal the general culture that pervades throughout Italian political life. Unfortunately, much of the outrage manufactured by the incident was generated by supporters of his rival, Demetrio Albertini – not as a campaign against racism but as political expediency. Significantly, Tavecchio's supporters, including Adriano Galliani, stood by their candidate.

The growth of international players has also contributed to racism in the stadiums. The Bosman ruling deregulated the national leagues' ability to control player numbers. This has seen an increase in the number of players from outside the national borders. This occurred at the same time as migration globalized with workers from Eastern Europe, Asia and Africa migrating to Italy for work. Although Italy has a long history of overseas players, many were *oriundi* players of Italian ancestry, while others were star players from Europe and South America. The deregulated player markets saw an increase in players from outside these 'traditional' markets. Players who were marked as being outside the 'norm' were targeted. The Japanese star, Shunsuke Nakamura, received racist abuse and suggested that this 'probably explains why so few Japanese players have made it here' (O'Henley 2008). African players have become particular targets. Certain black players are targeted with ritualistic 'buu buu' chants whenever they touch the ball. These expressions of racism are part of the culture of abuse. Fans see their role as helping their team. Abusing rivals is a way of attacking them psychologically and giving their team an advantage (Doidge 2013b). Referring to the colour of a player's skin is seen as the equivalent of deriding them for their lack of hair or fitness levels. What is lost in these situations is that people who are bald or fat have never been systematically enslaved for these reasons.

Abuse aimed at Mario Balotelli illustrates the complicated constructions of racism in the *curve* (Doidge 2013b). Balotelli was born to Ghanaian parents in Palermo but health problems early in his life meant that they could not fully care for him. Two years later he was adopted by an Italian family and raised in Brescia. He began his career at Inter before transferring to Manchester City in 2011 at the age of twenty. Two years later he moved to his boyhood team of AC Milan. Balotelli has been subjected to widespread abuse, including chants of 'There are no black Italians' and 'If you jump up and down, Balotelli dies'. Rival fans claim that the abuse is not against racism, but against the attitude of the player. Balotelli provokes fans when he scores, and has an insolent attitude to training which has seen him attract criticism from his managers, Jose Mourinho, Roberto Mancini, and Cesere Prandelli. Balotelli has also hit the headlines with a number of 'off-the-field' escapades, including setting fire to his bathroom after releasing fireworks from his bathroom window, giving a homeless person £1,000 after winning at the casino, and helping a young child deal with a bully at school. Balotelli has come to symbolize the ostentatious celebrity player whose petulant attitude and extravagant lifestyle embody the economic transformation of football. But he also embodies the demographic change in Italy. International migration has challenged some groups' conceptions of the nation. *Ultras* groups aligned to the right, like groups in Lazio or Verona, utilize this instrumental racist abuse to make political points. In addition to these political factors, Balotelli is also a significant asset to his team. The colour of his skin also adds to this construction as black men are frequently seen as naturally gifted. Consequently, Balotelli is denigrated for being a celebrity footballer, un-Italian and simultaneously a threat. The culture of abuse on the *curve* permits this symbolic desecration in the name of inter-club rivalry.

The reaction to Mario Balotelli should not be taken in isolation. After being subjected to abuse from Inter's fans in 2005, the Côte d'Ivoire player

Marco Zoro attempted to walk off the pitch during a game between his team Messina, and Inter. Other players have taken a stand eventually. In February 2010 players from the amateur club of Casteltodino in Umbria walked off the pitch. Castelodino had two players with Nigerian parents and were labelled 'Dirty Negroes' by an opposition player. A similar incident garnered worldwide attention in January 2013. Kevin-Prince Boateng marched off the pitch after being subjected to sustained abuse from Pro Patria fans during a friendly with his club AC Milan. Explaining the extent of the abuse, Boateng said:

> I could hear the first monkey calls after five minutes when I was on the ball. At first, I didn't think anything of it but then it happened over and over again. I went to the referee and told him that if I hear it again, then I'd quit. He tried to calm me down. When it started again in the 26th minute with the monkey calls, then I thought: 'That's it, I'm not carrying on'. (Drayton 2013)

Boateng was supported by his teammates, who refused to continue the game. Consequently, as with the Casteldino incident, it is the players who are taking action, rather than the authorities. Pro Patria were ordered to play one game behind closed doors as a punishment.

Unfortunately abuse is not restricted to opposition players. After Juventus' victory against Atalanta in March 2010, a Juventus fan slapped the French player Jonathan Zebina who played for the Turin club. In response to this Zebina said:

> Definitely it is racism ... it is an ugly thing for the image of Italian football that does not deserve this. The Federation must do something. I will probably stay and live in Italy, however, these images must be fought with much force, Italy deserves better. (*La Repubblica* 2010b)

Zebina's situation illustrates the contrast between black Italians and foreigners. As a French player, Zebina is free to return 'home' after his contract with Juventus expires, even though he expressed a wish to remain in Italy. For players like Balotelli, who are Italian citizens, the abuse becomes more politically motivated. As Balotelli declared on the social media site twitter, in response to fans who declared that he was not Italian, 'I'm Mario Balotelli. I'm 23 years old and I didn't choose to be Italian' (*La Gazzetta dello Sport* 2014).

Ultimately, the players have undertaken to deal with the situation themselves. Zoro attempted to walk off the pitch, while the players of Casteldino and AC Milan supported their teammates and mounted a similar protest. However, some examples of team solidarity could be seen as misconstrued in the United Kingdom or United States. Akeem Omolade, a young Nigerian player for Treviso made his debut in May 2001 and was quickly subject to racist abuse from his own fans (Bandini 2013). This was part of a sustained period of racist chanting from Treviso fans that had resulted in fines and one of their players, the Brazilian Pelado, leaving the club. In the absence of an official attempt to stop the abuse by the club, the players formed their own response. One of Treviso's midfielders bought some black face paint and every player painted their face black to show their solidarity with Omolade. The Nigerian scored the winner in the dying minutes of the match. He was thankful for the support from his teammates and the Treviso fans applauded the action. The team won praise from the media and authorities, while Omolade won a UEFA fair play award for the way he handled the abuse. Once again, however, the onus is on the victims to be stoic, rather than concerted efforts being made to tackle the perpetrators.

The FIGC has instigated some initiatives to counter these regular episodes of racism. After the Marco Zoro incident, they requested that players enter the pitch holding 'No to Racism' banners. They also sanction clubs whose fans participate in racist chanting. For example Juventus has been ordered to play a match behind 'closed doors' and fined €20,000 for the various episodes of abuse directed at Mario Balotelli. However Jose Mourihno, the manager of Inter, was fined €40,000 and suspended for three games for making a crossed-arm 'handcuffs' gesture after two Inter players had been sent off. He was insinuating that the authorities were contriving to prevent Inter from winning their fourth league title. When accusations against the Federation are punished more severely than widespread racist abuse, there is little surprise that the problem continues. Furthermore, the equivalent of the 'Kick it Out' campaign in the English Premier League does not have a counterpart in Italy and this illustrates the continued lack of legitimacy of the FIGC.

The problem in Italy is that there are few grassroots, fan-led initiatives against racism (Doidge 2014). Putnam (1993) suggests that political engagement comes from areas with traditions of civic participation. Yet this has not automatically translated to football fans. Mainly this is because the focus of fans and *ultras* has shifted to tackling the *repressione* of the Pisanu Law (which will be discussed later in the chapter). There was an attempt to deal with the growing problem of racism in the 1990s. *Progetto Ultrà* was an organization that tried to work with *ultras* and educate them about racism and fascism. It was established by Carol Balestri, a project worker in the Emilia-Romagna section of the Italian NGO, UISP (Unione Italiana Sport Per tutti) that attempts to make sport inclusive. *Progetto Ultrà* established the *Mondialli Antirazzisti* in 1997 to bring rival *ultras* groups together in a carnivalesque festival atmosphere (Sterchele and Saint-

Blancat 2013). This creates a powerful space for promoting anti-racism but tends to appeal to groups and individuals who are already interested in anti-racism. There is also the challenge of maintaining the focus after the event (Sterchele and Saint-Blancat 2013). Despite this, it provides a powerful model that can be used at other events and acts as a space to share ideas and strategies.

Some *ultras* groups are reverting to their political origins in order to tackle racism and discrimination. The *Mondialli Antirazzisti* has helped encourage and foster inclusion for groups interested in diversity in football. A good example is 'Rude Boys and Girls' from Sampdoria. They were originally called 'Rude Boys', but changed their name after reading a leaflet decrying sexism in football at the *Mondialli* (Sterchele and Saint-Blancat 2013). They also organize anti-racism football tournaments:

> In Italy the focus of the newspapers and politicians is on repressive regulations, not on social interventions because that is more laborious to change the behaviour of fans. There are no 'community schemes' in Italy, like in England. They would only do, or think to do, if they were told by UEFA. Instead these approaches come from certain fan groups, like Rude Boys and Girls at Sampdoria on racism and anti-racism. For thirty years they have organised a football tournament with schools to create a culture of anti-racism. They ask the fans for their ideas to work with the kids at this tournament'. (Carlo Balestri, UISP and Progetto Ultrà, personal interview, January 2014)

The 'Rude Boys and Girls Tournament' is run under the banner of 'Love Samp, Hate Racism'. It is important because it works with schoolchildren to create a culture of understanding around racism. It is also very important because it links anti-racism to the club, not to some abstract concept from outside the city. It is the importance and quality of the interaction that facilitates understanding (Sugden 2006). For the schoolchildren, anti-racism and Sampdoria are one and the same.

The focus on Balotelli highlights how players symbolize football clubs. The rituals around football elevate certain players as the embodiment of the club. These are either valorized by the home fans or denigrated by rivals. They are incorporated into the culture of abuse that fans and *ultras* engage in. At Livorno, Cristiano Lucarelli famously took a pay cut to transfer from Torino to play for his hometown club. He stated that 'some players buy themselves a Ferrari or a yacht, for a billion lire, I bought myself a Livorno shirt' (Pallavicino 2004). After transferring, he assigned himself the number '99' shirt in homage to the date of formation of BAL ('*Brigate Autonome Livornesi*'), the dominant Livorno *ultras* at the time. He also had the badge of BAL 99 tattooed on his forearm to denote his affiliation to the *ultras* group. As a member of BAL, Lucarelli was friends with many of the leading *ultras*, such as Lenny Bottai. As a consequence of increased global migrations of players, local players became inflected with increased significance (King 2003). Lucarelli became a potent player-symbol for Livorno; a totemic object for the fans. Max, a director of a supporters' club in Livorno, exclaimed, 'Lucarelli is our Maradona' (Personal interview, June 2009). Consequently, Lucarelli attracted much media attention, including becoming the subject of a documentary, '*99 Amaranto*'.[5]

Much of Lucarelli's totemic appeal was political. He stood in stark opposition to the mercenary image of contemporary footballers. In addition, he was open about his political identity. He announced his arrival on the national and international scene during a under-21 match against Moldova that was played at Livorno's Stadio Armando Picchi in 1997. After stroking the ball into the net in front of the *Curva Nord*, Lucarelli ran towards the Livornesi in the stand and lifted his Azzurri shirt to reveal a Livornesi *ultras* T-shirt. The T-shirt said 'Livorno is a faith and the *ultras* its prophets' and its centrepiece was a picture of Che Guevara. For Lucarelli this was a show of solidarity with the fans. Yet for the authorities this was seen as a political statement. Lucarelli suggests that this was the reason that he did not play for the national team again until 2005. Lucarelli answered allegations that he was a Communist with 'definitely I am a Communist, like all Livorno. So want? Where is it written that a Communist cannot play football?' (Pallavicino 2004). Lucarelli was belligerent about his political beliefs and this reflected the fans on the terrace.

Consequently, Lucarelli also became a target for abuse. Where a player like Mario Balotelli was targeted for the colour of his skin, Lucarelli was targeted for the colour of his politics. The same song that has been sung at Balotelli was chanted at Lucarelli; 'if you jump up and down, Lucarelli dies'. Lucarelli sits outside rival fans conceptions of themselves. Back et al. (2001) have highlighted how racism is situated in a complex ritual of inter-club rivalry. Fans valorize specific characteristics in their symbolic players, from playing style to politics and ethnicity. These characteristics form a conceptual hierarchy of traits that structure how fans interact with others. Lucarelli reflected the dominant characteristics of a particular section of the fan base and was valorized as a symbolic player. The reverse of this is that he also became counter-symbol for rivals who wished to desecrate the symbols of their opponents. For example, when Lucarelli was facing his former club of Torino in March 2004, he was subjected to 'Communist Lucarelli', 'Lucarelli Livornese of shit' and 'Lucarelli Jew' (Pallavicino 2004, p. 253). Each of these monikers reflects where Torino fans placed Lucarelli in their conceptual hierarchy of politics and identity. Situated at the bottom of their hierarchy were Jews, Communists and Livornesi. By being attributed with all of these traits, Lucarelli was beneath their contempt and worthy of derision.

Lucarelli can be contrasted with another potent player-symbol; Paolo Di Canio of Lazio. Prior to the match between Livorno and Lazio in 2005, both players were the subject of a parallel interview on Mediaset's television show, *Le Iene*, based on their image as player-*ultras*.[6] Di Canio was famed for his support of Lazio's far-right tendencies and expressed an admiration for Mussolini. He has celebrated scoring goals with a fascist salute to the crowd. In 2005, he made the same gesture as he was substituted against Livorno. In contrast, when Lucarelli scored a goal, he held aloft his clenched fist as a goal celebration, in allusion to the Communist symbol of solidarity. With actions and interviews, Lucarelli and Di Canio show solidarity with their 'comrades' on the *curva*. Di Canio confirmed this after the fascist salute against Livorno. He said afterwards, 'I will always salute as I did yesterday because it gives me a sense of belonging to my people' (*The Independent* 2005). His 'people' are the *ultras* on the *curva*. He is highlighting that he understands the *ultras* and what is important to them. By behaving in the same way, he is claiming membership of the group, just as Lucarelli did with his Che Guevara T-shirt. A similar incident occurred in March 2010 when the Argentine striker Mauro Zarate was photographed performing the fascist salute with Lazio fans in the home *curva*, although he subsequently claimed that he had never heard of Mussolini. The subsequent media furore around incidents such as these helps reinforce the outsider status of the groups and reinforces members' solidarity (Testa and Armstrong 2008). Thus players that empathize with the fans become signified with greater meaning and importance.

## *Ultras* and owners: Patronage and legitimacy

The actions of Di Canio and Lucarelli reaffirm the strong legitimacy *ultras* groups hold. As a result they have not been immune to the patrimonial approach of Italian political and business life. As we have seen, club owners utilize their clubs in the same way they use their business connections. Just as Moggi dispensed favours to those who helped him, club owners do the same. *Ultras* operate within this sphere of influence. This grants the *ultras* a degree of legitimacy as the club owners utilize them for their own ends. Some clubs provide free tickets or merchandising rights to *ultras*, who in turn sell them through their organizations (Dal Lago and De Biasi 1994; Kington 2007; Scalia 2009). Originally these concessions were in return for favours to the owners. Owners realized that empty stadiums were not good for the clubs and, in contrast to the commercial approach of British clubs, provided free tickets to stimulate interest. Other scenarios have seen presidents looking for justification to sack a manager, who would call on the *ultras* to start chanting against the manager and get the other fans to support the decision. Similarly, if the club wants a star player to sign a new contract, then the *ultras* would perform a similar task (Vialli 2007). In 2014, it was disclosed that the president of Bologna, Albano Guaraldi, took the head of Bologna's ultras as an advisor to negotiations about the sale of the club (De Carolis 2014).

Reflecting the wider patronage exhibited by politicians and entrepreneurs, club presidents also purchase players as 'gifts' to fans. For example Berlusconi signed Robinho as a gift to AC Milan's fans and permitted Marco Borriello to transfer at a reduced price to Roma, because he 'wanted to give a gift to our friends' (Bandini 2010; Colombo 2010). Yet this also reflects the power imbalance in the networks. It is not clear if fans asked for these players, nor how they are expected to repay the generosity of the owner. What is clear is that the *ultras* are incorporated into the wider strategies of owners and authorities. As Gramsci argued, hegemony is maintained through coercion and consent; it is an act of constant negotiation.

Owner neo-patrimony emerged during the 1980s as owners sought to utilize the power of the *ultras* to leverage purchases and control in the boardroom. Once again, Berlusconi is central to these changes in Italian football as Scalia (2009, p. 46) highlights:

> The first example of this dynamic dates back to 1986. As AC Milan was suffering a deep financial crisis, the old owners tried to sell the team. Many entrepreneurs and businessmen made their bid, and among them the TV tycoon Silvio Berlusconi, who promised to bring the team back to the glories of the recent past. His offer was not considered as the best by the incumbent owners. *Ultras* organised a snap protest in the stadium, and they were backed by some prominent politicians who supported the then-rampant entrepreneur. The result of this action proved to be successful, and in February 1986 Berlusconi became the boss of AC Milan.

In addition to introducing business and media practices into football, through his ownership of AC Milan, Berlusconi helped incorporate the *ultras* into the legitimate football network. Similar scenes occurred at Roma where the co-owners of Franco Sensi and Pietro Mezzaroma battled for complete control. The *ultras* campaigned for Sensi, which helped him obtain full ownership.

As a result, the *ultras* have been incorporated into the owners' patrimonial networks and this creates a paradoxical relationship between the clubs and the fans. Portelli (1993) has highlighted how Italian fans support and valorize the owner who provides them with success. Yet at the same time, they are also resentful of the fact that they are dependent on this owner. The concessions offered to the *ultras* simultaneously justify and reinforce the crisis of legitimacy. Providing concessions to *ultras* undermine the clubs' opportunities to deal with the crises and introduce measures that will allow them to compete in Europe. The *ultras* are faced with supporting a club owned by someone who does not feel the same emotional attachment and often resist attempts to remove their privileges. Accordingly, they draw on these traditions and campaign vociferously to maintain their special status. An official at Palermo reportedly received a goat's head after ending free ticketing. Similarly, Lazio *ultras* threw bombs into the grounds of Lazio owner's offices after he withdrew their 800 free tickets per match (Kington 2007). Silvio Berlusconi used the *ultras* propensity for violence as a reason for his debtspreading decree, *salva-calcio*. He stated that clubs could not be allowed to fail as 'there will be a revolution' (Foot 2006, p. 349). Once again Berlusconi utilized the image of the *ultras* to justify his actions relating to football and, by extension, his own football club. Rather than use this as an opportunity to fix the problem, he used it as a reason to maintain the *status quo*. This had the dual action of undermining the integrity of the league and the bodies seeking to regulate it, while simultaneously legitimating the *ultras*.

Having gained legitimacy from the clubs, the *ultras* of some clubs have grown in strength. This has led Fabio Capello, the former manager of England, Real Madrid, AC Milan, Roma and Juventus to state that 'In Italy the *ultras* are in charge' (*La Gazzetta dello Sport* 2009). This was powerfully demonstrated at the Rome Derby of 2004 when rumours circulated during the match that police had killed a child. The leading *ultras* of both sides pleaded with the players to stop the match. Indeed, the Roma *ultras* entered the pitch unobstructed by the authorities. This led to the haunting image of leading *ultras* telling the Roma captain, Francseco Totti, that a child had been killed and that they should stop the match. Totti walked away suggesting to teammates and management that they would be killed if they played on, and the game was abandoned. The Lazio players also addressed their fans to ascertain the truth. Meanwhile the referee phoned the head of the League, Adriano Galliani, for advice. Galliani permitted the game to be suspended. A riot ensued outside the stadium that resulted in over 200 police officers being injured.

Similar scenes occurred in 2012 when the Genoa fans that stage such spectacular choreographies also demonstrated the power of the *ultras* (*La Repubblica* 2012). Genoa was losing 0-4 at home to Siena. A group of approximately eighty *ultras* broke into the family stand at Genoa's Marassi Stadium and began throwing fireworks on the pitch. Amid the smoke and confusion the referee abandoned the game and escorted the Siena players off the pitch to an ovation from the Genoa *ultras*. The police were unable to negotiate with the *ultras* and did not resort to force. In the meantime, the Genoa players approached the *ultras* to negotiate, led by the captain, Marco Rossi. The players were instructed by the *ultras* that they were not fit to wear the shirt of Genoa, and were ordered to remove them. After consultation with the police and the club president, Enrico Preziosi, Rossi removed his shirt, followed by his teammates. Some of the players were in tears as they did so. Yet one player refused and strode towards the *ultras*. Giuseppe Sculli pushed past the stewards who tried to prevent him from making the situation worse. Sculli was the grandson of a 'Ndrangheta organized crime leader and one of the players photographed dining with Genoa's *ultras*, a Bosnian criminal and Domenico Criscito, the player investigated for match-fixing before the 2012 European Championships. As Sculli remonstrated with the *ultras*, the *capi-ultras* of Genoa descended onto the pitch. Sculli refused to remove his shirt saying that he gave everything for the shirt. Eventually the *ultras* backed down, and the players put their shirts back on. Despite the Genoa president saying that he would 'not hide from my responsibilities', he still sacked the manager after the match, which legitimated the actions of the *ultras*. Similarly, they are well connected with leading players, which reaffirms this legitimacy.

The themes of legitimacy and negotiations reoccurred during the *Coppa Italia* final in May 2014. Since 2008, the final has been played in the Stadio Olimpico in Rome in order to create a showcase event. The 2014 final between Napoli and Fiorentina began in harrowing circumstances. One of the *ultras* who invaded the pitch to talk to Francesco Totti in the 'derby of the dead child' in 2004, Daniele De Santis, was involved in an altercation with some Napoli fans a few kilometres from the stadium (*Il Fatto Quotidiano* 2014). He shot three of the Napoli fans, one of them critically. When the Napoli *ultras* heard the news, they attempted to have the final called off by throwing fireworks onto the pitch. In scenes reminiscent of the Olimpico in 2004, the captain of Napoli, Mario Hamsik, went to the *curva* and negotiated with the *capi-ultrà* Gennaro

De Tommaso. The wonderfully nicknamed Genny 'a Carogna (Genny the swine) was the son of a member of Naples' organized crime organization the Camorra (*La Repubblica* 2014). He relented and the game was allowed to continue. The media and political fallout was predictable. Genny 'a Carogna was given a Daspo and banned from the stadium for five years. Interestingly, Genny 'a Carogna was wearing a T-shirt saying 'Speziale Libero' ('Free Speziale'), which was declaring solidarity with Antonino Speziale who was convicted of killing the policeman Filippo Raciti. This T-shirt highlights a new form of solidarity that is connecting *ultras* from rival teams.

## *Mentalità Ultras*: A collective identity

The transition from homogenous political *ultras* to fragmented violent groups was marked by the death of Vicenzo Paparelli. Similarly, another death marks the emergence of a new form of *ultras* identity. *Ultras* were beginning to understand that they had more in common with each other than their rivalries suggested. Significantly, the *mentalità ultras* is proving to be an overarching identity:

> The *ultrà* mode of participation is encoded in the notion of '*La Mentalità*' (the mentality or mind). La Mentalità dictates that the *ultrà* must be an active spectator, overtly display identity, and confront authority and other *ultras* within the limits of an honour code. (Guschwan 2007, p. 254)

Maffesoli (1996) has argued that individualization has occurred simultaneously with the formation of new wider collectives, or 'neo-tribes'. These 'neo-tribes' are increasingly 'tied by culture, communication, leisure or fashion, to a commodity' (Maffesoli 1996, p. 81). Meanwhile, Touraine and Melucci have illustrated that new forms of political identity are forming around consumption, which sees socially diverse groups unifying around singular political issues. These new social movements can often be temporary; emerging and coalescing around a singular contemporary issue. Football has become this site of consumption as *ultras* temporarily unite around singular issues. The transformation of football has politicized fans in new ways. In England this was related to economic changes, stadium restructuring, and changing ownership (King 2003; Millward 2011). In Italy, new forms of political action have emerged as a result of the authorities *repressione* of the activities of the *ultras*. As Podaliri and Balestri (2000, p. 191) argue, the stadium has become the focus of this political debate, due to 'the disintegration of many places of assembly and socialisation outside stadium'. The result is that the stadium becomes an important 'public sphere' where the politics of the day is discussed (Guschwan 2013b).

Much of this collective action can be traced back to events in Genoa twenty years ago. On 29 January 1995, a Genoa fan was stabbed to death before their game with AC Milan (De Biasi 1996; Podaliri and Balestri 2000, 2002; Foot 2006; Ferreri 2008; Stefanini 2009; Contucci and Francesio 2013). Vincenzo Spagnolo was a twenty-four year old football fan who was part of a group that was confronted by a small band of AC Milan *ultras*. This faction was a splinter group from the main *ultras*, the *Fossa dei Leoni*, and called themselves 'The Barbour Gang', to reflect their interest in English hooliganism. A fight ensued and Simone Brasaglia stabbed Spagnolo, who died in the street. Brasaglia went to the stadium and held aloft the knife to his fellow *ultras*. Some AC Milan *ultras* even included a chant declaring that there was 'one fewer' of the Genoa fans; '*uno di meno, voi siete uno di meno*'. News of Spagnolo's death circulated around the stadium and led to the Genoa fans demanding that the game be halted. After initial rebuttals, the referee and players decided to abandon the game; the first time that a match had been stopped in this manner. Meanwhile, the Genoa *ultras* attempted to storm the AC Milan *curva* to exact revenge on the culprit. This led to a seven-hour standoff with police that resulted in a riot outside the stadium. Such was the shock of the murder that *Lega Calcio* abandoned all of the following week's matches.

Fans had been killed in incidents at football matches since Paparelli's death in 1979. It was, however, the first to be followed directly by the media (Stefanini 2009). The reactions from the authorities were similar to those employed after Paparelli and Raciti. They introduced swift measures to ban offensive items into the stadiums and reinforced the use of the Daspo banning order that was introduced in article 6 of Law 401 in 1989,[7] (as discussed in the previous chapter).

The reaction from the *ultras*, however, was unprecedented. On 5 February 1995, a week after Spagnolo's death, *ultras* from groups from across Italy held a conference. This was co-organized by *ultras* of Genoa and Sampdoria, traditional local rivals. The following statement was issued after the conference:

1) On Sunday Vincenzo Spagnolo, an *ultrà* of Genoa, died. This umpteenth absurd attack leads us to say: Enough! Enough of these people who are not *ultras* who try and make the news by using the *ultras* world to gain importance and by

ignoring the evil of what they do (as in this case irreparably). Enough with this trend of twenty against two or three and Molotovs or knives.

2) *Ultras*: once the championship starts again we will be faced with a difficult period. The police can now do what they like; the only people who will be blamed will be us, who have nothing to do with these cowards. If being an *ultras* is truly a way of life, we must have balls. On other occasions we ignored events, arguing that they were not our problem, now we must shout enough!

3) What is the alternative? We find ourselves caught between policemen who would like us to disappear and these filthy scum who don't care about anything and will continue with their cowardly 'attacks'. Let us unite against those who want to destroy the world of the *ultras*, a free and true world despite all its contradictions. (Ferreri 2008, pp. 40–1; Stefanini 2009, pp. 126–7)

The statement, or peace treaty, highlights some significant developments. While it utilizes the language of the oppressed, there is little self-criticism (Foot 2006). More importantly, it calls for unity. In the creation of this collective identity, it draws on the invented masculine traditions of the movement by insinuating that there is no honour in using knives or outnumbering rivals. The statement is an attempt to create a collective image of 'honourable' *ultras*.

It should be stated that *ultras* converging around shared politics is not a new phenomenon. The tradition of *gemellagio* demonstrates a long-standing cooperation between groups of different clubs. This was built upon by Livorno's leading *ultras* group, BAL, who established the *Fronte di Resistenza Ultras*, a pan-European network to challenge global capitalism and rising fascism (Doidge 2013a). What is important is that the Spagnolo conference was independent of ideological politics of left and right and focused on the collective identity of the *ultras*. Drawing on extensive fieldwork with Roma and Lazio fans, Testa (2008, 2009) and Testa and Armstrong (2010) highlight how the traditional rivalry between Roma and Lazio has become blurred. Roma groups like 'The Boys' have cooperated with the *ultras* of Lazio over far-right political issues. Post-Spagnolo, many *ultras* groups have engaged in various forms of charity work to demonstrate their importance to the local community (Podaliri and Balestri 2000; Testa and Armstrong 2010; Doidge 2013a). A new collective mentality is emerging, *mentalità ultras*, that is being performed through consumption and politics.

An apposite example of the production and consumption of an identity is demonstrated with the brand 'Mentalità Ultras'.[8] This clothing company was formed in 1995, the year of Spagnolo's death, and produces a range of clothing and designs to exploit the *ultras* identity. In addition to having a brand name and logo, 'Mentalità Ultras' also has created a logo that presents the image of the perfect *ultra*. The 'Cheeky Boy' logo depicts the head of an *ultra* in a hooded sweatshirt, fully zipped up. The hood is designed to completely cover the face, and has a pair of goggles covering the eyes. These 'goggle jackets' completely remove any individuality from the *ultra*. The result is a character that resembles a ninja or militaristic individual who cannot be identified and prosecuted. What is taking place, as Maffesoli (1996) argued, is a de-individualization of the *ultras*. The individual is being absorbed into the collective identity of the *ultras* through consumption of specific commodities and the adoption of specific practices.

The *mentalità ultras* encourages the consumption of clothing and merchandise produced independently of 'official' club products. This is an act of resistance to the growing commercialization of football. This conflict has manifested itself in relation to the growing movement called '*No al Calcio Moderno*' ('No to Modern Football'). These slogans are displayed on banners at grounds or printed on T-shirts that are sold in the same online stores as the 'Mentalità Ultras' brand. It is illustrative that these slogans are always written in English, except in Italy. The phrase originated with Italian *ultras* as the political, economic transformations occurred in Serie A first. Elsewhere, global business and the internet have done much to expand the use of English internationally. Despite the desire to enforce a local form of support, groups are using a global language to make their point. It also underplays the impact that countries like Italy, and individuals like Berlusconi, have had on football. The 'No to Modern Football' trope draws on a global movement of young masculine fans who see commercial football as barring them from the game, which they consider their own.

'No to Modern Football' and clothing from brands like 'Mentalità Ultras' draw on a specific form of wilful nostalgia. A range of 'Mentalità Ultras' merchandise includes the maxims 'Support your local team' and 'From Father to Son: Support your local team'.[9] The latter depicts an iconic representation of a white male holding his young son in his left arm. The image is evocative of post-war golden age of football. The father is sporting a 1940s football strip made of heavy-duty cotton, unadorned by badges or commercial logos. In his right hand he holds a brown leather football, similarly unadorned with logos. This highly masculine image depicts a specific image of *ultras* support: masculine, un-commercial and local. Drawing on this wilful nostalgia can be an important unifying approach.

> The transformative potential of protests can be reinforced through iconic representations, shared language, emotional investments, and collective memory of struggles ... at the same time, the transformative potential of the opposition initiatives risks being weakened as the protests become ends in themselves. (Numerato 2014, p. 13)

The danger with the *ultras* collective identity in the twenty-first century is that it becomes a self-reifying image that legitimates sexism, racism, homophobia, abuse and violence.

## 'All Cops are Bastards': Another unifying element

Although the *ultras* are engaged in political and charity work, the fragmentation of *ultras* has witnessed a reframing of key aspects of the *mentalità ultras* political identity. Ironically, the weakness of the state is facilitating the creation of this collective identity. As the state has attempted, and failed, to impose itself on the ultras, they have inadvertently reinforced the self-image of the *ultras*. As Contucci and Francesio (2013, p. 1) argue, 'they are trying to chase the violent people from the stadium. They have chased away everyone but the violent people.' The various bureaucratic measures imposed by the Pisanu Law have made it harder for the average fan to attend a match.

> In Italy only the hardest fans go to the stadium. And this is the problem and the difference with England. Because we had so many years of stronger rules and we have difficulty to get tickets and we have difficulties of every kind ... All the matches on the TV screen. I can see that my daughter, who is a big Roma fan, but sometimes she prefers to see it on the TV. And you don't risk anything and you can shout at the television and you don't get a banning order. You spend a lot less. (Lorenzo Contucci, AS Roma and lawyer, personal interview, January 2014)

The result is that the *ultras* are the only ones left attending the stadium. They see themselves as the 'authentic' fans and this strengthens their resolve 'Against Modern Football'.

As the state's representatives on the ground, the police have become the focus of conflict with the *ultras*. The origins of this shift in focus appeared the year before Spagnolo's death. On 13 November 1994, the deputy head of Divisional Police and the chief inspector of the State Police were injured in a confrontation after a game between Brescia and Roma (De Biasi 1996, Curro 2009). Reports indicated that around fifty ultra-right militants travelled from Rome with the specific intention of attacking the police. A similar incident occurred two weeks later when Lazio and Roma fans united during the Rome derby to attack the police, injuring eight officers. Ten years later Lazio and Roma fans united during the 'derby of the dead child'.

The media, politicians and police also help create the image of the *ultras*. The sporadic acts of violence that have accompanied the *ultras* have been amplified in the media who have constructed them as a 'folk devil' (Marchi 2005). In the case of the 'derby of the dead child', much of the media speculated that the *ultras* had pre-planned the move to protest against laws that would force many clubs into administration. The police assist in this construction. The Rome chief of police, Achille Serra, corroborated the media by saying that he suspected that the violence was premeditated. The police and media construction of the *ultras* as folk devils legitimates the requirement for a hard-line approach. When combined with the emotion of a 'hot' derby, the *ultras* were confronted with large numbers of police. This provided all of the ingredients for 'forward panic', as the police pre-empted violence from the fans and the *ultras* would anticipate this. On the night of the Rome derby the police took aggressive action against all fans because they anticipated that violence would occur. When the match was initially suspended, fans threw flares towards the police. The police responded with tear gas. This heightened the emotion of the situation and caused increased confusion as fans tried to navigate through the smoke of the flares and the clouds of tear gas. In addition to the scenes witnessed by the fans, the police response contributed to an atmosphere that could lead to fans at the ground to genuinely believe that the police could have killed a young fan. The unintended consequences of the repression tactics were that they were having the effect of making the situation worse.

The creation of the *ultras* folk devil is assisting in the creation of the *mentalità ultras*. Although powerful established groups enable the formation of 'outsider' groups, the groups themselves reinforce this construction (Becker 1963; Elias and Scotson 1965). Fans expecting a negative police response will have constructed themselves as Outsiders who will be treated in a different manner to other groups (Stott and Pearson 2007). This would make them more susceptible to perceived negative policing and therefore more likely to further embed themselves as Outsiders. Action against the police becomes legitimized when the Outsider imagined community has been created between 'us', the fans, and 'them', the police. This reinforces the Outsider identity. This feeling of persecution is reflected in the slogan *'libertà per gli ultras'* ('Liberty for the *ultras*') that appears on T-shirts and graffiti. This was highlighted after 2,000 Napoli fans without tickets visited Rome for their match against Roma on 31 August 2008. They were confronted with 'zero tolerance' from the police. The situation was exacerbated by the fact that the police allowed the fans to travel even though they knew they did not have tickets. Any resulting management of the Napoli fans in Rome would have been greeted with confusion and tension. Unsurprisingly, the situation saw violence around the stadium and at the train station. The police reinforced their stance, and the folk devil image, by releasing figures stating that 800 of the 2,000 fans had criminal records. This included twenty-seven who had connections with the Neapolitan-organized crime networks, the Camorra. The Napoli fans subsequently demonstrated their 'Outsider' identity at the next Napoli fixture through an act of consumption, by wearing T-shirts stating, 'I've got a criminal past' (Hawkey 2008).

The death of the policeman Filippo Raciti in 2007 marks a symbolic moment in the reinforcement of the *mentalità ultras* collective identity. Following Raciti's death, all Serie A games were cancelled for the following weekend. For the following round of matches, a minute's silence was held to commemorate the policeman. However, a different approach was taken nine months later when a fan was shot dead by a policeman. In November 2007, Lazio fans had an altercation with Juventus fans at a service station in Tuscany as both sets of fans were travelling north to attend matches. The situation resolved itself, in a case of self-policing, until a policeman in the service station on the opposite carriageway fired his gun in the air to try and calm the situation. The bullet hit Gabriele Sandri, who was asleep on the back seat of a car (and who was not part of the clash). He was fatally wounded. After Sandri's death, only the Lazio-Inter game was officially cancelled. The Atalanta-Milan game was also cancelled, but that was as a result of fan violence. A banner displayed at Parma prosaically stated the thoughts of the fans: 'Death is the same for all' (Bandini 2007). The following conversation between *ultras* of the *Livornesi* group highlights and reinforces the perceived injustice of Sandri's death:

> Roberto: 'A policeman, Spaccarotella, fired at Gabriele Sandri ... he shot Sandri. In order to kill. He has never visited prison ... too many people saw it and too many people said that he aimed ...'
> Gianni: 'He will not go to prison' (Personal interview, June 2009)

Conversations such as this one help reinforce a feeling of persecution among *ultras* and fuel the perception that the authorities are unaccountable. The authorities and the police acted differently depending on who was killed which was deemed unfair by *ultras* and consequently reinforced their 'Outsider' identity.

This *mentalità ultras* identity transcends existing club and political rivalries in circumstances like Sandri's death. These hostilities are abandoned when confronted with a perceived police threat (Stott and Pearson 2007). This was witnessed during the 'derby of the dead child' as Lazio and Roma fans united against the police aggression and succeeded in suspending the game before joining together to attack the police after the match. Likewise *ultras* from various groups attended the funeral of Gabriele Sandri. This included fans of Livorno and Roma, groups who traditionally would be sworn enemies of Lazio. Parma fans reinforced this solidarity on the anniversary of Sandri's death. Before their match with Livorno in November 2008, they attached a banner to the railings alongside the main roundabout approaching the Tardini stadium that read 'A year has passed, but we have not forgotten: justice for Gabriele'.

The creation of *ultras* as folk devils has given them an outsider status and reinforces their opposition to the central authorities. As a consequence of a number of similar events, the police have become the target for fan violence. This has created what Stefanini (2009) calls 'ACAB syndrome', named after the English term 'All Cops Are Bastards'. Consumption is being used to reinforce this aspect of the performance of the *mentalità ultras* identity. The abbreviation can be seen on a number of T-shirts worn by fans and is also exhibited in graffiti around stadiums and cities. For example, at Livorno, two of the three *ultras* groups utilize the acronym. One group is simply called 'ACAB'; the other is called 'Visitors 1312'. The latter was formed from the amalgamation of two groups, '1312' and 'Visitors'. '1312' is significant because it refers to the numerical positions in the alphabet of the letters comprising 'ACAB'. In contrast to the Livornesi *ultras*, the two ACAB groups are younger and in the 16–24 age bracket. This highlights a demographic shift in the *ultras*.

The performance of the anti-police attitude was witnessed in fan reactions to various commemorations for Carabinieri. The year 2003 saw an attack on a military base in Iraq which resulted in the death of twenty-eight people, including nineteen Italians, mostly Carabinieri. Serie A matches were cancelled in honour of the dead, but Serie B games continued. The depth of feeling towards the police was illustrated in the minute's silence before kick-off. Mantova fans whistled throughout the silence, whereas in Livorno the fans continued singing (Francesio 2008). Meanwhile, attacks on police increased dramatically in the 2006-7 season (Popham 2007). The zenith of this antipathy towards the police was reached after Raciti's death in Catania. During the minute's silence held to commemorate him, Torino fans sang through the silence, while at Roma, the fans whistled throughout (Francesio 2008). It is for this reason that Genny 'a Carogna was wearing a T-shirt saying 'Speziale Libero' to show solidarity with the Catania *ultrà* who was convicted of killing Raciti. It is significant that this feeling of persecution and anti-police attitude is spreading, as European *ultras* also are wearing 'Speziale Libero' T-shirts.

The *mentalità ultras* is also being reinforced through the government's actions to contain the violence. As mentioned in the previous chapter, after Raciti's death, the government quickly enforced 'the Pisanu Law'. This restricts certain articles inside the stadium. Regional autonomy, however, permits the local authorities and police to have discretion over which items are restricted.

> Some T-shirts, for example ... I am a free citizen; I can go around with Che Guevara T-Shirt, no? However, the moment in which I go to the stadium I am no longer a free citizen because there is a police officer who says: 'No, the T-shirt of Che Guevara cannot enter ... The moment you become a fan, that is on a Saturday or Sunday, you lose your civil rights, because no police officer can say in Viale Mameli [a general domestic street in Livorno] 'Remove the shirt!'. (Francesco, Livorno *ultras* member, Personal interview, June 2009)

The perceived injustice is helping to reinforce the 'Outsider' status of the *ultras*. Stefano's comments echo Cristiano Lucarelli's comments earlier about it not being illegal for a communist to play football. Wearing a T-shirt with the image of Che Guevara is not illegal, except at some (but not all) football stadiums when the police deems it political. The diverse approaches taken by different communes and police officers is helping to undermine the authority of the state and contributes to the overall crisis of legitimacy in the Italian state.

The use of the Daspo banning order also provides a similar narrative. Examples of inconsistent policing strengthen the *ultras* feelings of persecution. The police, not magistrates, issue these legal instruments and this simply reinforces the police as orchestrators of the repression. Confusion results from inconsistent regulation. For example, five Pisa fans were given Daspos for carrying toilet rolls because they were classed as 'inflammable material' (Lo Bianco and Messina 2008). In 2012, a Daspo was given to a player after he raised his shirt to show solidarity to two fans that were imprisoned for killing Raciti. Pietro Arcidiacono, a player for Consenza, was banned from attending a stadium for three years (Russo 2012). After the *Coppa Italia* final debacle, Genny 'a Carogna was given a Daspo for five years for wearing a T-shirt expressing support for Antonino Speziale. These examples reinforce the notion that *ultras*, and those who support them, are persecuted. The problem is not that fans are banned for violent or abusive acts. The issue is that Daspos are given by police and fans have no practical legal recourse.

The lack of state legitimation is reinforced through their approach to stadiums. Despite the stadium restrictions and Daspos, fans are still operating within the liminal space of the stadium. Despite the heavy police presence outside of Italian stadiums, the police are conspicuous by their absence inside. As witnessed at Genoa when the *ultras* stopped the match and ordered the players to remove their shirts, the police did not intervene. The same was true at the *Coppa Italia* final in 2014. Police do not enter the *curve* for fear of causing more trouble. A police officer interviewed after the riot in Catania that resulted in the death of Raciti, stated that they dare not enter the *curva* as 'it would have been considered an act of war. That's another country in there, outside the Italian Republic' (Richardson 2007). The police sanctify the sacred space of the *ultras* and permit an anarchic *mentalità ultras* to continue. In addition to the wide use of marijuana in the *curve*, banned objects are still smuggled into the stadium. This spectacularly occurred in May 2001 when Inter fans stole a scooter from an Atalanta fan before the game. They smuggled it into the top tier of the *curva*, set it alight and pushed it into the tier below.[10] Even though stadium regulations were tightened after the death of Raciti, Roma and Lazio fans still used homemade *carta bomba* and flares during their derby in December 2009. Smoke bombs and flares are continuously used at matches despite being banned by the Pisanu Law. During the game between Livorno and Bologna in February 2010, a rocket was fired across the pitch and landed in the Hippodrome next door to Livorno's stadium. The perpetrator could not be identified as it was launched from underneath the stand where there are no CCTV cameras. Their use is given tacit support by the authorities. Despite fireworks being banned by the Pisanu Law, firefighters are stationed in front of Livorno's *Curva Nord* at every match. They soak the running track that encircles the pitch so that it will not catch fire and they fill the long jump pit with water. This allows them to 'rescue' flares from the pitch and extinguish them quickly.

### 'The Pact of the Ultrà' the *mentalità ultras* is reinforced

The *mentalità ultras* was unintentionally reinforced by the authorities during the 2013-14 season. At the start of the season, the FIGC announced that it was going to clamp down on the racism that was occurring in the stadium.

They were going to start imposing partial and full stadium closures on clubs that participating in this form of abuse. While this was positive and long overdue, they also decided to use the same set of sanctions to tackle another form of abuse, 'territorial discrimination'. As was outlined earlier, the 1980s saw an increase in the amount of anti-Southern insults. This was incorporated into the *campanilistic* culture of abuse that existed between local rivals and extended to incorporate the anti-Southern rhetoric that was creeping into daily political life. Anti-Southern abuse took racialized form. In this way, it could be seen in the same pattern of abuse as xenophobia. Southerners were seen as being from outside of the nation, and were demonized for being poor, dirty and criminal, not unlike other immigrant groups in Italy. Therefore, the FIGC should have been applauded for attempting to tackle this problem. By linking it with racism, however, they spectacularly misread the situation and failed to understand the culture of the *ultras*.

*Ultras* have unified in the face of the 'repression' they feel that they are experiencing. Successive legislation and decrees, especially since the Pisanu Law, have given the *ultras* a persecution complex. This has manifested itself in 'ACAB syndrome'. The *ultras* were further unified after the imposition of stadium closures for 'territorial discrimination'. In October 2013, AC Milan were forced to play a match 'behind closed doors' after their fans chanted anti-Neapolitan songs and displayed a banner stating 'Napoli Colera' (Naples Cholera-sufferers). The implication was that Naples was dirty and disease-ridden. Moreover it was backward and uncivilized which is why it was suffering from a disease that was commonplace before the twentieth century. What the authorities did not expect was that AC Milan's rivals would come out in support.

This led to the headlines of the *Corriere dello Sport* declaring that there was 'The Pact of the Ultrà'. *Ultras* from clubs across the country planned coordinated action to resist these sanctions. The *ultras* of Inter and Juventus supported their rivals. More striking was the response of Napoli fans after AC Milan's punishment. They had been the original targets of the abuse that prompted the punishment from the Federation. Rather than welcome the sanctions, they showed solidarity with the *ultras* of AC Milan. They unfurled a similar banner to the AC Milan *striscione* stating, 'Naples cholera-sufferers. Now close our curva!', the Napoli fans directed abuse at themselves. At the same time, they called for the Federation to close their stadium. This pact reaffirms Maffesoli's notion that new collective forms are emerging despite the fragmentation of old groups. The *ultras* were unifying around a feeling of common '*repressione*'.

A further unintended outcome of the clampdown on 'territorial discrimination' was that it expanded beyond the *ultras*. In February 2014, AS Roma had their two ends closed as punishment for anti-Neapolitan chants. During this match, against Sampdoria, fans in the remaining two stands started the same chants that had led to the closure of the *curve*. They called for Vesuvius to erupt and 'wash [the city] with fire' (Bandini 2014). The following week only one stand was allowed to have fans. Non-*ultras* were showing solidarity. Not only did this give tacit support to the *ultras*; it also helped reinforce their self-belief that they are the 'legitimate' fans.

The problem with measures like this is that they punish *all* fans, not just the perpetrators. Unfortunately, many fans support their fellow fans. So when they are punished they come out in solidarity. This is further complicated by the lack of understanding of this type of abuse. Many fans do not see it as a problem. They see it as part of the culture of football fandom in Italy. *Campanilismo* is so embedded in Italian culture that football fans adopt it into their culture of abuse.

> And actually what is happening is that you can't have any more *campanilismo* because if you insult Napoli fans then you make this discrimination – you make a territorial discrimination. But the same doesn't happen if Milan fans insult our fans … there are not certain rules well written. If I know a rule I can respect it. If the rule is not written then it is impossible. (Lorenzo Contucci, AS Roma and lawyer, personal interview, January 2014)

*Ultras* are finely tuned to the hypocrisy of the authorities. Contucci highlights how the rule on 'territorial discrimination' is open to interpretation; there is no clear definition. As a lawyer, Contucci would like a clear definition to ensure understanding. He also illustrates the double standards of the rule. It is perfectly acceptable for Milan fans to chant anti-Roman songs, but not for them to sing the same songs about Naples. This point was also made by another Roma fan:

> The system in Italy is unclear. Juventus fans can make banners against Superga, the aircrash, but in Rome if we make chants against Napoli, we get fined. (Riccardo Bertolin, myRoma, personal interview, January 2014)

The hypersensitivity of fans and *ultras* to hypocrisy undermines the federation's attempts to stop this type of abuse. The lack of clarity from the authorities is reinforcing its own sense of illegitimacy while simultaneously providing a focus for the *mentalità ultras* to coalesce.

## Summary

The *ultras* operate in a strange paradox. They are both valorized and demonized. They have been labelled as 'folk devils', but still hold strong legitimacy. They have been incorporated into the patrimonial networks of the presidents, and in some cases they have been granted the concessions to run merchandising for the football club, or are given free tickets. Likewise, the police and authorities have granted them a degree of respect that elevates their role. All public order attention is focused on them as a problem. Unintentionally, this exalted position has been reinforced through the draconian measures of the Pisanu Law. Increased bureaucracy has made it harder for all fans to attend the stadium. This leaves the *ultras* at the vanguard of fandom in the stadium. Consequently, they have assumed the role as the guardians of football. They see their position as preserving a particular image of football in opposition to the new globalized commercial brand of the sport. Yet they are also seeking to preserve a particularly masculine image of the sport that excludes women and those from outside the local area. In extreme forms this has encouraged instrumental racism directed at players and fans. The choreographies of the *ultras* adds the colour and carnival to the spectacle of Italian football. Yet as Italian football struggles to compete in the global marketplace, aggressive masculine fans also alienate large sections of the global audience and damage the reputation of the league. When combined with frequent match-fixing scandals, Serie A becomes tarnished.

The globalization of football has created new sites for the articulation of identity. Simultaneously, local identity is reasserted while a broader national and pan-European collective *ultras* neo-tribe is forming: the *'Mentalità Ultras'*. Greater fragmentation and greater collective identification is occurring in parallel. The growth of consumer capitalism is also impacting the *ultras* identity. Again, it is a creating a space for resistance, as the 'No to Modern Football' movement shows. But it is also fuelling an alternative form of consumption. *Ultras* are producing and selling their own merchandise that is becoming a self-reifying image of the perfect form of the *ultras*-style of support. It is important not to continue to privilege the *ultras* position as other fans are equally important to the culture of football. The following chapter details other forms of fandom, including supporters' trusts and the official supporters' clubs that offer an alternative form of association for football fans. In doing so, they simultaneously reflect the continued decline of political involvement in Italy.

# 8

# Other Forms of Fandom

The argument was getting heated. Passions were rising along with the volume of the voices. In a small unit on the edge of Livorno, members of a supporters' club were debating the virtues of A.S. Livorno's president, Aldo Spinelli. On one side were those who supported Spinelli and all that he had achieved for the club. They argued that the football club had come from nothing, and that he had helped them win two promotions, and a return to Serie A for the first time in forty years. Furthermore, Livorno had played in a European competition for the first time in the club's history. Although they had been relegated two years later, they were in a strong position to return to Serie A. Meanwhile those in disagreement were getting more vociferous. The football club was underperforming on the field. Many fans felt that the team should have been challenging for the title, but they were struggling to win games. The team had been on a run of five straight draws and was losing ground on Parma and Bari above them. They blamed the president as he did not have the resources to fund new players, and even worse, he was not as well connected politically as the owners of Bari and Parma were. He had taken Livorno as far as he could and someone else needed to purchase the club to take it further. The debate raged for the duration of the club's opening hours. Other members who visited for various enquiries were drawn into the debate and asked for their opinion, which only added fuel to both sides. When the club closed at eight o'clock, neither side had come to a resolution and ultimately nothing had changed; the president was still in charge.

Football invokes strong emotion in its followers. It has long been seen as an avenue for a predominantly localized masculine form of identity. Yet this identity takes many different forms as fans have different motivations for their support (Bromberger 1995). Fans come from a range of backgrounds and bring a variety of views and ideas from their wider social milieu. Consequently, sport in general and football in particular, provide apposite vehicles to observe the minutiae of social life. In the mundane surroundings of the social spaces where fans congregate, it is possible to observe the wider dynamics taking place in society. In Italy, football provides the 'deep play' of society that permits a deeper understanding of society. Debates like the one above articulate specific interactions and help create and recreate these dynamics over time. Much of the academic focus of football fans in Italy has centred on the *ultras*. Yet there are many other fans who 'live and breathe' football and see it as an important part of their identity but do not participate in the same ritual space. Across the country there are many official supporters' clubs that are run by thousands of dedicated volunteers and these clubs provide another space for the performance of identity. There are also new supporters' trusts forming, which give a different type of engagement with the football club. The following chapter will detail the features of these official supporters' clubs and supporters' trusts. In doing so, it moves the debate away from the *ultras*, who occupy a privileged position in academic literature and political discourse, thanks to their roots in the visual, direct action of the 1970s. Yet there are other forms of political engagement in Italian football. Yet despite Robert Putnam's assertion that local associations automatically generate political involvement, the wider power networks that operate in Italian football still limit political engagement.

## Official supporters' clubs

Official supporters' clubs provide an alternative form of supporter association, alongside the *ultras*. They have been around since the 1950s, with the *ultras* emerging from these organizations. Official supporters' clubs are, as their name suggests, affiliated to the football club and they operate within the patrimonial networks of the football clubs. Fundamentally, the difference between the groups is demographic. Most *ultras* are young males, whereas the official supporters' clubs encompass all ages and genders. Anyone can become a '*socio*', a member, upon paying their membership fees. Membership is through a different set of rituals to the *ultras*. Consequently, the official supporters' clubs do not replicate the focus on choreographies, politics and violence of the *ultras*, although members may still participate in the activities of the *ultras*. Likewise there is no spatial demarcation between groups. Although the *ultras* would restrict themselves to the *curve* at the ends of the pitch, official supporters' club members can be found in the *curve*, the tribunes along the length of the pitch or in the grandstand. Therefore, discussion of the official supporters' clubs presents an alternative view of Italian football supporters. This section will detail the organization and activities of these associations and locate them within the broader argument illustrating the decline in social capital and political participation in Italy.

Official supporters' clubs are central to a number of fans. Like many other aspects of Italian football, the commercial activities have been decentralized away from the football club. As highlighted earlier, some *ultras* organizations like Lazio's *Irriducibili* were granted the rights to sell tickets or merchandising. Despite many Italian clubs establishing dedicated ticket outlets, official supporters' clubs still operate as ticket outlets and local distributers for merchandise and information related to the football club. Official supporters' clubs also organize away travel for fans and arrange social events. When important matches approach, these clubs become focal points for local fans trying to obtain tickets. As Guschwan (2011, p. 1996) argues:

> In eras past, neighborhood fan clubs were an essential link between professional teams and ticket buyers, that is, fans. While fan groups are no longer the primary distributor of tickets, organized fan clubs remain a vital part of local social life for many Italians.

Many of these are situated in bars, while others are in dedicated club headquarters. Either way, they are located in the heart of the community that they serve.

Official supporters' clubs are set up by fans independently of the football club. In this manner they are not dissimilar to the *ultras*. However, supporters' clubs can choose to become affiliated to the football club, which the *ultras* would never do:

> Everyone can found a Club Amaranto [supporters' club]; later on one can ask to have relations with the football club and can be a member of associated clubs … Innumerable clubs can exist. There is no limit and the football club of AS Livorno does not have a voice in this and cannot influence the clubs. (Max, official Livorno supporters' club director, personal interview, June 2009)

Official status grants these clubs concessions to sell merchandise, and to use the football club's logo on the supporters' clubs details. Although the football club does not dictate the activities of the official supporters clubs, they provide concessions over merchandise and access to players. In this way, they are incorporated into the football club's patrimonial network.

In order to access these activities, fans become a *socio*, a fee-paying member. In return they often receive membership gifts, opportunities to meet players and invites to end-of-season dinners. They can also access discounted rates for travel to away games. Official supporters' clubs also provide financial benefits for their members. Berlusconi provided a range of incentives to join the AC Milan supporters' clubs after he took over AC Milan. The extent of this patrimonial network facilitated his move into politics as he utilized the same practices when he set up *Forza Italia*, his political party. Other official supporters clubs negotiate benefits for their members, as they have access to a wide network of fans. These can include cheaper cinema tickets or special deals on hotels.

The clubs are the embodiment of the history, personality and social capital of the football club, supporters' club and member. Here the image of the city, supporters' club and football club are entwined. As Guschwan (2011, p. 1998) argues:

> The clubhouse functions as a museum devoted to the exposition and celebration of culturally significant artefacts … Roma Club Testaccio's 'shared vision of history, identity and heritage' is literally taped, painted, and tacked onto the walls of the clubhouse as selection of highlights from Roman History.

Although Guschwan was focusing on one club in the heart of Rome, this is typical of other club headquarters. Throughout Livorno, clubhouses will be decorated with significant moments in Livorno's history, both as a city and as a football club. They will have scarves, pennants and posters. Frequently they will have club jerseys signed by star players like Igor Protti or Cristiano Lucarelli. Significantly, they will frequently have many photos that show the directors and members of the supporters' club with star players. The social capital of the club is clearly visible for all members to see.

The independent nature of the supporters' clubs is reflected in the naming conventions of the clubs. Unlike the *Ultras* who name their groups after political groups or violence, names of official supporters' groups are more sedate. Some are named after the area of the city in which they are located, such as Sampdoria Club Rapallo, or Roma Club Testaccio. Others are named after prominent players, such as Club Igor Protti in Livorno, or Juventus Club Langa Bianconera Alessandro Del Piero in Cortemilia near Turin. Local history can also influence the nomenclature of the clubs as in the case of the Roma Club Impero Romano, named after the Roman Empire. A female supporters' club at Livorno is called B52s, and is named after the Second World War American bombers that were stationed at Camp Darby, an American airbase located between Livorno and Pisa. Some clubs are also named after family members in order to preserve their memory.

The clubs come to embody their operators and become a space to perform their identity. The B52s is located in a bar in Livorno and this provides for a more socially orientated approach to their club. Like other headquarters mentioned above, it is decorated with memorabilia of A.S. Livorno, such as team shirts, posters and photographs. This club is also more frivolous as it embodies the personality of the director. This was evident from my first meeting with her as she responded to my interest in the club and the city with, 'Why Livorno? We are all pirates and prostitutes.' This Livornese performance reaffirmed the history of the city and the 'earthy' character of its inhabitants. The B52s club provides other opportunities to perform this Livornese character through the consumption of a range of products that were produced by the club. T-shirts were sold in the deep-red colours of the city and the football team and were emblazoned with the passage, 'Better to be unemployed in Ardenza [the suburb of Livorno near the beach where the stadium is located] than a worker in Milan.' Similarly, they also produced a range of stickers with similar amusing and vulgar quotations, with many directly reflecting *campanilismo* and directed at Pisa.

The physical proximity of these clubs to the local residential area allows for ease of access for the members and opportunities to meet other fans. Simmel (1950) highlighted the mundanity of social interactions. With his theory of sociability, he argued that people come together for the sheer pleasure of having shared interests. For many fans, there is no greater desire than to be with other people who have a common outlook. For Simmel, sociability was an end in itself – it was mundane. The symbol of the group is themselves. The mutual and everyday pleasure of the meeting friends and acquaintances is a symbol of themselves. While some groups and individuals seek wider meaning or action from themselves or their group, like politically active fan groups, it is not automatic that a group generates this. We cannot assume that broader social action emerges from social situations; this can only be defined within the group itself.

Official supporters' clubs create these sociable spaces by providing facilities in the local neighbourhood and by organizing social events. In this way they not only generate social capital among members but also help to provide a stronger attachment to the football club. Supporters' clubs organize football tournaments, Christmas parties and end-of-season dinners. Often the football clubs' players will attend to provide a 'star attraction' to entice participants. A major criticism of many football writers, from fans, journalists and academics, is that increased commodification of sport has led to an increased distance from fans. Taylor (1968, 1971) even proposed that this was a reason for hooliganism. Giulianotti and Robertson (2006), however, have demonstrated that members of Celtic and Rangers supporters' clubs in North America felt closer to the players of their respective football clubs than they would have done in Glasgow. This was because players and ex-players attended the clubs' social engagements and dinners, which would not have happened as regularly in Scotland. Likewise, the supporters' clubs in Italy provide this opportunity to interact with players and management of the football club, as well as allowing them to interact with fellow *soci*. This provides an environment for people to socialize and interact away from the family and work colleagues and allows them to build bridging social capital, trust and associations in a wider community.

## Supporters' clubs and political engagement

Although official supporters' clubs are sociable spaces, this does not automatically translate into wider political action. It is important to remember that football clubs rarely provide concessions to fans out of pure charity. As Merkel (2012) argues in relation to the Bundesliga, German fans have not achieved the '50 + 1' ownership model through the benevolence of owners and the DFB (German Football Federation). It was achieved by fans fighting for these rights. How this political activism grows among groups of fans is important. Putnam's (1993, 2000) central argument suggests that participation in voluntary associations contributes to increased political involvement and this underpins democracy. Likewise, Habermas (1989) suggested that debate undertaken in public created a 'public sphere' and this assisted in the formation of liberal political democracy. Although these clubs can create networks of social capital and they constitute a 'public sphere' where local and national politics are discussed, this does not automatically translate into further political engagement.

As previously noted, official supporters' clubs are recognized by the football club. This provides access to a wider network of supporters' clubs. In some of the smaller football clubs, this network is informal. The directors and members of supporters' clubs meet at matches, attend meetings with the football club, or organize end-of-season dinners together. Larger football clubs have official umbrella organizations. These *Centri di Coordinamento* (Coordination Centres) manage the various supporters' clubs and their activities. These coordination centres reflect the link between the fans and the club. Fiorentina's Associazione Centro Coordimento Viola Club ties the violet colours of the football team to the official supporters' clubs, many of whom will have 'Viola' in their nomenclature.[1] Meanwhile, Juventus Club DOC uses the abbreviation 'DOC' that is used on

Italian food and wine to verify that it is from a particular region and of the highest quality.²

These coordination centres are associated with the FISSC or *Federazione Italiana Sostenitori Squadre Calcio* (Federation of Supporters of Italian Football Teams).³ This federation was formed over forty years ago to unite the coordination centres nationally. It provides advice to coordination centres and tries to provide an alternative voice for supporters. It is important to note that this is not the equivalent of the independent Football Supporters Federation in Britain, or *Bundniss Aktiver Fussball Fans* (Association of Active Fans, BAFF) in Germany.⁴ These organizations are politically involved with various aspects of football, and the changes that have taken place since the 1990s in relation to policing, stadiums and commercialization. The FISSC does not engage in political activities in the same way, as will be discussed later.

It is helpful to trace the development of supporters' associations in England to illustrate the commonalities and differences in Italy. The National Federation of Football Supporters Clubs (NFFSC) was the earliest organization of football fans in England and originated in 1927. Like the current Italian FISSC, this represented the official supporters associations affiliated to football clubs. Taylor (1992) argues that these supporters' clubs, and the NFFSC, were seen as deferential to the football clubs, and were unofficial fund-raisers for the owners. Fans at Luton Town and Plymouth Argyle raised money for new stands; the entrance turnstiles that were built in the 1920s at Argyle's Home Park are still in existence today. After the war, fans at Oxford United raised money to buy the ground.

There were few attempts to mobilize this financial support into executive power in the boardroom. Although the chairs of some supporters' clubs, notably Aldershot, Plymouth Argyle and Southampton, gained access to the board, there is no indication that this was due to the benevolence of the directors, but probably due to the fans being from the same social network. As Taylor (1992, pp. 38–9) argues:

> The most typical pattern of supporter-club liaison throughout the period 1930–70 ... was the 'one-way' system which involved a Board member acting as president and/or Chairman of the Supporters' Club and its committee. There appears to be no examples of Supporters' Club members being given the opportunity even to elect which of the Board members should sit on their committees.

Despite the paternalistic approach of football club directors, there was at least some dialogue between fans and the board, even if it was one way. The situation in Italy has been very different and members of the football club may be *soci* of supporters' clubs, but purely on an individual basis.

By the 1980s, the NFFSC was seen as too official, undemocratic and lacking campaigning credentials (Brown 1998). The Heysel tragedy provoked many fans to challenge the status quo in football. Led by Rogan Taylor, the Football Supporters Association (FSA) was formed in 1985. With a younger and more politically astute membership, the FSA developed a more prominent media profile. It was initially successful in campaigning against racism and the treatment of England fans abroad. Its most notable success was in challenging the introduction of identity cards for all fans. It is instructive that the resistance to the *tessera del tifoso* in Italy has not necessitated a national fan organization, and consequently, fan resistance has not completely eradicated the *tessera*. While national support is necessary to provide unity and strength in numbers, a lack of national focus can impede organizations like the FSA. As a result, the FSA was unable to sustain its power. The outcome was that 'the FSA is unable to mobilize fans because in an increasingly deregulated environment there are few national issues' (King 2003, p. 182). As Italy is the deregulated nation *par excellence* and local identification remains strong, this remains a major issue for fans of Italian football clubs. When fans do not unify nationally (or across Europe) it significantly weakens their ability to challenge the hegemonic authorities.

The demise of the FSA was due to an increase in Independent Supporters' Associations (ISAs). These ISAs were arising due to the increased commercialization of football during the 1990s. For Touraine (1981) and Melucci (1989), new social movements are often temporary, emerging and coalescing around a singular contemporary issue. Fans no longer mobilized around traditional class structures but formed new groups to challenge the changes to their clubs. Often these ISAs were established to challenge specific local issues, such as stadium redevelopments, relocations, or issues with boards of directors. The ISAs grew out of the fanzine movement that stimulated debate among fans (Jary et al. 1991). Italy, however, did not have a strong fanzine culture (Dal Lago and De Biasi 1994). The result is that the democratization of debate within football culture did not have the same stimulus as in the United Kingdom. The result is the polarized positions of the *ultras* and official supporters' clubs. While the *ultras* represent one form of new social movement, as Testa (2009) argues, alternative forms of political engagement have not taken hold in Italy.

The FISSC has become involved with specific transformations within football, specifically the Italian government's laws relating to identity cards. The FISSC promotes the *tessera del tifoso* along with the advantages associated with being seen as a positive fan of the football club.[5] However, by simply complying with government proposals, they risk being seen as part of the government's patrimonial network. The FISSC also promote specific initiatives, in particular 'Fair Play' projects. There are not, however, any anti-racism or anti-homophobia projects. While they publish a monthly newsletter, written by fans, entitled *La Voce del Tifoso* (The Voice of the Fan), this promotes the various initiatives of the Federation, as well as highlighting the transformations taking place in football from a fan's perspective. While the organization engages in a lot of very good work and tries to present itself as an alternative to the *ultras*, its relatively apolitical stance sees it remain relatively passive. In contrast to the strength and visibility of the *ultras*, this sees the FISSC struggle to provide an alternative voice for fans and further illustrates the decline of political engagement in Italy. Ultimately, it is suffering from the same problem as the NFFSC in England.

Despite the lack of national (or European) action, members of supporters' clubs do protest. The stadium permits fans to vent visceral expressions of anger or despair as part of the ritual of football. The boards of football clubs acknowledge some political protests, as Taylor (1971) highlighted. Unlike pitch invasions, members of the grandstand picketing the players' exit can elicit a response from the board. This was witnessed in Livorno in 2009 when the club hit a run of bad form. Members of various supporters' clubs, and independent fans, would wait outside the exit after every match. Often this was to wait for friends and family who were working as stewards or administrators. Significantly, these protestors are not *ultras*, as they engage in a very different form of protest. With the emotion of the game still strong, these fans wanted to vent their feelings at the players and management of the football club.

Much of the disagreement centred on the president Aldo Spinelli, as illustrated in the introduction to this chapter. Portelli (1993) has argued that there is a 'love–hate' relationship between Italian fans and presidents. From one perspective the fans are happy that their club has done well, thanks to the resources of the president. Yet they also resent the fact that they are reliant on the president and that that he will never love the club as much as the fans. Spinelli divided opinion whenever his name was mentioned in supporters' clubs, at the stadium or elsewhere in Livorno. The only time physical violence was witnessed in Livorno occurred after the match with Modena. An argument occurred between two fans. An elderly fan was vociferously supporting Spinelli and clearly disagreeing with a forty-year-old fan. Speaking in a manner that was audible to all those around him, the elderly fan pointed to the history of Livorno football club and reiterated that the club had had a difficult post-war history. He drew on his own experience of watching the club and argued that they had not played in Serie A for over fifty years. They went out of business in the 1990s and had to fight their way through the leagues. The elderly gentleman attributed the subsequent relative success of Livorno to Aldo Spinelli who bought the club in 1999. Since then the club had been promoted back into Serie A and played in the UEFA Cup for the first time in the club's history. In contrast, the forty-year-old fan spoke of the immediacy of the situation. He argued Spinelli had taken the club as far as he could. He did not have the financial or political resources to move the club forward. Furthermore, he was not from Livorno but from Genoa; he had no love of the club. Both sides reiterated their position and emotions increased until the elderly gentleman grew exasperated with his younger counterpart and pushed him away. At this point others joined in to prevent any further escalation. The overall mood was only abated when the players started to exit the ground and board the team coach. This gave the congregated fans an opportunity to express their feelings. They jeered and booed the players, with some fans shouting 'shame' or 'players of shit' or 'idiots' (using the more vulgar vernacular expression of *coglione*). Once the gates ahead opened, and the team coach had sped away, the focus for the ire of the crowd had gone, and they dispersed.

Like the *ultras* members of supporters' clubs also have strong legitimacy with the football club and players. As can be seen from the number of supporters' clubs' social events that are attended by the players, fans are part of a wider network. Players also act as intermediaries during the protests and arguments outside of the gates. Taylor (1971) highlighted how the authorities treated a pitch invasion differently than a protest by fans at the stadium gates. This was reflected in Livorno. After a 1-0 home defeat to AlbinoLeffe in April 2009, star players Alessandro Diamanti and Massimo Loviso talked to fans outside the gates to explain the situation. More significantly, the president Spinelli exited the stadium. He approached the fans, alongside the director of football, Francesco Ceravolo, and explained that he took the concerns of the fans seriously and that he saw promotion to Serie A as paramount. He told the fans that he would take decisive action. Spinelli was true to his word. With two games of the season to go he sacked the manager Leonardo Acori and installed a former player, Gennaro Ruotolo, as manager. He then 'supported' his inexperienced new manager by sitting next to him on the bench during the subsequent matches and providing motivational speeches in training.

Fans and *ultras* are seen as important aspects of the football club. Dialogue and communication takes place between protesting *ultras* and protesting fans from supporters' clubs. This grants both parties a degree of legitimacy within the overall power network. In this way both groups are incorporated into the hegemonic power of the football clubs. It helps the owners gain consent and limits the power of the fans. Yet this form of protest is informal and rests on the charisma and authority of the owners. It is instructive that Italian football clubs have had Referee Liaison Officers for decades, but only the clubs competing in European competition have Supporters' Liaison Officers due to this being imposed by UEFA. There are encouraging signs, however that this is being expanded, as Serie B clubs will begin to introduce this position in 2015. Italian fans need to challenge for more formal channels of communication with the football club. Yet political protest has been limited to such an extent that few fan groups are trying to get a voice on the board. There are signs, however, that this may be starting to change.

## Supporters' trusts

Potentially there is a middle ground between the official supporters' clubs and the *ultras*. As Brown (1998, p. 64) argues, 'It is extremely difficult for any fans' organization to legitimately claim that they represent the views of a majority of a clubs' support.' Football fans are incredibly heterogeneous. Supporters' Trusts, however, can provide a space to engage politically with the power structures of Italian football, without the confrontational approach of many *ultras*' groups. Likewise, they will not just acquiesce to the authorities' demands like the FISSC. Supporters' Trusts highlight the importance of political engagement and direction as a prerequisite for civic engagement rather than a by-product of it. This is not to say that political activism cannot come from pre-existing social networks, but that these forms of engagement derive from specific localized issues.

Supporters' Trusts emerged out of the ISA movement in England as a direct response to a series of financial crises hitting various clubs. The first trust was established in 1992 at Northampton Town after the football club started experiencing severe financial problems. The Northampton Town FC Trust was established to raise money to save the football club from bankruptcy. This has since become a model for other supporters' trusts in the United Kingdom as various clubs have encountered financial problems, like Portsmouth and Plymouth Argyle. Some trusts have managed to take a controlling interest in their club, with Brentford and Exeter City both being run by their trusts. It is also important to differentiate trusts from ISAs and official supporters' clubs. As Dunn (2014, p. 3) states,

A supporters' trust is not a supporters' club, but is a properly-registered company, mostly set up as an industrial and provident society, where one share is owned by each member, and governed by an elected board. Money made by IPSs is invested back into the organisation to further its aims and objectives; in practise, with supporters' trusts, this means buying shares in the club, or funding community projects related to the club.

Unlike ISAs, trusts have a specific role to raise funds to buy shares in the football club and engage in community work. ISAs had a political role to campaign against specific elements within football, such as inclusion policies, stadium redevelopment and commercialism. This does not mean that supporters' trusts do not engage in political campaigns. After Northampton Town's trust was elected onto the board, they were the first club to introduce an equal opportunities policy. Elsewhere, supporters' trusts have joined campaigns for safe standing to be reintroduced at English stadiums and to prevent the establishment of a League 3 comprising Premier League B teams.

The supporters' trust movement developed with the introduction of Supporters Direct. This was established with the support of the New Labour government in 1999. This reinforces the importance of securing governmental support in order to provide the financial and political security of the organization. Supporters Direct acts as a political body that is a repository for information assisting fans setting up trusts. It has since expanded outside of Britain with Supporters Direct Europe. It is important for fans to put aside personal egos and parochial rivalries. In this way they can start sharing information. With a cooperative movement and a coherent message, fans can begin to challenge the hegemonic position of the authorities.

Supporters in Campo became the first umbrella organization of Italian supporters' trusts in June 2013. It united the growing interest in fan involvement in Italy and was supported by an EU project looking at community and supporter involvement in football. The importance of European connections was reinforced as it affiliated to Supporter Direct Europe. It launched with a handbook declaring *Il Calcio senza Tifosi perde la propria anima* (Football without fans loses its soul). It attempts to make the case for supporters' trusts and also lays down practical and legal guidelines for establishing trusts. Significantly, this handbook also lays out the general guiding principle of trusts by declaring that 'The supporters trust is to design and implement the development and growth of community values and for a stronger social and economic presence of its relative territory' (Supporters in Campo 2013). These supporters' trusts were not simply to achieve democratization in the boardroom, but to be a social and economic benefit to the wider community.

In the short time they have been active, supporters' trusts in Italy have achieved a modicum of success. Five of these trusts have obtained a shareholding in their football club (Taranto, Modena, Arezzo, Ancona and Rimini). Meanwhile, four have achieved representation on the board of the football club (Taranto, Modena, Arezzo and Piacneza). It is significant that the early members have come from smaller clubs, as they did in England. One trust associated with a Serie A club, Hellas Verona, was also involved: Verona Col Cuore. Elsewhere, fans of A.S. Roma have also established a supporters' trust called MyRoma. Unfortunately, they have not joined Supporters in Campo. As Nash (2000) highlighted in relation to English ISAs, there is internal contestation both within and between organizations as they determine the direction of the organization. Ultimately, both organizations would be strengthened through sharing ideas and providing a powerful incentive to other trusts across Italy.

Perhaps the most interesting supporters' trust in Italy has been established in Taras in Puglia. The local football team, Taranto, has played in various leagues since its establishment in 1927, mainly between Serie B and Serie D. The club was declared bankrupt in 1993 after they suffered financial difficulties while in Serie B. They were re-established and allowed to compete in Serie D. The club continued to suffer financial difficulties and was insolvent another three times – the final time occurred in 2012. On this occasion the fans intervened and drew on the experience of supporters' trusts in Europe and founded l'Aps Fondazione Taras 706 a.C.[6]. They own over a quarter of the football club and have representatives on the board. This trust is the most active in Italy as it campaigns on a variety of football and local political matters. In May 2014, campaigners, including the trust, successfully fought to allow the sports field at the Naval Centre, Maricentro, to be used for football. Outside of football, members of the trust have also campaigned on local political matters. The largest local employer is the ILVA steelworks. This plant accounts for 83 per cent of Italy's pollution (Parliamentary Questions European Parliament 2007). The result is that many of the local inhabitants are dying from various diseases, including leukaemia and cancer. The conflict is that if the plant is closed, there would be no jobs, but if it stays open then the local population has a shortened life expectancy. Fondazione Taras is campaigning to clean up the steelworks and ensure its economic viability for the town.

Despite the emerging signs of wider political involvement by Italian supporters' trusts, the movement is still in its infancy. Part of this is related to the parochialism of football fans. Even though *campanilismo* is a strong cultural factor in Italy, this is a problem of all football fans. As King (2003, p. 184) argues:

> While it is possible that fans can be mobilised on a national level for certain critical developments such as the introduction of all-seater stadiums, it is almost impossible to sustain national fan groups beyond a period of crisis.

The focus on the local can hinder wider development. Although the *ultras* have developed a wider *mentalità ultras* in the face of opposition to draconian legislation and police repression, the supporters' trusts need to do the same. Groups like *Supporters in Campo* can provide the central resources and moral encouragement to support individual trusts and share information. It is also important for these organizations to connect to the wider European network of football fans that are engaged in comparable activities. Although the local contexts vary, football fans across Europe are experiencing similar impacts on their clubs. Football Supporters Europe (FSE)[7] potentially provides the wider umbrella organization that can facilitate the collaborative exchange of information and reinforce fan democracy. Only by sharing information can these new social movements develop. More importantly, only then can they begin to have an impact.

## Summary

Throughout this book it has been argued that a hegemonic elite utilize personal and political networks to maintain their position. Football is central to this, and fans operate within this network. Complex power networks operate between politicians, entrepreneurs and club presidents. In many cases, these exist within the same individuals. Football club presidents seek to maintain their power using football and seek to both legitimate and pacify *ultras* and fans in various ways. This creates a complex approach to political engagement by fans in Italy. Although football clubs cannot tell official supporters' clubs what to do, they have been incorporated into the patrimonial networks of clubs. The football club provides concessions to these supporters' clubs, allowing them to sell merchandise and tickets, as well as providing players with end-of-season dinners. While this helps build a strong local rapport between fans and football clubs, it also allows the authorities to minimize protest. When protest does occur, it is the manager that is removed, not the owner.

Some fans are starting to follow European forms of protest and are trying to gain a democratic voice within their football clubs. Currently, communication between football clubs, fans and *ultras* is informal and based on who is protesting the most vociferously. Supporters' trusts are attempting to formalize this communication and gain a voice for fans in the boardroom. Potentially they can also be powerful tools to make Italian football more inclusive. In doing so, they can provide an alternative to the *ultras* style of support. At the moment these trusts are operating in the lower league football clubs, but if a trust like MyRoma can join the wider Italian and European networks then it can lend the whole movement gravitas and help move Italian football forward.

# 9
# 'Year Zero'

On Tuesday 25 June 2013 Italy's tax police, the Guardia di Finanza, undertook a systematic raid across forty-one football clubs across Italy. This raid searched eighteen Serie A clubs, including AC Milan, Juventus, Inter, Roma and Lazio. Eleven clubs from Serie B were raided, including Livorno, Bari and Brescia, as well as a further twelve from the lower leagues. Dubbed *Calcio Malato* (Sick Football), these raids were ordered by prosecutors in Naples to investigate tax evasion and money laundering, which they suspected took place through the transfer of players. Echoing the financial problems of 2001, the Neapolitan magistrates also alleged that clubs had made 'systematic' billing for non-existent transactions. Further links to past scandals resurfaced when it was revealed that the Guardia were also investigating the agents Alejandro Mazzoni and Alessandro Moggi – the latter being a central figure in the *calciopoli* scandal of 2006. Many clubs declined to comment on the investigation. The president of Inter, Massimo Moratti, sought to defuse the situation and stated that 'It wasn't a search, just a request for past documentation. Nothing to be concerned about' (*La Gazzetta dello Sport* 2013a). The global financial crisis of 2008 and recession in Italy had led to a wholesale crackdown on tax evasion. These raids can be seen as an extension of this concerted effort to tackle the problem. High-profile athletes were also caught up in the crackdown, including Diego Maradona from his time at Napoli in the 1980s and 1990s.

Six weeks later, there was the culmination of two years of investigations into match-fixing. Stefano Mauri, the Lazio captain, was banned for six months for his failure to report match-fixing (*La Gazzetta dello Sport* 2013b). Mauri was one of eight other players who were fined and banned by the FIGC. In addition, Lazio and Lecce were also fined for the actions of their players. This was the third consecutive summer that clubs had been fined or had a points deduction for match-fixing. This followed the results of the *Calcioscommesse* scandal involving twenty-seven clubs, resulting in Sampdoria, Torino, Atalanta and Siena receiving penalties in 2012, and Atalanta and Lecce in 2011. Since *calciopoli*, only two seasons, 2008-9 and 2013-14, have not resulted in points deductions for clubs. In 2009, Cagliari was docked points (subsequently reversed) for filing an unauthorized lawsuit, while the following year Bologna was deducted points for unpaid taxes and wages. In a continuation of the arguments laid out in this book, these raids and scandals can also be seen as further evidence of the failure of the central authorities to impose itself over its citizens. They can, however, also be seen as an attempt by the federation to try and reassert its authority. Yet this continued weakness was further demonstrated by continued fan protests throughout the 2013-14 season in relation to the FIGC's attempt to stop 'territorial discrimination'. The disruption caused during the 2014 *Coppa Italia* final also revealed the serious structural problems within Italian football. After outlining the response of clubs and authorities to the current situation, this chapter will present some future directions for Italian football.

## The 'English Model'

The introduction to *Football Italia* highlighted the decline of Italian football in this era of globalization. This has been reinforced by comments from managers in Serie A. The Juventus (and current national team) manager, Antonio Conte said in April 2013 that 'Italian football has come to a standstill and that should be a concern for everyone' (*The Independent* 2013). This supports what Jose Mourinho stated when he coached in Italy: 'Italian football is not liked by the rest of the world' (Lawrence 2008). Italy has dropped below Germany and Portugal in the UEFA coefficient tables and is in danger of falling further, behind France. As the original globalized league, the English Premier League continues to be the benchmark upon which other leagues are measured. In Italy in particular, there has long been a neurotic relationship with the English game that was introduced in the nineteenth century. As a result it looks to England, for example, but continues to take an Italian approach to governance and organization.

One such trope that epitomizes this relationship is the term *modello inglese* (English Model). The Italian government and media talk about applying an 'English Model' to resolve the problems in Italian football, especially in relation to hooliganism and policing. Although putatively based on the Taylor Report, the 'English Model' was not actually explained or developed and had become rhetoric to symbolize a hard-line approach to violence (Bianchi 2005; Valdiserri

2008; *La Gazzetta dello Sport* 2008b; Francesio 2008; D'Auria 2009). As D'Auria (2009, p. 89) states, the 'English Model', as laid out in the Taylor Report, is:

> principally orientated to reaching four fundamental objectives: 1) reinventing the stadium as a public space and therefore re-evaluating the sporting community; 2) rediscovering the sense of spectacle of the footballing encounter; 3) to give attention to the customer satisfaction of the fans, pampered and handled as customers; 4) to introduce control measures for the regular attendees at the stadium.

As has been demonstrated throughout this book, an 'English Model' has not actually been implemented as there has not been wide-scale redevelopment of stadium safety, the implementation of wider commercial practices, nor reform of policing. If anything, the sense of spectacle and customer satisfaction has been diminished through the imposition of draconian legislation. Ironically the changes within the 'English Model' also provide an alternative symbol to fans. The commercialization and commodification of the game represents something for many fans to resist with the 'No to modern football' movement. Paradoxically, English fans represented the model of support for Italian *ultras* and hooligan groups across Europe (Dal Lago 1990; Dal Lago and De Biasi 1994; Podaliri and Balestri 1998; Spaaij 2006). As Francesio (2008, p. 73) states sardonically, 'evidently there is always an "English Model" to refer to'.

Central to the symbolism of the 'English Model' is the continuing crisis in Italian football. The first decade of the twenty-first century has seen Italian football rocked by financial scandals that have affected large Italian businesses and their football subsidiaries, such as Parma, Lazio, Fiorentina and Napoli. This has been compounded by scandals including forged passports, forged financial declarations and doping. The nadir of the crisis in Italian football was reached in 2006 when the *calciopoli* scandal was leaked to the Italian media. *Calciopoli* revealed the intricate patrimonial networks of politicians, businessmen and the football authorities that were operating in Italian football. Strategic charismatic leaders were extending their patronage across the network in order to favour their teams. *Calciopoli* was compounded by the *Calcioscommesse* scandal involving twenty-seven teams in match-fixing. The culmination of the years of scandal has not led to any widespread change within the game as existing practices have continued. Fan apathy has led to a decline in attendance at football stadiums and continued violence from the *ultras*. Less than a year after *calciopoli*, violence between Catania and Palermo fans led to the death of a policeman, Filippo Raciti. Nine months later, Gabriele Sandri, a Lazio fan, was shot and killed by a police officer. The government adopted the Pisanu Law in an attempt to enforce an 'English Model', and impose some regulation upon football, but without understanding the full details of the Taylor Report.

Throughout this book it has been argued that political debate has been marginalized as the hegemonic elite accumulate resources and power to maintain their position. The Pisanu Law reflect this lack of political dialogue. As Lorenzo Contucci argues,

> In Italy when there is *confusione* you know, when there is an accident in the stadium, after two or three days you have a new law. It is an emotional law and sometimes it is not fair and it is not correct. In Italy the *Daspo* it is done directly by the police and there is no control over it. While in England there is a proposal I think, by the police, and then there is the judge that gives the banning order. (Lorenzo Contucci, AS Roma and lawyer, personal interview, January 2014)

The problem with this emotional reactive legislation is that there is no significant public or parliamentary debate to work through all aspects of the regulations. Testa (2013) argues that as these laws are imposed using the *Decreto Legge* (Decree Laws), they have actually been used to bypass parliamentary debate, particularly during Berlusconi's administration. Because the *Decteri Leggi* are quickly introduced they require continued readjustment; a solution that was debated thoroughly in parliament would produce a more enduring and beneficial result (Contucci 2010).

The overarching argument of the Taylor Report was to improve the safety at stadiums through stadium reconstruction and reformed policing (Taylor 1990). Yet neither of these points have been addressed in relation to the Pisanu Law. Many of the Italian stadiums are antiquated and have poor facilities. After the death of Raciti, only four stadiums passed the safety review (Sanminiatelli 2007; Kiefer 2007b; Hamil et al. 2010). Despite this, there were no provisions to improve stadium infrastructure in the Pisanu Law. Fundamentally, the Taylor Report sought to prevent congestion at entrances to stadiums and on the terraces, which was a significant factor contributing to the Hillsborough tragedy. The Pisanu Law has not acknowledged this aspect. It has in fact added to the congestion at turnstiles by instigating an identity check to ensure hooligans do not enter the stadium. However, these checks are disregarded when there is excessive congestion at the turnstiles and fans have been admitted without checks at Parma and Livorno. Ticket sales are not adequately controlled as approximately 1,000 Napoli fans attended their match at Livorno despite the

*Osservatorio* banning all away fans. Furthermore, some of the features of the Taylor Report were never implemented in Britain. For example, membership cards for fans were never introduced in Britain after widespread opposition from fans, yet the equivalent in Italy, the *tessera del tifoso* was introduced in 2009. If an 'English Model' is to be implemented in Italy, studies must be undertaken to fully understand the situation in England.

A key element of the Taylor Report (1990) related to the architecture of the terracing within the stadium. The report required that perimeter fences should be dismantled to ensure that fans had a safe exit from the end in the event of an emergency. Within Italy, only Fiorentina and Juventus have removed the Perspex fencing that encloses the *curve*. In addition to the removal of the perimeter fences, numbered seating was installed in British stadiums, and followed by similar measures in the Netherlands. In combination with Foucauldian surveillance techniques, numbered seating permitted the identification of individual troublemakers. These surveillance techniques outside of Britain, in Germany in particular, have permitted the retention of terraces in certain circumstances. These practices have not been fully implemented in Italy. Although there are closed-circuit television cameras in Italy, perpetrators are not reprimanded. Objects are frequently thrown onto the pitch during games. For example, in Livorno's Armando Picchi stadium, no cameras are installed underneath the stand, and this permitted a fan to launch a rocket across the pitch in 2010. Inter fans have even launched an enflamed scooter, which they stole from an Atalanta fan, from a stand of the San Siro Stadium in 2001.[1]

The draconian measures imposed on all fans, and their piecemeal enforcement, only helps to reinforce the 'Outsider' identity of the *ultras*. They perform their identity within the liminal space of the stadium in opposition to the symbolic constructions of the police and the state. As the state does not infringe on the territory of the *ultras*, problems occur when the two sides re-enter the 'Italian' state outside the stadium. Consequently, the opportunities for a Hillsborough-style tragedy in Italy are manifest. The Pisanu Law is an Italian solution that imposes excessive regulation without improving the final result. Balestri argues:

> It is a harmful and punitive legislation because it assumes that all the fans are potential criminals and therefore are filed. The *Tessera del tifoso* is merely an example of a further bureaucratization and it seems to confirm a trend for some time by the biggest football clubs to move the interest of the matches to television viewing, focus on royalties and discourage participation in the stadiums. (Carlo Balestri, UISP and Progetto Ultra, personal interview, January 2014)

The laws affect all fans, rather than the small number of *ultras* it is designed to target. The result is that many fans are not watching the matches on the television at home. As Lega Serie A permits all matches to be pay-per-view then there is no incentive to attend the stadium. In contrast, no game may be broadcast live on a Saturday afternoon in England so as to encourage fans to physically attend the match.

The perceived lack of legitimacy of the central authorities ensures that it does not impose safety regulations onto the clubs. The Taylor Report (1990) placed the obligation for safety of fans within the stadium on the clubs. In abdicating responsibility for fan safety, the British state reaffirmed its legitimacy. It advocated individual clubs' accountability for their consumers, and the individual responsibility of the fans. Surveillance assumed that all fans were potentially being observed. In doing so, the state imposed neo-liberal economics by placing the economic burden on the clubs. Consequently, English clubs employed third-party security firms to maintain order, which restricted the police to a public order role away from the stadium. The poor infrastructure of the stadiums and the Outsider identity of the *ultras* have necessitated increased police presence at Italian stadiums; the police operate as the lynchpin that maintains the *status quo*. As the police operate within the political patrimonial system they become active agents in constructing the *ultras* as the only cause of the problem in Italy (Della Porta 1998; Marchi 2005; Testa 2013). The weakness of the central state to impose reform permits the maintenance of existing patterns of policing. The heavy police presence operating around the stadium, combined with the regulations related to the stadium security check and the *tessera del tifoso*, criminalizes all fans. This is apparent from the police presence afforded to *all* fans travelling to away games. Without fully understanding the key aspects of the 'English Model' the Italian authorities are perpetuating the vicious cycle of decline in Italian football.

The incorporation of football into the patrimonial system permits the presidents of football clubs to abstain from the responsibility of stadium safety. As local councils, or state institutions like CONI, own most stadiums, presidents do not take responsibility for their maintenance. Consequently, this prevents Italian clubs from capitalizing on their stadiums. An unintended consequence of stadium redevelopments in Britain led to football clubs increasing their commercial and matchday revenues. Corporate boxes were enhanced and augmented with catering facilities, merchandising outlets and special events. In addition, stadiums host conference and restaurant facilities, club superstores and various leisure facilities to extend the profitability of the stadium over the course of the week, rather than restrict their facilities to matchdays. In contrast, a few Italian stadiums include facilities to purchase club merchandise and even fewer have adequate catering facilities. Fan comfort is restricted to inadequately maintained *curva*. Poor seating and temporary stands create an unsatisfactory fan experience that is compounded by poor toilets and catering. The former England, Juventus, Roma and AC Milan manager, Fabio Capello, has echoed this point. As he collected a career award at Parma University in February 2010, Capello stated that

> Italian teams are well equipped but English sides are on top right now. Players prefer to go to England and Spain and it is not just for the money. They see Italian stadiums are half empty and realise we've got problems. (Kington 2010)

The lack of revenue-generating facilities is compounded by the failure to implement improved stadium safety. This contributes to fan apathy and falling attendances, which impact the financial viability of the clubs. Consequently, matchday revenue constitutes the smallest percentage of overall revenue for many Italian clubs (Deloitte and Touche 2013). The vicious circle is complete as the restricted revenue further reduces the clubs' ability to improve the facilities of the stadium.

Television revenue has been a key driver of transformation within football. Deregulation of television networks saw the inauguration of new broadcasters. These networks had more freedom over content and sport became a key market opportunity. In Britain, the satellite broadcaster, Sky, was central to the transformations within the English Premier League. Similarly, television income from the Champions League helped transform European and national competition. Within Italy, Silvio Berlusconi's Mediaset made extensive use of entertaining neo-television and utilized these television networks to publicize and transform his football club, AC Milan. The complete deregulation of the football television rights in Italy permitted individual clubs to negotiate their own television contracts. This has seen the popular and powerful clubs in Italy maximize their revenue, accumulate the most resources and lengthen the economic distance between them and the provincial clubs. Consequently, television revenue constitutes most of the overall revenue for Italian football clubs. For example, Italy's most popular club, Juventus, generated nearly a half of its revenue from television in 2010 (Deloitte and Touche 2010). This ratio has significantly improved since the construction of their new stadium

(Deloitte and Touche 2013). Until then two-thirds of their revenue came from television. The neo-patrimonial system had permitted the over-reliance of television revenue to the detriment of other aspects of the football experience. This practice came to an end in 2010 as Serie A clubs signed a new deal to have a more equitable distribution of television revenues. This is one small step in making Serie A more competitive, both at home and abroad.

Football requires referees to arbitrate between the sides. In the wider political economy, the state should act as this arbitrator. Within the global neo-liberal economy, the authority and power of the state as arbitrator has been challenged, changed and, in many cases, diminished. In the absence of a powerful arbitrator, such as the state, influential actors operating across business, politics and football can accumulate resources to the detriment of other groups. The Italian political economic system encourages the incorporation of football clubs into the wider patrimonial network. The 'deep play' of football within Italian society sees the sport as a major contributor of social and symbolic capital to charismatic individuals. As the British novelist and cultural commentator of Italy, Tim Parks states 'In Italy, you haven't really arrived until you own a football club' (cited in Arie 2004). This permits dense interdependencies between football clubs, television, business and politicians that frame the production and consumption of Italian football. The deregulation of the 1980s resulted in connections thickening between the media, politics and football. Silvio Berlusconi utilized television to promote his football club before using this as a paradigm to 'enter the field' of politics. Italian family capitalism and thicker personal connections permitted clubs like Parma and Lazio to be incorporated into wider family businesses. The lack of regulation and transparency, however, resulted in the clubs being affected when the parent companies went bankrupt. The problems affecting Parma and Lazio exposed widespread financial irregularities across Italian football and saw many clubs operating under incredible debt. Top clubs such as Parma, Fiorentina and Napoli have all been relegated due to financial complications. The neo-patrimonial system then saw the government attempt to pass the *salva-calcio* law to allow clubs to delay repayment of their tax debts (Porro and Russo 2004). Furthermore, the lack of regulation also resulted in several clubs utilizing fraudulent paperwork or doping in order to gain an advantage. Personal connections across a neo-patrimonial network were exposed spectacularly with the *calciopoli* scandal in 2006. This permitted a successful club with the right connections to influence the outcomes of football matches. *Calciopoli* became a metaphor for the wider Italian state; personal connections influenced the operation of the system for individual gain at the expense of the wider interest. The accumulation of resources by strategic individuals, facilitated by personal networks, permitted the elite clubs to dominate Italian football and empty out wider involvement.

## The future of Italian football: 'Year Zero'?

At the start of the 2009-10 season, Carlo Verdelli (2009) of the *Gazzetta dello Sport* suggested that it was 'year zero' for Serie A and Italian football. The season passed without any major scandals or incidents and finished with Inter's triumphant Champions League victory in Madrid. The success of Inter had demonstrated that Italian football could still compete on the global stage. Much of this, however, was down to personal wealth and ambition of Massimo Moratti, as well as to the economic weakening of rivals. Despite this brief moment of optimism, Italian football continues to the struggle. It is instructive that *Gazzetta dello Sport* also declared that Italian football was at 'year zero' in July 2014 (Monti 2014). Italy had just been defeated in the World Cup finals and did not qualify for the second round. They presented research that showed that Italy was bottom of a list detailing the percentage of players trained in the academies of clubs in European national leagues A day later, the death of Ciro Esposito was announced. Esposito was the Napoli fan who had been shot before the Coppa Italia final. Italian football was again blighted by failure on the pitch and violence off it.

In order for Italian football to build upon its past successes it needs to understand the changing global economic system. After two decades of deregulation, King (2010) has highlighted that the worldwide recession of 2007-10 could constitute a renewed process of regulation. UEFA sounded this signal when they announced that from the 2011-12 season they will enforce 'financial fair play' rules to ensure that all clubs who play in UEFA competitions comply with strict financial regulations. As Michel Platini, the president of UEFA states, 'The clubs will comply, or they will not play' (Conn 2010). It is instructive that a transnational body is imposing regulation in the absence of state regulation. Furthermore, UEFA will need to enforce the regulations to ensure legitimacy – a problem that has dogged the Italian federation since its inception.

There are signs that Italy is beginning to adapt to this global situation. In 2009, all but one of the twenty Serie A clubs voted to create a separately administered league, along the lines of the English Premier League. Lega Serie A became operational at the start of the 2010-11 season and signalled the start of a collective television deal for the league. This represents an opportunity to make the league more competitive and appealing to a global market. In the short term, it dramatically affected the revenue of the elite clubs who had previously received a substantially larger share of the television revenue during the last twenty years. How these clubs manage this transition will be crucial. Juventus, for example, initially struggled after *Caliciopoli* with relegation and the loss of television money. Their financial and footballing fortunes were strengthened, however, with the construction of the Juventus Stadium in 2011. Since its inauguration, Juventus' matchday revenue has trebled (Deloitte and Touche 2013). Other clubs in Italy may have to follow their lead in order to compete both nationally and across Europe. Promotion of other revenue streams will also mitigate the revenue reduction from television.

Since Lega Serie A was inaugurated in 2010, every league has been affected by points deductions due to financial irregularities or match-fixing, except in 2013–14. Although this is evidence of the entrenched corruption within the patrimonial networks of Italian football, it also highlights how the league is beginning to assert authority. Any form of regulation must be adequately policed. There has been a long history of patrimonial networks used to circumvent regulations. The 'Rosetta Case' in 1923 resulted from Juventus providing Virginio Rosetta an accountancy job in addition to his salary. Similarly, the restrictions on foreign players resulted in passports being forged to 'prove' Italian ancestry. These scandals are in addition to the opportunities taken by presidents and players to profit from their positions. Betting scandals and match-fixing payments have beset the Italian league since 1926 when Torino was found guilty of bribing a player from Juventus. Brian Glanville highlighted systematic bribery in Italian football during the 1960s and 1970s. *Totonero, calciopoli* and *Calcioscommesse* are further examples of individuals utilizing their networks to organize football results. Economic profit is not always the prime driver for these scandals. Symbolic capital and prestige are equally important. The history of Italian football is a history of pushing the boundaries of authority, and Lega Serie A will need to assert its legitimacy.

The football authorities and the elite Italian clubs have highlighted the need for improved stadiums. In their book, *Ripartenza ('Reboot)*, which calls for Italian football to 'reboot', Gianfranco Teotino and Michele Uva (2010) highlight that Serie A was the only league in Europe to witness a fall in the average number of spectators per match in the first decade of the twenty-first century. In addition to calling for a new governance model, and a respect for the regulations, they argue that Italy needs new stadiums. The Italian Football Federation acknowledged this and made a bid for the 2012 European Championships to act as a driver for stadium renovation. Fan violence and *calciopoli*, however, saw the Championships granted to the Ukraine and Poland (Praverman 2007). The Federation subsequently bid for the 2016 tournament, yet this was awarded to France. The new Italian Prime Minister, Enrico Letta of the Partito Democratico, reiterated the importance of renovating stadiums in May 2013. In the senate he argued that 'we need new stadiums or the Italian decline will not stop' (*Corriere dello Sport* 2013). Significantly, however, Letta made no governmental provisions for financial support given the global economic crisis.

As a result, the Federation and the clubs will need to seek alternative funding for any redevelopment. Stadium redevelopment is vital in order for these clubs to offset the short-term loss of television income, as Teotino and Uva argue. This situation is complicated by the continuing communal control of football stadiums in Italy. This restricts opportunities for revenue generation for the clubs. Some clubs have begun the process of stadium redevelopment. Juventus lead the way with their club-owned Juventus Stadium. The two Milan clubs and Roma have also announced plans to renovate their stadiums. In Florence, Fiorentina announced plans to build a new stadium, alongside a modern art gallery, hotels, and conference facilities. Yet disputes with the commune resulted in their plans stalling. More importantly, Fiorentina have experimented with new policing techniques to minimize confrontation and violence at the stadium. Only time will tell if the new stadium and reformed policing constitute a 'Fiorentina Model' for Italian football (Giudici 2010).

Despite the changes to the structure and administration of the leagues, there has been little widespread reform in the governance of the federation and this will impact the wider success of the league. Guschwan (2007, p. 264) succinctly summarizes this problem:

> The difficult task facing Italian government, soccer league and fans is to balance the requirements of safety and civility with the passion and expression that makes Italian soccer matches so compelling.

One of the enduring features of Italian football has been its vibrant spectator culture; it was part of the unique selling point when Channel 4 first broadcast *Football Italia* in 1992. Unfortunately, the bureaucracy imposed by the Pisanu Law has dramatically impacted the matchday experience of *all* fans. It is for this reason that Contucci and Francesio (2013) are more pessimistic and suggest that these as 'the last days of Italian football'. As they argue, 'they [the government] are trying to chase the violent people from the stadium – they have chased away everyone but the violent people'. The unintended consequence of the 'repression' has been a strengthening of the *mentalitá ultras*. They are the only ones continuing to go to the stadium so feel legitimated in their actions as 'authentic' fans.

Any form of governance or transition to an 'English Model' needs to incorporate an understanding of fan culture. As Merkel (2012) argues, German fans have fought to maintain their position within 'their' clubs and 'their' game. The result is a number of concessions to fans that maintains significant levels of order, but permitting the performance of fan culture. One of the major criticisms from fans in England has been the suppression of matchday atmospheres in all-seater stadiums. The Football Supporters' Federation has launched the 'Safe Standing Campaign' and 'Away Fans Matter' for lobby clubs to acknowledge the contribution to the atmosphere that safe terraces and away fans bring.[2] Something similar would be beneficial for Italian football.

One final danger of following an 'English Model' too closely relates to power. Although power is more evenly distributed among English Premier League clubs, there still exists a hegemonic bloc within the league. Clubs that compete in Europe have access to greater resources than those who do not and this helps maintain their position. A dual process occurs where the income of the overall league increases, but the resources are accumulated by the powerful. Those with less power have encountered a growing financial crisis, especially among lower league clubs, such as Plymouth Argyle, Leeds United and Portsmouth. Despite these financial problems, there remains an active fan involvement in rescuing and supporting their club. Independent Supporters' Associations and Supporters' Trusts have emerged in England in order to try and effect a change within supporters' football clubs. This is one area that differs from English fans' counterparts in Italy.

## Political participation in Italian football

Despite Robert Putnam's (1993, 2000) assertions that social capital accumulated through associations contributes to national democracy and national economic success, this has not been demonstrated in Italy. The restructuring of the global political economy has also led to the restructuring of local communities. Deregulation of the economy and the movement of capital have also had a direct impact on individuals who have less time to attend associations, or have moved away from their community. This has been facilitated by increased consumption where traditional associations have been supplanted with new forms of association. Although social capital is generated at all levels of society and within every social network, it operates in accordance with economic capital; those with the resources to accumulate it generate capital in greater quantities. As Skidmore et al. (2006) suggested, 'Those already well connected tend to get better connected ... community participation tends to be dominated by a small group of insiders who are disproportionately involved in a large number of governance activities.' Economic and social capital is intimately entwined, as Bourdieu (1986) argued. So as individuals accumulate these stocks of capital, it reinforces their position. This allows patrimonialism to flourish. Consequently, we must make a clear distinction between the Bourdieu concept of 'social capital' that is a resource that is used by individuals within a group and the more generic theory proscribed by Putnam. While stocks of social capital may increase with certain individuals participating in community life, this does not automatically translate to a wider benefit for the community in general. Many fans are participating for the sociability, not for any wider political or national involvement.

The restructuring of the global economy has opened up the football economy for new entrepreneurs. These have exploited existing connections to make the most of the transformations in the global political economy. Individuals like Silvio Berlusconi extend their wide social networks and, in doing so, win acclaim and favours from their supporters. This facilitates the accumulation of economic capital and sets in motion a self-reinforcing cycle. This in turn has accumulated and reinforced patrimonial networks. Personal patrimonial connections were retained within the new structure of Lega Serie A.[3] Adriano Galliani, the vice president of AC Milan, was also the first vice president of Lega Serie A. Galliani was a former president of the Italian League until he resigned due to *calciopoli*. Even more disconcerting was the place of Massimo Cellino on the board of Lega Serie A. The president of Cagliari moved his team's home matches to Trieste, over 1,000 kilometres from Sardinia, after a dispute with the commune over their imposition of safety regulations. He then decided to move the club to a smaller stadium in the city, but was arrested in February 2013 over an investigation into fraud and embezzlement. As part of this investigation, the prosecuting magistrate described Cellino as having 'marked criminal tendencies' (Masu 2013). The central authorities have to impose a regulatory framework upon Italian football in order to mitigate the patrimonial networks. Yet the individuals are part of the same patrimonial networks that have systematically undermined the league.

The crisis of authority has contributed to player and fan malaise and this is contributing to the decline in Italian football. The culture of mistrust towards the authorities has been highlighted by the changes to the league structure in the 2010-11 season. These changes have necessitated a new collective agreement between the players and the clubs. In September 2010, the players of the Italian Footballers' Association (AIC) voted to strike (which they subsequently suspended) in opposition to a new agreement proposed by the clubs. In particular, they were protesting against the suggestion that footballers should not have additional jobs outside football, that salaries should be tied to performance and, significantly, that a club could force the sale of a player in the last year of his contract to any club that agreed a transfer fee.

Challenges to central regulation have also affected fan involvement. Stadium regulations have not been enforced, and years of scandal, violence and crisis have resulted in fan apathy, resulting in decline in attendances at the stadium. This has been compounded by the introduction of the *tessera del tifoso*. The imposition of this card has galvanized the collective identity of the *mentalità ultras*. The *tesserae*, 'for the *ultras*', as Guschwan argues, 'embodies police repression and commercialism – the two characteristics of modern day football that *ultras* most detest' (Guschwan 2013a, p. 224). *Ultras* have protested against the imposition of this card, and this saw a dramatic reduction in attendances at Italian stadiums for the 2010-11 season. For example, Roma only had 18,600 fans for their opening match against Cesena in the 80,000 capacity Stadio Olimpico. As Contucci and Francesio (2013, p. 1) argue, 'they [the authorities] are trying to chase the violent people from the stadium. They have chased away everyone but the violent people.' This impacts the spectacle, both in the stadium and on television. Draconian legislation has directly impacted the one area that made Italian football unique, and has simultaneously created a symbol of resistance for the *ultras*.

The fans have a key opportunity to turn the patrimonial networks to their advantage. The supporters' clubs and *ultras* groups represent excellent avenues of social capital creation, which Putnam (1993, 2000) argues would overcome this decline. Instead, they also represent the emptying out of politics from public life (Sennett 1976; Habermas 1989; Putnam 1993, 2000). Richard Sennett (1998) suggested in *The Corrosion of Character* that the way to overcome individualization and to manage changes brought about by the global deregulated economy are to form small collectives. As Maffesoli (1996) argues, new collectives or neo-tribes are forming around consumption. In Italy, the supporters' clubs and *ultras* already constitute these collectives. Yet they need to reframe their political outlook. Historically, *ultras* have reflected the politics of the *piazza*. Political symbols of the extreme left and right emerged in the *curve* during the 1970s. This has been replaced by a localized communist identity in the case of Livorno, or anti-immigration and secessionist politics of the *Lega Nord* and Berlusconi's centre-right governments in the north. There needs to be more social movements like *Projetto Ultrà* to present an alternative image of the fans. Although there is the FISSC (Federation of Supporters of Italian Football Teams), this does not have the activism of their equivalents in England, such as the Football Supporter's Federation and Kick it Out, or fan-projects and BAFF in Germany.[4]

Potentially, Supporters' Trusts could occupy this third position between the *ultras* and official supporters' clubs. Supporters Trusts can provide a critical eye to football governance, but also an active approach to issues such as anti-racism, and other forms of discrimination. Supporters Trusts should be supported, where possible, in their endeavours so they can become the critical friends of clubs. Yet in order to nurture and develop these ideas, fans must put aside their parochial rivalries. Just as the *ultras* are uniting in the face of common political and police pressure, other fans need to do the same. In this way they can share ideas and develop collaborative approaches to tackle the repressive measures in Italian football. Organizations like Supporters in Campo can potentially operate as this umbrella organization. Linking in with wider fan activism across Europe can help stimulate these actions. Organizations like Football Supporters Europe are potentially vital to maintain a vibrant fan culture across Europe.

Italy stands on the precipice. 'Year Zero' and the newly formed Serie A constitute a new beginning for Italian football. Yet Italy has been adept at *gattopardismo*; this has permitted change while remaining the same. For Italian football to reach the echelons they once occupied, all parties must adopt a controlled strategy to compete across Europe. Alternatively, Serie A will fade away and become a chapter in the history of football. For those who succumbed to the glamour and style of Channel 4's *Football Italia*, this will be a sad loss to world football.

# Glossary

**Allianza Nazionale (AI)** – The National Alliance Party formed after the dissolution of the MSI.
**Calcio** – The Italianized word for 'Football'.
**Calciopoli** – Match-fixing scandal that emerged in 2006 involving Juventus, AC Milan, Fiorentina, Lazio and Reggina.
**Campanilismo** – Literally, the love of one's bell tower. Reflects the feelings of attachment and belonging to one's hometown or city.
**Carabinieri** – Corps of armed police with the standing of armed forces (along with Air Force, Army and Navy).
**Catenaccio** – Literally 'padlock'; a style of defence popularized by Hellguera in Italy in the 1950s–60s and specialized in preventing the opposition from scoring.
**Comitato Olimpico Nazionale Italiano (CONI)** – The Italian National Olympic Committee. This is the umbrella organization which administers and manages all national sporting federations.
**Covisoc (Commissione di Vigilanza sulle Società Calcistiche)** – Literally, 'Vigilancy Commission on Football Clubs'. This body operated as the financial regulator for CONI to ensure that football clubs had the financial assets to complete a full season.
**Curva (pl. Curve)** – The ends behind the goals in Italian stadiums, similar to the terrace in Modern British stadiums.
**Daspo (Diffida ad Assistere alle Manifestazioni Sportive)** – Literally 'Prohibition to attend sport events'. This is the equivalent of a football banning order in Britain. It prevents the holders of this quasi-legal order from attending football matches.
**Democrazia Cristiana (DC)** – The Christian Democratic Party.
**Federazione Italiana Giuoco Calcio (FIGC)** – The Italian Football Federation. Responsible for the administration and management of Italian Football.
**Fideiussione** – Financial guarantees provided by clubs to guarantee the financial eligibility for the season.
**Forza Italia (FI)** – The political party started by Silvio Berlusconi in 1992 after the *tangentopoli* scandal.
**Gattopardismo** – From the novel entitled *Il Gattopardo* by Giuseppe Tomasi di Lampedusa. It reflects the continuance of existing practices despite change.
**Lega Calcio (Lega Nazionale Professionisti)** – The Italian Football League; the governing body for the professional leagues in Italy, principally Serie A and Serie B.
**Lega Nord** – The Northern League. A secessionist political movement which originates from the north of Italy. Occasional supporter of Silvio Berlusconi.
**Mani Pulite** – Literally 'clean hands'. This is the investigation by magistrates.

**Movimento 5 Stelle (M5S)** – The Five Star Movement, a new social movement created by the comedian Beppe Grillo.
**Movimento Sociale Italiano (MSI)** – The Italian Social Movement (MSI), a neo-fascist, then national conservative right-wing party.
**Moviola** – The slow motion replay performed on sports broadcasts.
**Oriundo (pl. Oriundi)** – Foreign-born players of Italian descent.
**Osservatorio Nazionale sulle Manifestazioni Sportive (Osservatorio)** – Quasi-political body initiated to review safety at football matches.
**Partito Comunista Italiano (PCI)** – The Italian Communist Party.
**Partito Socialista Italiano (PSI)** – The Italian Socialist Party.
**Plus-valenze** – An accounting system that spread the profit made on the sale of players over an accounting term
**Il Popolo della Libertà (PdL)** – The 'People of Freedom' Party formed after the merger of *Forza Italia* and the *Allianza Nazionale*.
**Questore** – The Chief of State Police.
**RAI** – The state television and radio station. Originally called *Radio Audizione Italiana* it changed its name in 1954 to *Radio Televsione Italiana* to reflect the new medium of television. The acronym remained unchanged.
**Risorgimento** – The political and social movement that led to the unification of the Italian peninsula.
**Scudetto (pl. Scudetti)** – Literally 'little shield'. The winner of the Serie A championship. Champions are entitled to wear a small shield with the Italian tricolour on their jerseys in the following season. The winner of ten *scudetti* is entitled to place a gold star above their badge. Only three clubs have won this gold star: Juventus (twice), AC Milan and Inter.
**Settore Ospiti** – The area for away fans. This is an area for parking, congregation and confinement for fans travelling to away games. Occasionally these areas are adjacent to the stadium. Alternatively, they are located at the edge of the city.
**Striscione** – Banners held up at games that make political, insulting or humorous comments on the players, opposition or politicians. Usually written on white sheets, or rolls of white paper.
**Tangentopoli** – Political scandal of 1992 which resulted in the *Mani Pulite* investigation and the subsequent demise of the First Republic, the DC, PCI and PSI.
**Tessera del tifoso** – The identity card imposed by the FIGC on fans to reduce the requirement for identity checks at football matches. It also operates as a loyalty card and MasterCard.
**Trasformismo** – The practice of Italian politicians to switch political support in return for personal support. Personal patrimony was utilized to ensure that political support endured. This maintained a stable form of government without ideological shifts to the right or left. It dates to the pre-fascist period, after unification.
**Tribunale Amministrativo Regionale (TAR)** – Regional Administrative Courts which exercise regional judicial autonomy.

# Methodological Note

In order to gain an understanding of Italian football, its operation and fan culture, it was important to undertake a variety of methods. Three principal methods were used: participant observation; interviews; and documentary research.

## Participant observation

In order to develop an appropriate understanding of Italian football fans and the political climate in Italy, it was important to spend time with Italians, fans and those with an interest in the sport. I carried out a period of participant observation in the city of Livorno, ten miles south of Pisa, on the Tuscan coast. I spent six months in Livorno at the end of 2008-9 season. Livorno was chosen for two reasons. A.S. Livorno represents a typical provincial football club in Italy; it has enjoyed minor success, financial crisis and continued difficulties compared to larger football clubs. In 2003 the club returned to Serie A after a fifty-five-year hiatus. The major reason for the choice of Livorno was that their fans have distinctive left-wing identity that is the product of the city's unique history (Doidge 2013a). After the port at Pisa began to silt up, the Medici in Florence established a new port ten miles south at Livorno. To populate this new town, Florence passed the *Leggi Livornine* in 1593, which welcomed anyone, regardless of background. As a result the city was home to a number of merchants encouraged by the absence of tax. It was also populated with criminals and those fleeing religious persecution, including Catholics from Britain, Huguenots from France, and Jews from across Europe. The religious tolerance was highlighted by the fact that city did not ghettoize the Jewish population. This unique history and the identity of Livorno's fans made for an apposite case study.

Participant observation was chosen so I could gain an insight into Italian culture and football. Using this type of interpretative method allowed me to immerse myself in the local culture and gain a deeper understanding of the fans themselves. During the period, I stayed with two Italian families, which gave me extensive insight into Italian culture. Through these families, I made many acquaintances with whom I could familiarize myself with Livornese culture and Italian football.

Gaining access to rival fan groups can prove problematic. Alberto Testa's (2010) excellent ethnographic account of key *ultras* groups of Roma and Lazio highlighted the difficulties in gaining access to important members. Serendipity was central to finding significant opportunities to participate in Livornese life. As an English researcher, who spoke Italian with a clear accent, it was not possible for me to operate covertly, regardless of any ethical issue this represented. My first piece of luck occurred when my former Italian teacher, who was from Livorno, discussed my project with her husband. He was a close friend of someone who organized local charity football tournaments. Through these tournaments, he knew a local supporters' club and the directors of the supporters' club invited me to meet with them. After this, I became a *socio* and regularly attended the club's headquarters and travelled with them to away matches. The other significant piece of luck came from the livorno now website. I had written some match reports for this site and when I arrived in Livorno I met who webmaster. She introduced me to a journalist for *Il Tirreno* newspaper, who interviewed me. Through these interviews I was approached directly by a number of Livorno fans. One particular fan, 'Levriero' was particularly useful as he provided many newspaper archives and helped unpick some of the intricacies of local culture.

Participant observation took place at a number of locations, not all of them football related. Most of these were in public settings, where all members of the public were able to attend. Specifically linked to football matches, participant observation took place at the football-related spaces, namely the stadiums and football supporters' clubs. I attended every match I could, both home and away. And always stood in the *Curva Nord,* home the Livornese *ultras*. Various spaces en route to the match were also included, such as supporters' coaches, trains (and stations), Autogrills and car trips. Broader locations were also incorporated, such as bars, nightclubs, restaurants and parties (Livorno has a number of outdoor parties and festivals during the spring and summer). I also attended several football-related political protests. Some of these sites were less public, or 'closed', such as the supporters' coaches, and some supporters' clubs' meetings. Most fans were 'ordinary' fans, as opposed to *ultras*. Participant observation was not only a way of obtaining data but also a means to develop a 'feeling' for the Livornese, and to understand the themes and approaches which the Livornese took to everyday life and football in particular.

## Interviews

To embellish the participant observation, semi-structured interviews were undertaken with various fans. Fifteen interviews were conducted with supporters' club members. Many of these came from the club where the majority of the participant observation was undertaken. The director of this club facilitated others; through his social network he introduced me to other clubs, including the B52s, females supporters' club. Additionally, a focus group was conducted with leading members of one of Livorno's *ultras* groups, *Livornesi*. This was conducted in the bar that they used as their headquarters.

Interviews were also undertaken as part of a research project investigating anti-racism initiatives by fans across Europe in 2013–14 (supported by UEFA). Only part of this project was linked to Italy, but some interviewees that were particularly pertinent to *Football Italia*, namely, Lorenzo Contucci, a lawyer who supports AS Roma, is a member of MyRoma supporters' trust, and provides widespread support to *ultras*, particularly through his asromaultras. org website. Focusing on supporters' trust, I interviewed Riccardo Bertolin, another member of MyRoma (and a member of the Football Supporters Europe committee). I also travelled to Bologna to interview Carlo Balestri, a project worker with UISP and the founder of *Progetto Ultrà*.

## Documentary research

Four types of documentary research were undertaken: newspapers; books; fanzines; and social media.

### Newspapers

As mentioned in Chapter 2, Italy does not have a truly national press. It is no coincidence that the biggest national daily newspaper is *La Gazzetta dello Sport*, which is dedicated to sport, and football in particular. I have been a regular reader of *La Gazzetta dello Sport* for many years, either online or whenever I could obtain a physical copy. The other national sport daily, *Corriere dello Sport* was also used for a wider understanding of Italian football. National dailies, in particular *La Repubblica* and *Corriere della Sera* were read in cafes and online.

## Archival work

Any piece of academic research requires an understanding of wider academic and theoretical literature. In addition to the usual range of academic research, archival research was undertaken in football and Italian social history. The city library of Livorno housed a significant collection of works on the city and with the cooperation of the local library staff, a significant proportion of my early work in Livorno was based there. Wider academic research of football literature was also undertaken at the libraries of the University of Pisa, University of Bologna, *La Sapienza* (the University of Rome), and the British School at Rome. Unlike Britain, Italy does not have a culture of films about hooliganism and 'hoolie-lit' (Poulton 2008). Because these events still take place, there is no nostalgic demand for stories about masculine identity and violence. Ricky Tognazzi's 1991 film *Ultrà* provided an interesting insight.

## Fanzines

Fanzine culture within British football fan cultures is particularly strong and this has provided a valuable insight into the outlook of particular fan communities and worthy of academic attention (Jary et al. 1991; King 1998; Giulianotti 1999; Millward 2008). Fanzines have also been adopted across Europe, particularly in Germany and the Netherlands (Spaaij 2006). However, there is no similar fanzine culture within Italy which Dal Lago and De Biasi (1994) ascribe to the intense coordination of the matchday choreographies. There are two national fanzines for *ultras*: *Supertifo* and *Fan's Magazine*. The fanzine *Supertifo* (Superfan) started in 1985 and has recommenced publishing in 2010. *Supertifo* conforms to the British notion of a fanzine, in that it contains a large number of 'comment' features, where *ultras* recount their experiences of football; from nostalgic stories of away games to recent problems. The fanzine also provides an 'agony aunt' column called '*L'avvocato risponde*' (The lawyer replies) where the well-known solicitor and *ultras* of AS Roma, Lorenzo Contucci, responds to a question relating to legal issues relating to football fandom. The majority of *Supertifo* is devoted to fans' photos of choreographies. This is replicated in the other national fanzine, *Fan's Magazine*. This is produced by *ultras* of Salernitana and principally operates as a medium to further display *ultras* choreographies. These magazines highlight the sophisticated ways that the *ultras* identity is produced and consumed. Despite being predominantly photographic, they include commentary and discussion related to government measures and police actions, so operates as an important method to investigate *ultras* viewpoints.

## Internet and social networking

The internet has produced a number of instruments for *ultras* identity to be re-performed and re-articulated. In particular, the website www.asromaultras.org provides extensive information on the *ultrà*, in addition to information on AS Roma and its fans. This website is maintained by Lorenzo Contucci, the lawyer who defends *ultras* and provides legal advice for the fanzine *Supertifo*. YouTube also proved to be a valuable resource. Fans and *ultras* actively post videos and clips displaying their activities, in particular their choreographies and confrontations. Although these videos are not unbiased, they provide a useful example of how *ultras* actively perform their identity and re-perform it through the internet. YouTube, and other internet sites, provide extensive platforms for *ultras* to actively choose the image they want to portray. Other forms of social networking, in particular Twitter and Facebook, were used to ascertain conversations, ideas, and analysis of key aspects of Italian football.

# Notes

## Chapter 1

1. The European Cup was instituted in 1955 to provide a European competition in order to create a clear mechanism to affirm European Champions. This was in response to the British Press' assertions that Wolverhampton Wanderers were the 'Champions' based on a number of friendly matches. The English FA prevented Chelsea from entering the first tournament in 1955, although Manchester United were allowed to enter in the following year. King, A. (2003), *The European Ritual: Football in the New Europe*. Aldershot, England; United Kingdom, Ashgate.
2. English Premier League (€1562 m), Ligue 1 (France) (€337 m) and Bundesliga (€1038 m). Hamil, S., S. Morrow, et al. (2010), 'The governance and regulation of Italian football'. *Soccer & Society* 11(4): 373–413.
3. http://www.uefa.com/memberassociations/uefarankings/country/index.html.

## Chapter 3

1. http://www.assocalciatori.it/.
2. http://www.acmilan.com/InfoPage.aspx?id=41293.

## Chapter 4

1. Jean-Pierre Papin moved from Marseilles to Milan for £10 million, before Gianluca Vialli signed for Juventus from Sampdoria for £12 million. This was followed by Gianluigi Lentini's move from Torino to Milan for £13 million.
2. http://www.gruppospinelli.com/home.htm.
3. http://www.comune.milano.it/portale/wps/portal/CDM?WCM_GLOBAL_CONTEXT=/wps/wcm/connect/contentlibrary/In+Comune/In+Comune/Il+Sindaco/In+Comune_Il+Sindaco.
4. The G-14 was a lobby group of Europe's largest and most powerful clubs. It was formed in 2000 and included Milan, Inter and Juventus from Italy, Liverpool and Manchester United from England, Real Madrid and Barcelona from Spain, Bayern Munich and Borussia Dortmund from Germany, Marseilles and Paris

Saint-Germain from France, Ajax and PSV Eindhoven from the Netherlands, and Porto from Portugal. In 2002, four additional clubs were incorporated, including Arsenal from England, Bayer Leverkusen from Germany, Valencia from Spain and Lyon from France. The G-14 agreed to disband in 2008, and in its place a European Club Association containing over 100 teams from every UEFA federation was formed. To date, only one club (Chelsea) from outside of this elite group of clubs has won the Champions League since its inception in 1992, which highlights the hegemonic position of these elite clubs.

5  For example, see the following from 16 September 2013: http://www.gazzetta.it/Calcio/Squadre/SerieA/15-09-2013/moviola-terza-giornata-fiorentina-rossi-rigore-2-2-torino-milan-gioco-andava-fermato-201171206604.shtml.

# Chapter 5

1  http://www.asbari.it/societa/stadio.html
2  http://www.asbari.it/societa/stadio.html
3  http://www.fcparma.com/citta-e-stadio/il-tardini.html
4  http://www.osservatoriosport.interno.it/Daspo/index.html
5  www.osservatoriosport.interno.it
6  see http://www.dailymotion.com/video/x6mupk_ultras-napoli-direction-la-roma_sport
7  http://www.osservatoriosport.interno.it/allegati/determinazioni/2010/osservatorio_21.pdf
8  http://www.osservatoriosport.interno.it/allegati/determinazioni/2010/osservatorio_13.pdf
9  http://www.osservatoriosport.interno.it/allegati/determinazioni/2010/osservatorio_02_10.pdf
10 www.osservatoriosport.interno.it/allegati/determinazioni/2009/osservatorio_16.pdf
11 http://www.video.mediaset.it/mplayer.html?sito=iene&data=2007/02/26&id=2316&from=iene
12 http://cuorerossonero.acmilan.com/main/?menuId=1.146
13 http://www.livornocalcio.it/home/triglia_card.pdf

# Chapter 6

1  http://www.carabinieri.it/Internet/Multilingua/EN/HistoricalReferences/01_EN.htm

2. The forces of order also comprise the Guardia di Finanzia who deal with tax and customs matters. Additionally, there are the Municipal Police, who deal with motoring and local regulations, and the Provincial Police, who deal with country laws such as hunting and fishing regulations. There are also Coast Guard and National Park Police.
3. http://www.video.corriere.it/?vxChannel=Roma%20Cronaca&vxClipId=2524_d07ccb4c-5acd-11df-903e-00144f02aabe
4. This clip from Danish TV talks to a young Danish Manchester United fan and highlights the events after Roma fans surge: http://www.uk.youtube.com/watch?v=gIfgEwL2QMo.
5. http://www.osservatoriosport.interno.it/pubblicazioni/steward_new.html
6. For example, in Britain, Wigan (in the Premiership) incurred a cost of £240,000 for policing in 2007–8; for Hereford, the cost was £80,000. HOUSE OF COMMONS HOME AFFAIRS COMMITTEE 2009. The Cost of Policing Football Matches.

# Chapter 7

1. http://www.youtube.com/watch?v=s09wQzTSTSU&feature=fvwrel (Accessed Tuesday 13th May, 2014).
2. See http://www.youtube.com/watch?v=L_lvUbCPYwc&feature=related (Accessed Tuesday 13th May, 2014)
3. A Uruguayan urban guerrilla group.
4. For example, the fan website tifonet details the various twinnings and rivalries with other teams under it's 'war and peace' section: http://www.tifonet.it/guerraepace/.
5. http://www.99amaranto.it/en/index.html
6. See http://www.youtube.com/watch?v=kblqsUPWLMw (Accessed Saturday 27 October 2012).
7. http://www.sportgoverno.it/focus/stop-alla-violenza/daspo.aspx
8. http://www.hooligan.de/en/shop/manufacturer/10-mentalita-ultras (Accessed Tuesday 13 May 2014).
9. http://www.distantecho.co.uk/products/mentalita-ultras-from-father-to-son (Accessed Tuesday 13 May 2014).
10. See http://www.youtube.com/watch?v=L_Nu6HKVSmk

# Chapter 8

1. http://www.accvc.it
2. http://www.juventusclubdoc.it

3 www.fisscitalia.eu
4 http://www.fsf.org.uk/; http://www.aktive-fans.de
5 http://www.89.97.230.138/carta_tifoso.htm
6 http://www.fondazionetaras.it
7 www.fanseurope.org

# Chapter 9

1 See http://www.youtube.com/watch?v=L_Nu6HKVSmk
2 See http://www.fsf.org.uk/campaigns/
3 See http://www.legaseriea.it/it/lega-calcio/il-governo-della-lega
4 http://www.fsf.org.uk/; http://www.kickitout.org; http://www.kos-fanprojeckte.info

# Bibliography

AGEM (2007), IC27 - Settore Del Calcio Professionistico.

Agnew, P. (2006), *Forza Italia: A Journey in Search of Italy and its Football,* London: Ebury.

Alegi, P. (2007), 'The Political Economy of Mega-Stadiums and the Underdevelopment of Grassroots Football in South Africa'. *Politikon: South African Journal of Political Studies,* 34, 315–31.

Anderson, P. (2014), 'The Italian Disaster'. *London Review of Books,* 36, 3–16.

Andrews, G. (2005), *Not a Normal Country: Italy After Berlusconi,* Ann Arbor, MI: Pluto Press.

Archetti, E. (1998), 'The Spectacle of a Heroic Life: The Case of Diego Maradona'. In D. Andrews and S. Jackson (Eds), *Sport Stars: The Cultural Politics of Sporting Celebrity,* London: Routledge.

Arie, S. (2004), 'Parma Fc Face Ruin as a Dynasty Crashes'. *The Observer,* 11 January 2004.

Arvidsson, A. (2003), *Marketing Modernity: Italian Advertising from Fascism to Postmodernity,* New York: Routledge.

Axford, B. and Huggins, R. (1998), 'Anti-Politics or the Triumph of Postmodern Populism in Promotional Cultures?' *Telematics and Informatics,* 15, 181–202.

Bagnasco, A. (1977), *Tre Italie. La Problematica Territoriale Dello Sviluppo Italiano,* Bologna: Il Mulino.

Bakhtin, M. M. (1984), *Rabelais and his World,* Bloomington: Indiana University Press.

Bale, J. (1990), 'In the Shadow of the Stadium: Football Grounds as Urban Nuisances'. *Geography,* 75, 325–34.

Bale, J. (1993a), 'The Spatial Development of the Modern Stadium'. *International Review for the Sociology of Sport,* 28, 121–33.

Bale, J. (1993b), *Sport, Space, and the City,* London; New York: Routledge.

Bandini, P. (2007), 'Fan Tragedy Sends the Fight Against Ultras Back to Square One'. *The Guardian,* 12 November 2007.

Bandini, P. (2010), 'Milan's Frailty Laid Bare by Cesena'. *The Guardian,* 13 September 2010.

Bandini, P. (2013), 'Remembering Treviso's Controversial 2001 Anti-Racism Gesture'. *The Score* [Online]. Available: http://blogs.thescore.com/counterattack/2013/01/08/bandini-remembering-trevisos-controversial-2001-anti-racism-gesture/ [Accessed 30 September 2013].

Bandini, P. (2014), 'Internazionale's Mauro Icardi Begins to Make Right Headlines in Fiorentina Win'. *The Guardian,* 17 February 2014.

Banfield, E. C. (1958), *The Moral Basis of a Backward Society,* Glencoe, IL: Free Press; [Chicago] Research Center in Economic Development and Cultural Change, University of Chicago.

Barbagli, M. and Sartori, L. (2004), 'Law Enforcement Activities in Italy'. *Journal of Modern Italian Studies,* 9, 161–85.

Barker, M. (2012), 'One Livorno Fan's Lonely Journey Across Italy'. *When Saturday* [Online]. Available: http://www.wsc.co.uk/wsc-daily/1153-october-2012/9120-one-livorno-fan-s-lonely-journey-across-italy [Accessed 21 January 2015].

Baroncelli, A. and Lago, U. (2006), 'Italian Football'. *Journal of Sports Economics,* 7, 13–28.

Bartali, R. (2006), 'Allende, Berlinguer, Pinochet ... and Dario Fo'. In A. Cento Bull and A. Giorgio (Eds), *Speaking Out and Silencing,* Leeds: Legenda.

Bayley, D. H. and Shearing, C. D. (1996), 'The Future of Policing'. *Law and Society Review,* 30, 585–606.

Becker, H. S. (1963), *Outsiders; Studies in the Sociology of Deviance,* London: Free Press of Glencoe.

Bernini, S. (2010), 'Family Politics, the Catholic Church and the Transformation of Family Life in the Second Republic'. In A. Mammone and G. A. Veltri (Eds), *Italy Today: The Sick Man of Europe,* London; New York: Routledge.

Bianchi, F. (2005), 'Hooligans, Gabbie E Steward Ecco La Verità Sul "Modello Inglese"'. *La Repubblica,* 11 February 2005.

Bianchi, F. (2012), 'Il Maxi-Spezzatino Nel Gelo La Lega: "Ecco La Verità..."'. *La Repubblica,* 11 December 2012.

Boissevain, J. (1966), 'Patronage in Sicily'. *Man,* 1, 18–33.

Boykoff, J. (2013), *Celebration Capitalism and the Olympic Games,* London: Routledge.

Bromberger, C. (1995), Football as World-View and as Ritual. *French Cultural Studies,* 6, 293–311.

Brown, A. (1998), *Fanatics! Power, Identity, and Fandom in Football,* London: Routledge.

Brusco, S. (1982), 'The Emilian Model: Productive Decentralisation and Social Integration'. *Cambridge Journal of Economics,* 6, 167–84.

Burke, J. (2006), 'Paradiso To Inferno'. *The Observer,* Sunday, 30 July 2006.

Carminati, N. (2009), 'Cissokho Deal Collapses'. *Sky Sports* [Online]. Available: http://www1.skysports.com/football/news/12003/5387202/ [Accessed 30 September 2013].

Carroll, R. (2001), Genoa Raid was Police 'Revenge'. *The Guardian,* 24 July 2001.

Carroll, R. (2007), The Dark Side of Italy's Paramilitary Force. *The Guardian,* 27 July 2001.

Cellini, L. (2009), *Questore Di Firenze 'Ultrà? Qui Siamo Un Modello'* [Online]. Available: http://www.calciomercato.com/index.php?c=5&a=149364&archive=archive [Accessed 19 May 2010].

Ceniti, F. (2011), 'Maxi-Investigation on Betting. "Match-Fixing in Serie B and C"'. *La Gazzetta Dello Sport,* 1 June 2011.

Cento Bull, A. (2010), 'The Legacy of the Strategy of Tension and the Armed Conflict in a Context of (Non)Reconciliation'. In A. Mammone and G. A. Veltri (Eds), *Italy Today: The Sick Man of Europe*. London; New York: Routledge.

Cento Bull, A. and Corner, P. (1993), *From Peasant to Entrepreneur: The Survival of the Family Economy in Italy*, Oxford: Providence.

Clegg, J. (2010), 'Italian Football Faces Tough Times'. *Wall Street Journal*, 21 April 2010.

Collin, R. O. (1999), 'Italy – A Tale of Two Police Forces'. *History Today*, 49(9).

Collins, R. (2008), *Violence: A Micro-Sociological Theory*, Princeton: Princeton University Press.

Colombo, M. (2010), 'Milan Brasiliano'. *Corriere Della Sera*, 1 September 2010.

Conn, D. (2010), 'Michel Platini Will Expel Debt-Laden Clubs from the Champions League'. *The Guardian*, 26 August 2010.

Contucci, L. (2010), 'L'avvocato Del Diavolo'. In S. Cacciari and L. Giudici (Eds), *Stadio Italia - I Conflitti Del Calcio Moderno*, Florence: La Casa Usher.

Contucci, L. and Francesio, G. (2013), *A Porte Chiusi: Gli Ultimi Giorni Del Calcio Italiano*, Milano: Sperling & Kupfer.

Cooke, P. (2006), 'Collective Memory and Childhood Narratives: Rewriting the 1970s in the 1990s'. In A. Cento Bull and A. Giorgio (Eds), *Speaking Out and Silencing*, Leeds: Legenda.

*The Godfather* (1972), Directed by Coppola, F. F. [Film]. USA: Paramount Pictures.

*Corriere Della Sera* (2006), 'Le Intercettazioni «Ad Amsterdam Ti Ho Messo Meier: Lo Vedi Che Io Mi Ricordo Di Te?»' *Corriere Della Sera*, 4 May 2006.

*Corriere Della Sera* (2010), 'Gugliotta Scarcerato, Indagato Agente. Vito: Se Colpevole, Viminale Parte Civile'. *Corriere Della Sera*, 12 May 2010.

*Corriere Della Sera* (2014), 'Zanzi: "La Partnership Con Disney È Una Parte Importante Del Nostro Impegno"'. *Corriere Della Sera*, 21 May 2014.

*Corriere Dello Sport* (2013), 'Letta: Stadi Sono Vecchi. Fermi Da Troppo Tempo'. *Corriere Dello Sport*, 30 April 2013.

Croci, O. (2001), 'Language and Politics in Italy: From Moro to Berlusconi'. *Journal of Modern Italian Studies*, 6, 348–70.

Curro, E. (2009), 'I Bamboccioni Di Mou Balotelli E La Gioventù Viziata È Il Problema Di Una Generazione'. *La Repubblica*, 24 October 2009.

D'auria, S. (2009), 'Gli Ultras: Analisi Globale Del Fenomeno E Delle Politiche Di Contrasto Allo Stesso'. *Rassegna Penitenziaria E Criminologica*, 57–98.

Dal Lago, A. (1990), *Descrizione Di Una Battaglia: I Rituali Del Calcio*, Bologna: Il Mulino.

Dal Lago, A. and De Biasi, R. (1994), 'Italian Football Fans: Culture and Organisation'. In R. Giulianotti, N. Bonney and M. Hepworth (Eds), *Football, Violence, and Social Identity*, London: New York.

Damascelli, T. (2010), 'Mou Si Mangia Ancelotti Perde Solo Supermario'. *Il Giornale*, 17 March 2010.

Davies, N. (2008), 'The Bloody Battle Of Genoa'. *The Guardian*, Thursday 17 July 2008 [Online]. Available: http://www.theguardian.com/world/2008/jul/17/italy.g8 [Accessed 21 January 2015].

De Biasi, R. (1996), '*Ultra*-Political: Football Culture in Italy'. In V. Duke and L. Crolley (Eds), *Football, Nationality and the State*, New York: Harlow.

De Carolis, G. (2014), 'Guaraldi Da Zanetti Con Un Ultras. Così Ha Partecipato Alla Trattativa'. *Il Corriere Di Bologna*.

Della Porta, D. (1995), 'Political Parties and Corruption: Reflections on the Italian Case'. *Modern Italy*, 1, 97–114.

Della Porta, D. (1998), 'Police Knowledge and Protest Policing: Some Reflections on the Italian Case'. In D. Della Porta and H. Reiter (Eds), *Policing Protest: The Control of Mass Demonstrations in Western Democracies*. Minneapolis: University of Minnesota Press.

Della Porta, D. and Reiter, H. (2003), *Polizia E Protesta*, Bologna: Il Mulino.

Della Porta, D. and Vannucci, A. (2007), 'Corruption and Anti-Corruption: The Political Defeat of 'Clean Hands' in Italy'. *West European Politics*, 30, 830–53.

Deloitte and Touche (2010), *Deloitte Football Money League 2010*, Manchester: Deloitte.

Deloitte and Touche (2013), *Deloitte Football Money League 2013*, Manchester: Deloitte.

Dickie, J. (1996), 'Imagined Italies'. In D. Forgacs and R. Lumley (Eds), *Italian Cultural Studies: An Introduction*, Oxford; New York: Oxford University Press.

Dickie, J. (2013), *Mafia Republic*, London: Sceptre.

Doidge, M. (2011), 'La Vecchia Signora non Sfigurerà all'estero', *Il Giornale dell'Architettura*, October 98.

Doidge, M. (2013a), '"The Birthplace of Italian Communism": Political Identity and Action Amongst Livorno Fans', *Soccer and Society*, 14(2), 246–61.

Doidge, M. (2013b), '"If You Jump Up and Down, Balotelli Dies": Racism and Player Abuse in Italian Football', *International Review for the Sociology of Sport* [Online First].

Doidge, M. (2014), *Anti-racism in European Football: Report to UEFA*, Brighton: University of Brighton.

Doidge, M. (2015), Il Calcio as a Source of Local and Social Identity in Italy. In U. Merkel (Ed.), *Identity Discourses and Communities in International Events, Festivals and Spectacles*, Basingstoke: Palgrave Macmillan.

Drayton, J. (2013), 'I'm Ready to Go: Boateng Considers Quitting Italy for Good After Racial Abuse'. *The Daily Mail*, 5 January 2013.

Dunne, F. (2006), 'Makings of a Scandal: Juventus' Match-Fixing System Copied by Their Rivals'. *The Independent*, Saturday, 15 July 2006

Eco, U. (1990), 'A Guide to the Neo-Television of the 1980s'. In Z. Baranski and R. G. Lumley (Eds), *Culture and Conflict in Postwar Italy: Essays on Mass and Popular Culture*, New York: St. Martin Press.

Eisenstadt, S. N. (1973), *Traditional Patrimonialism and Modern Neopatrimonialism*, Beverly Hills: Sage Publications.

Elias, N. and Scotson, J. L. (1965), *The Established and the Outsiders; A Sociological Enquiry into Community Problems*, London: F. Cass.

Eve, J. and Goodbody, J. (2004), 'Juventus Guilty of Drug Abuse'. *The Times*, 27 November 2004.

Farrell, J. (1995), 'Berlusconi and Forza Italia: New Force for Old?' *Modern Italy*, 1, 40–52.

Feltri, M. (2006), 'Da Mani Pulite a Piedi Puliti'. *La Stampa*, 24 May 2006.

Ferrarella, L. (2012), 'Gli Manteniamo Moglie E Figli. Se Lo Sanno I Militanti È Finito', *Corriere Dello Sport*, 6 April.

Ferreri, A. (2008), *Ultras, I Ribelli Del Calcio: Quarant'anni Di Antagonismo E Passione*, Milano: Bepress.

Foot, J. (2001), *Milan Since the Miracle: City, Culture, and Identity*, Oxford: New York.

Foot, J. (2003), *Modern Italy*, Basingstoke: Palgrave Macmillan.

Foot, J. (2006), *Calcio: A History of Italian Football*, London: Fourth Estate.

Foot, J. (2007a), 'Italian Police Beating Up Fans? Big Deal. It's What They Do'. *The Independent*, 8 April 2007 [Online]. Available from: http://independent.co.uk/opinion/commentators/john-foot-italian-police-beating-up-fans-big-deal-its-what-they-do-443746.html [Accessed 1 August 2014].

Foot, J. (2007b), *Winning at All Costs: A Scandalous History of Italian Soccer*, New York: Nation Books.

Foot, J. (2011), 'A Qaddafi Son, Italian Soccer and the Power of Money'. *New York Times*, 25 February 2011.

Foucault, M. (1990), *The Will to Knowledge: The History of Sexuality Volume I*, London: Penguin.

Foucault, M. (1991a), *Discipline and Punish: The Birth of the Prison*, Harmondsworth; Middlesex: Penguin Books.

Foucault, M. (1991b), 'Governmentality' In G. Burchell, C. Gordon and P. Miller (Eds), *The Foucault Effect: Studies in Governmentality: With Two Lectures by and an Interview with Michel Foucault*, Chicago, IL: University of Chicago Press.

Francesio, G. (2008), *Tifare Contro: [Una Storia Degli Ultras Italiani]*, Milano: Sperling & Kupfer.

Gamble, A. (1994), *The Free Economy and the Strong State: Politics of Thatcherism*, Basingstoke: Palgrave Macmillan.

Ginsborg, P. (1990), *A History of Contemporary Italy: Society and Politics, 1943–1988*, London; New York: Penguin.

Ginsborg, P. (1996), 'Explaining Italy's Crisis'. In S. Gundle and S. Parker (Eds), *The New Italian Republic: From the Fall of the Berlin Wall to Berlusconi*, London: New York.

Ginsborg, P. (2003), *Italy and its Discontents: Family, Civil Society, State, 1980–2001*, London; New York: Penguin.

Ginsborg, P. (2004), *Silvio Berlusconi: Television, Power and Patrimony*, London; New York: Verso.

Giudici, L. (2010), 'Il "Modello Firenze": Un Laboratorio Del Calcio Moderno'. In S. Cacciari and L. Giudici (Eds), *Stadio Italia – I Conflitti Del Calcio Moderno*, Florence: La Casa Usher.

Giulianotti, R. (1999), *Football: A Sociology of the Global Game,* Cambridge: Polity Press.
Glanville, B. (1999a), *Football Memories,* London: Virgin.
Glanville, B. (1999b), 'Obituary: Italo Allodi'. *The Guardian,* 8 June 1999.
Goldblatt, D. (2007), *The Ball Is Round: A Global History of Football,* London: Viking.
Gould, D. and Williams, J. (2011), After Heysel: How Italy Lost the Football 'Peace'. *Soccer & Society,* 12, 586–601.
Gramsci, A. (1971), *Selections From the Prison Notebooks of Antonio Gramsci,* New York: International Publishers.
Gramsci, A. F. D. (2000), *The Gramsci Reader: Selected Writings, 1916–1935/Uniform Title: Selections. English,* New York: New York University Press.
Guastella, G. (2011), 'Ruby, Le Telefonate, I Bonifici', *Corriere Della Sera,* 17 February.
Gundle, S. and Parker, S. (1996), *The New Italian Republic: From the Fall of the Berlin Wall to Berlusconi,* London; New York: Routledge.
Guschwan, M. (2007), 'Riot in the Curve: Soccer Fans in Twenty-First Century Italy'. *Soccer & Society,* 8(2–3), 250–66.
Guschwan, M. (2013a), 'La Tessera Della Rivolta: Italy's Failed Fan Identification Card'. *Soccer & Society,* 14(2), 215–29.
Guschwan, M. (2013b), Stadium as Public Sphere. *Sport in Society,* 17(7), 884–900.
Habermas, J. (1989), *The Structural Transformation of the Public Sphere: An Inquiry into a Category of Bourgeois Society,* Cambridge, MA: MIT Press.
Hamil, S., Morrow, S., Idle, C., Rossi, G. and Faccendini, S. (2010), The Governance and Regulation of Italian Football. *Soccer & Society,* 11, 373–413.
Hanretty, C. (2010), 'The Media Between Market and Politics'. In A. Mammone and G. A. Veltri (Eds), *Italy Today: The Sick Man of Europe.* London; New York: Routledge.
Harding, T. (2001), 'Carabinieri had a High Profile and Low Tactics'. *The Telegraph,* 28 July 2001.
Harvey, D. (1989), 'From Managerialism to Entrepreneurialism: The Transformation in Urban Governance in Late Capitalism'. *Geografiska Annaler. Series B, Human Geography,* 71, 3–17.
Hawkey, I. (2006), 'Italy Takes a Dive'. *The Sunday Times,* 14 May 2006.
Hawkey, I. (2008), Hooligan Hell for Shamed Napoli. *The Times,* 5 October 2008.
Hill, D. (2008), *The Fix: Soccer and Organized Crime,* Toronto: M&S.
Hobsbawm, E. J. and Ranger, T. O. (1983), *The Invention of Tradition,* Cambridge; New York: Cambridge University Press.
Hooper, J. (2010), 'Silvio Berlusconi Ally had no Mafia Links After 1992, Court Rules'. *The Guardian,* 29 June 2010.
Horncastle, J. (2012), *Udinese's Dedicated Lone Away Supporter Against Sampdoria Reveals Turnout Issues in Serie A* [Online]. Available: http://blogs.thescore.com/counterattack/2012/12/12/horncastle-udineses-dedicated-lone-away-supporter-against-sampdoria-reveals-turnout-issues-in-serie-a/ [Accessed June 2013].

Horne, J. (2011), 'Architects, Stadia and Sport Spectacles: Notes on the Role of Architects in the Building of Sport Stadia and Making of World-Class Cities'. *International Review for the Sociology of Sport*, 46, 205–27.

Horne, J. and Whannel, G. (2012), *Understanding the Olympics*, London: Routledge.

House of Commons Home Affairs Committee (2009), *The Cost of Policing Football Matches*, London: The Stationery Office.

Ignazi, P. (2006), 'Listening and Silencing. Italian Feminists in the 1970s: Between Autocoscienza and Terrorism'. In A. Cento Bull and A. Giorgio (Eds), *Speaking Out and Silencing*. Leeds: Legenda.

*Il Fatto Quotidiano* (2014), 'Spari A Roma, Tifoso Giallorosso Arrestato Per Tentato Omicidio: È Daniele De Santis'. *Il Fatto Quotidiano*.

*Il Giornale* (2008), 'Ultras, Matarrese: "Celle Negli Stadi"'. *Il Giornale*, 12 September 2008.

Jackson, G. (2008), Safety and Security First. Available: http://www.uefa.com/uefa/keytopics/kind=1048576/newsid=689264.html [Accessed 5 November 2008].

Jary, D., Horne, J. and Bucke, T. (1991), 'Football "Fanzines" and Football Culture: A Case of Successful "Culural Contestation"'. *Sociological Review*, 39, 581–98.

Johnston, B. (2001), 'Berlusconi Defends Tactics of Riot Police'. *The Telegraph*, 28 July 2001.

Jones, T. (2007), *The Dark Heart of Italy*, London: Faber.

Jones, T. and Newburn, T. (2002), 'The Transformation of Policing? Understanding Current Trends in Policing Systems'. *The British Journal of Criminology*, 42, 129–46.

Kiefer, P. (2007a), 'Hooligans Kill a Policeman, Throwing Italy Soccer into a Void'. *International Herald Tribune*, 4 February 2007.

Kiefer, P. (2007b), Italian Authorities Propose Barring Fans. *New York Times*, 6 February 2007.

Kiefer, P. and Fisher, I. (2006), 'Leader of Italy's Most Revered Soccer Club Takes a Spill'. *New York Times*, 21 May 2006.

King, A. (1998). *The End of the Terraces: The Transformation of English Football in the 1990s*, London; New York: Leicester University Press.

King, A. (2003), *The European Ritual: Football in the New Europe*, Aldershot: Ashgate.

Kington, T. (2007), 'Italy's Mr Clean Bids to Save Football from Fascist Thugs'. *The Observer*, 11 February 2007.

Kington, T. (2009), 'Berlusconi's Wife Seeks Divorce'. *The Guardian*, 3 May 2009.

Kington, T. (2010), 'Fabio Capello Tells Italy the Premier League Puts Serie A to Shame'. *The Guardian*, 10 February 2010.

Kington, T. (2012), 'Serie A Players in Fear as Fan Violence and Spectre of Match-Fixing Return'. *The Guardian*, 28 April 2012.

*La Gazzetta Dello Sport* (2008a), 'La Juventus Patteggia Esce Da Calciopoli 2', *La Gazzetta Dello Sport*, 18 June 2008.

*La Gazzetta Dello Sport* (2008b), 'San Paolo: Chiusura Ridotta Matarrese: "Celle Allo Stadio"'. *La Gazzetta Dello Sport*, 11 September 2008.

*La Gazzetta Dello Sport* (2009), '"In Italia Comandano Gli Ultrà" Polemica Capello-Petrucci'. *La Gazzetta Dello Sport,* 26 October 2009 [Online]. Available from: http://www.gazzetta.it/Calcio/26-10-2009/polemica-capello-petrucci-601752727016.shtml [Accessed 21 January 2015].

*La Gazzetta Dello Sport* (2010a), 'Berlusconi: "Milan Sfortunato Incontriamo Arbitri Di Sinistra"'. *La Gazzetta Dello Sport,* 12 September 2010.

*La Gazzetta Dello Sport* (2010b), 'Rai, Addio Moviola! Ecco La Cassazione'. *La Gazzetta Dello Sport,* 26 July 2010.

*La Gazzetta Dello Sport* (2013a), 'Blitz Della Guardia Di Finanza Nelle Sedi Di 41 Società Dalla Serie A Alle Serie Minori'. *La Gazzetta Dello Sport,* 25 June 2013 [Online]. Available from: http://www.gazzetta.it/Calcio/25-06-2013/guardia-di-finanza-blitz-serie-a-20651609632.shtml [Accessed 21 January 2015].

*La Gazzetta Dello Sport* (2013b), 'Calcioscommesse, Deferiti Mauri, Milanetto, Lazio, Genoa E Lecce'. *La Gazzetta Dello Sport,* 10 July 2013.

*La Gazzetta Dello Sport* (2014), 'Mondiali 2014, Balotelli: "Ho La Coscienza A Posto. I 'Negri' Non Mi Avrebbero Mai Scaricato Così"'. *La Gazzetta Dello Sport,* 24 June 2014.

*La Repubblica* (2006a), Calcio Shock, 21 Indagati a Napoli in 6 Nella Cupola Che Decideva. *La Repubblica,* 12 May 2006.

*La Repubblica* (2006b), '"Consigli" Agli Arbitri e Minacce Le Telefonate Dei Potenti Del Calcio'. *La Repubblica,* 12 May 2006.

*La Repubblica* (2010a), 'Caso Gugliotta, Interviene Manganelli Disposta Una "Rigorosa" Inchiesta'. *La Repubblica,* 10 May 2010.

*La Repubblica* (2010b), 'Zebina: "E' Razzismo. Voglio Essere Difeso"'. *La Repubblica,* 28 March 2010.

*La Repubblica* (2012), Il "Miracolo" Di Sculli: Convince Gli Ultras E Genoa – Siena Riprende [Online]. Available from: http://video.repubblica.it/edizione/genova/il-miracolo-di-sculli-convince-gli-ultras-e-genoa-siena-riprende/93291/91685 [Accessed 1 August 2014].

*La Repubblica* (2013), 'Paolo Berlusconi: "Balotelli, Il Negretto Della Famiglia"'. *La Repubblica.*

*La Repubblica* (2014), 'Coppa Italia: Ultrà Ha Dato Ok A Match, È Il Capo Della Curva A Del Napoli Ed È Figlio Di Un Boss Del Rione Sanità'. *La Repubblica.*

Lane, D. (2004), *Berlusconi's Shadow: Crime, Justice and the Pursuit of Power,* London: Allen Lane.

Lapalombara, J. (1987), *Democracy, Italian Style,* New Haven: Yale University Press.

Lawrence, A. (2008), 'Serie A on the B-List'. *The Observer,* 23 November 2008.

Leroux, M. (2008), 'Fabio Capello, the High-Profile Victim Caught in Crossfire as Italy Takes Aim at Corruption'. *The Times,* 1 April 2008.

Liguori, G. and Smargiasse, A. (2003), *Calcio E Neocalcio: Geopolitica E Prospettive Del Football in Italia,* Roma: Manifestolibri.

Liguori, M. (2007), 'Spinelli: Meno Tasse; Il Fisco: "Paghi Quello Che Non Ha Versato"'. *Quotidiano,* 25 June 2007 [Online]. Available from: http://qn.quotidiano.net/conti_

del_pallone_2007/2007/06/25/1964-spinelli_meno_tasse.shtml [Accessed 21 January 2015].

Lipow, A. and Seyd, P. (1996), 'The Politics of Anti-Partyism'. *Parliam Affairs*, 49, 273–84.

Lo Bianco, G. and Messina, P. (2008), 'Stadio, Spranga E Ultras'. *L'espresso*, 8 September 2008 [Online]. Available from: http://espresso.repubblica.it/palazzo/2008/09/08/news/stadio-spranga-e-ultras-1.9882 [Accessed 21 January 2015].

Macaskill, E. and Elliot, L. (2001), 'Protester Killed in Summit Chaos'. *The Guardian*, 21 July 2001.

Macleod, A. (2005), 'Scotland Yard Back-Up for Edinburgh G8 Protesters'. *The Times*, 29 January 2005.

Maffesoli, M. (1996), *The Time of the Tribes: The Decline of Individualism in Mass Society*, London: Sage.

Maguire, J. (1999), *Global Sport: Identities, Societies, Civilizations*, Cambridge; Malden, MA: Polity Press.

Malcolm, D. and Waddington, I. (2008), '"No Systematic Doping in Football": A Critical Review'. *Soccer & Society*, 9, 198–214.

Marchi, V. (2005), *Il Derby Del Bambino Morto: Violenza E Ordine Pubblico Nel Calcio*, Roma: Deriveapprodi.

Marcotti, G. (2006), 'You are the Boss! You Own Serie A'. *The Times*, 15 May 2006.

Marcotti, G. (2007), United Fans Pay in Blood for Italy's 'Loose Dogs'. *The Times*, 6 April 2007.

Martin, S. (2004), *Football and Fascism: The National Game Under Mussolini*, Oxford: Berg.

Masu, A. (2013), 'Cagliari Owner Cellino Arrested Together with the Mayor of Quartu'. *La Gazzetta Dello Sport*, 14 February 2013.

Mauss, M. (1967), *The Gift: Forms and Functions of Exchange in Archaic Societies*, New York: Norton.

Mcmahon, B. and Buckley, K. (2006), 'Scandal Hits Italy World Cup Plans'. *The Observer*, 14 May 2006.

Melucci, A., Keane, J. and Mier, P. (1989), *Nomads of the Present: Social Movements and Individual Needs in Contemporary Society*, Philadelphia: Temple University Press.

Menduni, E. (1996), *La Più Amata Dagli Italiani: La Televisione Tra Politica E Telecomunicazioni*, Bologna: Mulino.

Mensurati, M. (2007), Funzionava Così Il Sistema Moggi: 107 Partite Sospette Nel (2004–05). *La Repubblica*, 22 April 2007.

Merkel, U. (2012), Football Fans and Clubs in Germany: Conflicts, Crises and Compromises. *Soccer & Society*, 13, 359–76.

Monti, A. (2014), 'Alla Ricerca Del Talento Perduto: Cambiare O Sparire'. *Gazzetta Dello Sport*, 27 July 2014.

Monti, F. (2005), 'Arbitri Nel Caos: Carraro Perde La Pazienza'. *Corriere Della Sera*, 8 May 2005.

Monti, F. and Valenti, G. (2014), 'Figc. Bufera Tavecchio, Adesso Faccia Un Passo Indietro'. *Gazzetta Dello Sport*, 27 July 2014.

Morrow, S. (1999), *The New Business of Football: Accountability and Finance in Football*, Basingstoke: Macmillan.

Nowell-Smith, G. (1979), 'Television – Football – The World'. *Screen*, 19, 45–59.

Nowell-Smith, G. (1990), 'Italy: Tradition, Backwardness and Modernity'. In Z. G. Baranski and R. Lumley (Eds), *Culture and Conflict in Postwar Italy: Essays on Mass and Popular Culture*, New York: St. Martin Press.

O'henley, A. (2008), 'Nakamura's Magic Touch'. *Uefa Magazine*, 11 January 2008 [Online]. Available from: http://www.uefa.com/news/newsid=643756.html [Accessed 21 January 2015].

O'malley, P. (1997), 'Politics and Postmodernity'. *Social and Legal Studies: An International Journal*, 6, 363–81.

Padellaro, A. and Tamburrano, G. (1993), *Processo A Craxi*, Milan: Sperling & Kupfer.

Pallavicino, C. (2004), *Tenetevi Il Miliardo: La Sfida Di Lucarelli Che Portò Il Livorno in Serie A*, Milano: Baldini Castoldi Dalai.

Palmeri, T. (2010), 'Il Blob Della Settimana. Drogba Redento Dal Figlio'. *Gazzetta Dello Sport*, 8 February 2010.

Paramio, J. L., Buraimo, B. and Campos, C. (2008), 'From Modern to Postmodern: The Development of Football Stadia in Europe'. *Sport in Society*, 11, 517–34.

Parliamentary Questions European Parliament (2007), *Answer Given by Mr Dimas on Behalf of the Commission* [Online]. Available: http://www.europarl.europa.eu/sides/getallanswers.do?reference=p-2007-5221&language=en [Accessed 1 June 2014].

Piore, M. J. and Sabel, C. F. (1984), *The Second Industrial Divide: Possibilities for Prosperity*, New York: Basic.

Podaliri, C. and Balestri, C. (1998), The Ultras, Racism and Football Culture in Italy. In A. Brown (Ed.), *Fanatics! Power, Identity, and Fandom in Football*, London: Routledge.

Poli, E. (2001), The Revolution in the Televised Soccer Market. *Journal of Modern Italian Studies*, 5, 371–94.

Popham, P. (2003), '"Kiss of Honour" Between Andreotti and Mafia Head Never Happened, Say Judges'. *The Independent*, 26 July 2003.

Popham, P. (2007), 'The Big Question: Will Italian Football Recover from its Hooliganism Crisis?' *The Independent*, Wednesday, 7 February 2007.

Porro, N. (2008), *Sociologia Del Calcio*, Roma: Carocci.

Porro, N. and Russo, P. (2000), 'Sport and Society in Italy Today – Berlusconi and Other Matters: The Era of "Football-Politics"'. *Journal of Modern Italian Studies*, 5, 348–70.

Porro, N. and Russo, P. (2004), 'Italian Football Between Conflict and State Aid'. *Italian Politics*, 19, 219–34.

Praverman, F. (2007), 'Violence in Italy Hands Euro 2012 to the Eastern Bloc'. *Times Online*, 18 April 2007.

Putnam, R. D. (2000), *Bowling Alone: The Collapse and Revival of American Community*, New York: Simon and Schuster.

Putnam, R. D., Leonardi, R. and Nanetti, R. (1993), *Making Democracy Work: Civic Traditions in Modern Italy*, Princeton, NJ: Princeton University Press.

Reiner, R. (1992), Policing a Postmodern Society. *Modern Law Review*, 55, 761–81.

Richardson, J. (2007), 'The End of the Old Ultras Violence'. *The Guardian*, 9 February 2007.

Riesman, D. (1961), *The Lonely Crowd; a Study of the Changing American Character*, New Haven: Yale University Press.

Robinson, M. J. (1976), 'Public Affairs Television and the Growth of Political Malaise: The Case of "The Selling of the Pentagon"'. *The American Political Science Review*, 70, 409–32.

Robson, G. (2000), *No One Likes us, we Don't Care: The Myth and Reality of Millwall Fandom*, Oxford: Berg.

Rowe, D. (2004), *Sport, Culture and the Media*, Maidenhead: Open University Press.

Russo, A. (2012), Arcidiacono Può Giocare. Il Questore Modifica Il Daspo. *La Gazetta Dello Sport*, 22 November 2012.

Russo, P. (2005), *L'invasione Dell'ultracalcio: Anatomia Di Uno Sport Mutante*, Verona: Ombre Corte.

Sanga, G. (1996), Campane E Campanili. In M. Isnenghi (Ed.), *I Luoghi Della Memoria. Strutture Ed Eventi Dell'italia Unita*. Roma-Bari: Laterza.

Sanminiatelli, M. (2007), 'Officials: Only Six Italian Soccer Stadiums Meet Security Requirements'. *Usa Today*, 2 August 2007.

Sapelli, G. (1995), *Southern Europe Since 1945: Tradition and Modernity in Portugal, Spain, Italy, Greece and Turkey*, London, New York.

Sarzanini, F. (2006), 'Pisanu Chiamò Moggi: Aiuta La Torres'. *Corriere Della Sera*, 16 May 2006.

Sarzanini, F. (2009), 'Topolanek Nudo Nel Giardino Della Villa E Nei Viali Bionde E Brune Mazzafiato', *Corriere Della Sera*, 31 May 2009.

Sassen, S. (2001), *The Global City: New York, London, Tokyo*, Princeton: Princeton University Press.

Sassoon, D. (1986), *Contemporary Italy: Politics, Economy, and Society Since 1945*, London; New York: Longman.

Scalia, V. (2009), 'Just a Few Rogues?: Football Ultras, Clubs and Politics in Contemporary Italy', *International Review for the Sociology of Sport*, 44(1), 41–53.

Schimmel, K. S. (2001), 'Sport Matters'. In C. Gratton and I. P. Henry (Eds), *Sport in the City*, London: Routledge.

Schimmel, K. S. (2006), 'Deep Play: Sports Mega-Events and Urban Social Conditions in the USA'. In J. Horne and W. Manzenreiter (Eds), *Sports Mega-Events: Social Scientific Analyses of a Global Phenomenon*. Oxford: Blackwell Publishing; Sociological Review.

Schlesinger, P. (1990), The Berlusconi Phenomenon. In Z. Baranski and R. G. Lumley (Eds), *Culture and Conflict in Postwar Italy: Essays on Mass and Popular Culture*, New York: St. Martin Press.

Sennett, R. (1976), *The Fall of Public Man*, Cambridge: Cambridge University Press.

Silverman, S. (1965), Patronage and Community-Nation Relationships in Central Italy. *Ethnology*, 4, 172–89.

Silverman, S. (1975), *Three Bells of Civilization: The Life of an Italian Hill Town*, New York: Columbia University Press.

Simmel, G. (1950), *The Sociology of George Simmel*, London: Free Press of Glencoe.

Skidmore, P., Bound, K. and Lownsbrough, H. (2006), *Community Participation: Who Benefits?*, York: JRF.

Sklair, L. (2001), *The Transnational Capitalist Class*, Oxford; Malden, MA: Wiley-Blackwell.

Smith, A. D. (1987), *The Ethnic Origins of Nations*, Oxford; New York: Blackwell.

Spaaij, R. (2006), *Understanding Football Hooliganism: A Comparison of Six Western European Football Clubs*, Amsterdam: Vossiuspers Uva – Amsterdam University Press.

Stefanini, M. (2009), *Ultras: Identità, Politica e Violenza Nel Tifo Sportivo Da Pompei a Raciti a Sandri*, Milano: Boroli.

Stille, A. (1999), 'Emperor of the Air'. *The Nation*, 29 November 1999.

Stott, C. and Adang, O. (2003), Policing Football Matches with an International Dimension in the European Union: Understanding and Managing Risk. Liverpool: Liverpool University.

Stott, C. and Reicher, S. (1998), 'How Conflict Escalates: The Inter-Group Dynamics of Collective Football Crowd "Violence"'. *Sociology*, 32, 353–77.

Stott, C. J. T. and Pearson, G. (2007), *Football 'Hooliganism': Policing and the War on the 'English Disease'*, London: Pennant Books.

Sugden, J. P. and Tomlinson, A. (1998), *Fifa and the Contest for World Football: Who Rules the People's Game?*, Cambridge: Polity Press.

Supporters In Campo (2013), Il Manuele Di Supporters In Campo. Supporters In Campo.

Tavares, C. and Thomas, G. (2008), *Eurostat: Crime and Criminal Justice*, Luxembourg: Eurostat

Taylor, R. H. L. J. (1990), *The Hillsborough Stadium Disaster*, London: HMSO.

Testa, A. (2009), 'The Ultras: An Emerging Social Movement?'. *Review of European Studies*, 1(2), 54–63.

Testa, A. (2013), 'Normalization of the Exception: Issues and Controversies of the Italian Counter-Hooliganism Legislation'. *Sport in Society*, 16, 151–66.

Testa, A. and Armstrong, G. (2008), 'Italian Ultras and Neo-Fascism'. *Social Identities*, 14, 473–90.

*The Daily Telegraph* (2012), 'Udinese Fan Arrigo Brovedani the Only Supporter to Turn Up for Serie A Clash with Sampdoria'. *The Daily Telegraph*, 13 December 2012.

*The Independent* (2005), Di Canio In Trouble Again For Fascist Salute. *The Independent*, 13 December 2005.

*The Independent* (2013), 'Juventus Coach Antonio Conte Admits: 'I Can't See an Italian Team Winning the Champions League in the Coming Years''. *The Independent*, 11 April 2013 [Online]. Available: http://www.independent.co.uk/sport/football/european/juventus-coach-antonio-conte-admits-i-cant-see-an-italian-team-winning-the-champions-league-in-the-coming-years-8568231.html [Accessed 1 June 2014].

Tonelli, M. (2009), 'La D'addario Da Berlusconi Svelati Gli Audio Degli Incontri', *La Repubblica*, 20 July.

Touraine, A. (1981), *The Voice and the Eye: An Analysis of Social Movements/Uniform Title: Voix Et Le Regard. English,* Cambridge; New York: Cambridge University Press.

Tsoukala, A. (2009), *Football Hooliganism in Europe: Security and Civil Liberties in the Balance*, New York: Palgrave.

Urry, J. (1990), *The Tourist Gaze: Leisure and Travel in Contemporary Societies,* London: Newbury Park.

Urry, J. (2002), *Consuming Places,* London; New York: Routledge.

Valdiserri, L. (2008), Calcio Totale. *Corriere Della Sera*, 17 March 2008.

Verdelli, C. (2009), Campianato Anno Zero. *La Gazzetta Dello Sport*, 14 August 2009.

Vidal, J. (2001), 'The City Burns, a Young Man Lies Dead...'. *The Guardian*, 21 July 2001.

Von Beyme, K. (1996), Party Leadership and Change in Party Systems: Towards a Postmodern Party State? *Government and Opposition*, 31, 135–59.

Wagstaff, C. (2001), 'The Media'. In Z. G. W. Baranski and J. Rebecca (Eds), *The Cambridge Companion to Modern Italian Culture*. Cambridge: Cambridge University Press.

Wilcox, V. (2008), From Heroic Defeat to Mutilated Victory: The Myth of Caporetto in Fascist Italy. In J. Macleod (Ed.), *Defeat and Memory: Cultural Histories of Military Defeat in the Modern Era*. Basingstoke: Palgrave Macmillan.

Williams, R. (2007), 'The Loophole that Allowed Milan to Take Athens Road'. *The Guardian*, Monday, 21 May 2007.

Wilson, S. (2009), 'David Beckham Chews the Fat in the Milan Lab'. *The Telegraph*, 5 February 2009.

Withnall, A. (2013), 'Italy's First Black Minister Cécile Kyenge Likened to a Prostitute in Latest Public Insult'. *The Independent*.

Wodak, R., Khosravinik, M. and Mral, B. (2013), *Right-Wing Populism in Europe: Politics and Discourse,* London: Bloomsbury Academic.

Wood, S. and Farrell, J. (2001), Other Voices: Contesting the Status Quo. In Z. G. W. Baranski and J. Rebecca (Eds), *The Cambridge Companion to Modern Italian Culture*. Cambridge: Cambridge University Press.

Yorke, G. (2013), 'Lazio's Italian Cup Glory Marred by Crowd Trouble... They Even Booed Gangnam Style'. *The Daily Mail*, 26 May 2013.

Zinn, D. L. (2001), *La Raccomandazione: Clientelismo Vecchio E Nuovo,* Roma: Donzelli Editore.

# Index

ACAB   171, 174, 177
AC Milan   2, 3, 4, 9, 10, 14, 21, 22, 24, 26, 27, 28, 29, 31, 33, 35, 36, 37, 39, 40, 47, 48, 49, 50, 51, 52, 53, 54, 56–61, 64–6, 68–72, 74–5, 77, 83, 87–9, 91, 102, 106, 107, 117, 120, 121, 126, 145, 148, 149, 150, 151, 153, 154, 156, 157, 158, 159, 164, 165, 168, 173, 177, 178, 184, 185, 197, 203, 207, 209, 213, 214, 221, 222, 225
Adreotti, Giulio   30, 31, 234
Agnelli, Andrea   22, 48
Agnelli, Edoardo   48
Agnelli, Giovanni   21, 26, 71
Agnelli, Umberto   52, 90
AlbinoLeffe   190
Albo nazionale degli striscioni   116
Aldair   4
Allegri, Massimiliano   70
Allianza Nazionale   36, 213, 214
Allodi, Italo   54, 78
Ancona   69, 145, 193
anni di piombo   22
Argentina   1, 4, 75, 154
AS Livorno   7, 49, 51, 69, 70, 80, 90, 91, 101, 101, 103, 104, 106, 107, 108, 109, 112, 113, 114, 115, 116, 117, 118, 119, 120, 121, 123, 129, 130, 132, 133, 137, 138 141, 145, 149, 151, 154, 155, 161–3, 169, 174, 176, 181, 183, 184, 185, 189, 190, 197, 200, 201, 211, 217
Aspilla, Faustino   4
Atalanta   91, 102, 103, 139, 149, 154, 159, 173, 176, 198, 201
Azzurri   35, 91, 92, 162

Baggio, Roberto   2, 68
Baldas, Fabio   83–4
Balotelli, Mario   114, 157–62
Barcelona   10, 35, 52, 98, 99, 221
Bari   4, 40, 71, 92, 101, 103, 181, 197
Batitstuta, Gabriel   4, 69
Bayern Munich   9, 10, 221
BBC   1, 32
Benfica   9
Bergamo, Paolo   79–82, 89
Berlusconi, Paolo   28
Berlusconi, Silvio   3, 5, 14, 26–9, 31–8, 39–43, 44, 51, 55, 57–62, 63, 65, 68, 69, 70, 71, 72, 75, 76, 77, 87, 107, 111, 131, 157, 164, 165, 170, 184, 200, 203, 204, 209, 211, 213
Berthold, Thomas   2
Biscardi, Aldo   56, 82, 83
Boateng, Kevin-Prince   159
Boban, Zvonomir   4
Bologna   22, 24, 50, 51, 53, 71, 103, 120, 148, 149, 151, 164, 176, 198, 217, 218
Borselino, Paolo   30
Borussia Dortmund   10, 221
Bosman   3, 59, 75, 84, 157
Brazil   4, 67, 151, 154, 160
Brescia   103, 109, 132, 134, 158, 171, 197
Brigate Autonome Livornesi   141, 154, 161–2, 169
Brigate Rosse (Red Brigades)   23, 148
Brighton and Hove Albion   104
Britain   3, 18, 25, 26, 42, 47, 97, 98, 100, 104, 135, 136, 155, 187, 192, 201, 202, 203, 213, 215, 218, 223
Brolin, Thomas   4
Bundesliga   8, 9, 10, 59, 67, 68, 186, 221

Cagliari   53, 70, 83, 104, 198, 209
Calcio Fiorentino   16, 47, 49, 96
Calciopoli   68, 77–93, 102, 112, 139, 197, 198, 199, 204, 206, 207, 209, 213
calcioscommesse   90, 91, 197, 199, 206
Calleri, Gianmarco   84

Calleri, Riccardo   84
Campanilismo   16, 145, 146, 150, 156, 178, 185, 194, 213
Cannavaro, Fabio   61, 67, 74
Canniggia, Claudo   4
Capello, Fabio   165, 203
Capitalia   72, 84
Careca   1
Carnivalesque   110, 138, 143, 144, 153, 160
Carraro, Franco   72, 78, 84, 87, 89, 91
Casere, Prandelli   158
Catania   7, 51, 71, 110, 112, 149, 153, 174, 175, 176, 199
Catenaccio   52, 59
Catholic Church   15, 19, 86
Cecchi Gori, Mario   69
Cecchi Gori, Vittorio   69, 73
Cellino, Massimo   70, 101, 104, 209
Cesena   35, 210
Champions League   3, 9, 10, 35, 61, 62, 65, 68, 72, 77, 81, 88, 89, 102, 138, 203, 205, 207, 221, 222
Chelsea   10, 102, 221, 222
Chioggia   113
Cirio   69, 72, 73, 74, 84, 87
Collina, Pierluigi   82
Communitas   143, 144
Conte, Antonio   92, 198
corruption   21, 24, 30, 39, 40, 41, 43, 51, 54, 64, 68, 79, 89, 101, 109, 206
Cosmi, Serse   69–70
Couto, Fernando   4, 61
Covisoc   72, 74, 76, 124, 213
Cragnotti, Andrea   84
Cragnotti, Sergio   69, 84, 87
Craxi, Betino   25–30, 32, 39, 41, 42, 55, 111
Cremonese   91
Criscito, Domenico   92, 166
Crudelli, Tiziano   56
Cruyff, Johan   1, 52

Dalla Valle, Diego   87, 91
Davids, Edgar   61, 68, 86
Decreto Legge   111, 200
De Gasperi, Alcide   19
De Laurentiis, Aurellio   70
Dell'Ultri, Marcello   33–4
Democazia Cristiana   19, 20, 23, 25, 30, 31, 71, 213

Derby of the Dead Child   128, 135, 166, 172, 174
deregulation   2, 3, 4, 5, 11, 14, 20, 22, 24, 26, 27, 31, 32, 33, 43, 45, 55, 58, 65, 67, 68, 75, 78, 84, 92, 107, 110, 116, 117, 136, 203, 204, 205, 208
De Santis, Massimo   80, 88, 166
De Tommaso, Gennaro (Genny 'a Carogna)   167, 175
DiBenedetto, Thomas   62, 63
Di Canio, Paolo   86, 163
Diffida ad Assistere alle manifestazioni Sportive (Daspo)   111, 113, 117, 121, 175, 176
di Lampedusa, Tomasi   13, 213
Divisione Investigazioni Generali e Operazioni Speciali (Digos)   125, 127, 134
Doni, Cristiano   91
Drughi   152
Dunga   4

Elkann, John   21
Emilian Model   24, 26, 100
Empoli   103, 138
England   1, 2, 3, 4, 8, 9, 62, 99, 100, 105, 106, 108, 109, 111, 114, 130, 136, 137, 144, 152, 153, 161, 165, 167, 171, 187, 188, 189, 191, 193, 198, 200, 201, 202, 203, 208, 211
English Model   114, 198–205

Faccheti, Giacino   89
Falcone, Giovanni   30
Fascism   18, 22, 46, 49, 50, 103, 130, 160, 169
Federazione Italiana Sostenitori Squadre Calcio (FIISC)   113, 187, 188, 189, 191, 211
Fiat   21, 22, 24, 26, 27, 48, 52, 63, 69, 71, 75, 80, 149
fideiussione   74, 213
FIGC   47, 48, 49, 51, 53, 55, 58, 66, 71, 72, 75, 76, 78, 79, 80, 84, 87, 89, 90, 109, 124, 139, 157, 160, 176, 177, 197, 198, 213
Fini, Gianfranco   36, 37, 40
Fininvest   29, 33, 34, 35, 57

Fiorentina   4, 35, 53, 66, 69, 73, 74, 79, 83,
    87, 89, 91, 99, 102, 104, 137, 138,
    139, 148, 149, 151, 157, 166, 186,
    199, 201, 204, 207, 213, 222
Florence   4, 16, 24, 47, 49, 97, 106, 115,
    138, 148, 149, 150, 151, 207, 215
Folk Devils   127, 139, 172, 173, 174, 179
Football Supporters Europe   194
forward panic   127, 128, 129, 130, 132,
    133, 134, 172
Forza Italia   34–7, 184, 213
Fossa dei Leoni   148, 168
France   3, 4, 13, 18, 45, 50, 62, 67, 198, 207,
    215, 221, 222
Freak Brothers   154
Frosinone   114

Galante, Fabio   80
Galliani, Adriano   60, 70, 72, 88, 90, 91,
    157, 165, 209
game of the bridge   16
Garibaldi, Giuseppe   13, 15, 50, 95, 103
Gascoigne, Paul (Gazza)   1, 2, 4, 69
Gattipardismo   13, 14, 17, 211, 213
Gaucci, Luciano   63, 71, 77, 84
GEA World   78, 84, 86
gemmellaggio   150
Genoa   46, 106, 128, 129, 131, 135, 190
Genoa Cricket and Football Club   7, 47,
    49, 50–1, 53, 66, 84, 92, 103, 119,
    145, 147, 149, 150, 166, 168, 176
Germany   1, 3, 4, 6, 8, 10, 18, 22, 62, 67,
    80, 85, 100, 187, 198, 201, 211,
    218, 221, 222
Geronzi, Cesare   84
Geronzi, Chiara   84
globalization   5, 6, 10, 25, 44, 45, 46, 65, 67,
    97, 128, 131, 179, 198
Gramsci, Antonio   17, 18, 80, 164
Grillo, Beppe   41, 42, 44, 214
Grosseto   104
Guevara, Che   115, 133, 162, 163, 175
Gulli, Ruud   2, 4, 59, 68

Häßler, Thomas   2
Henry, Thierry   86
Herrera, Helenio   52
Heysel stadium disaster   2, 6, 8, 188
Hillsborough stadium disaster   2, 5, 6, 97,
    98, 100, 118, 121, 137, 139, 200, 201

I Moschettieri   148
Il Popolo della Libertà   36, 37, 39, 157, 214
Il Processo   56, 82, 83, 109
Ince, Paul   5
Independent Supporters'
    Associations   187, 188, 208
Ingargiola, Pietro   81
Internazionale (Inter)   2, 4, 5, 8, 10, 16, 18,
    21, 22, 24, 26, 30, 33, 35, 38, 40,
    42, 46–56, 58, 59, 61–5, 68–70,
    74, 75, 88–90, 102, 107, 114,
    117, 120, 130, 148, 149, 150, 154,
    156, 158, 159, 160, 173, 177, 197,
    201, 205, 214

Juventus   2, 4, 9, 10, 22, 35, 47, 48, 49,
    51–4, 59–65, 68, 69, 71, 74, 75,
    78–106, 108, 113–14, 120, 139,
    149–50, 152, 154, 156, 157, 159,
    160, 165, 173, 177, 178, 184, 186,
    197–8, 201, 203, 207, 223–4,
    221, 223

Kirch   3
Klinnsmann, Jürgen   2
Kyenge, Cecile   157

Lazio   4, 7, 53, 54, 66, 69, 72, 74, 75, 76, 84,
    87, 89, 91, 92, 104, 107, 109, 113,
    115, 116, 118, 120, 123, 129, 130,
    151, 152, 155, 156, 157, 158, 163,
    165, 169, 172, 173, 174, 176, 183,
    197, 199, 204, 213, 216
Lecce   92, 103, 120, 197, 198
Lega Nord   36, 37, 38, 44, 153, 156, 157,
    162, 176, 211, 213
Lentini, Gianluigi   4, 60, 221
Letta, Enrico   37, 207
Lima, Salvatore   30, 31
Lippi, Davide   85
Lippi, Marcello   85
Liverpool   2, 9, 62, 89, 97, 131, 137,
    138, 221
Livorno   16, 42, 46, 47, 215, 216, 218
Lotito, Caludio   72, 87, 91
lottizzazione   20
Lucarelli, Cristiano   141, 161–3, 175, 184

Mafia   23, 30, 31, 33, 38, 44, 125, 127
Manchester City   100, 158

Manchester United   9, 10, 98, 100, 131, 137, 138, 221, 223
Mancini, Roberto   158
Maradona, Diego   1, 52, 54, 60, 154, 162, 197
Mataresse, Antonio   71
Matthäus, Lothar   2
Mauri, Stefano   197
Meani, Leandro   87, 88
Mediaset   3, 28, 32, 33, 34, 39, 40, 55, 64, 82, 163, 203
Mentalità Ultras   167–71, 172, 173, 174, 175, 176, 178, 194, 208, 210
Messina   7, 90, 159
Milanello   60
Milla, Roger   1
Miracle, The   18, 21, 22, 29, 46, 51, 52, 63, 65, 122, 147
Moggi, Alessandro   85, 197
Moggi, Luciano   76, 78–92, 112, 163, 197
Mondadori   29, 33
Mondialli Antirazzisti   160–1
Moratti, Angelo   52
Moratti, Massimo   63, 70, 71, 88, 197, 205
Moro, Aldo   23
Morosini, Piermario   118
Mourinho, Jose   158, 198
Movimento 5 Stelle   41, 42, 44, 214
Mussolini, Benito   16, 18, 20, 22, 23, 36, 45, 47, 49, 50, 71, 100, 101, 103, 121, 163

Napoli   1, 7, 37, 42, 54, 60, 68, 70, 71, 73, 74, 78, 104, 112, 113, 117, 120, 153, 154, 166, 173, 177, 178, 197, 200, 204, 205, 222
Ndrangheta   166
Novara   103

official supporters clubs   11, 58, 124, 132, 179, 182–91, 194, 211
Olivetti   22, 29, 48
Omolade, Akeem   159–60
Oriundi   50, 75, 157, 214
Osservatorio Nazionale sulle Manifestazioni Sportive   112, 113, 114, 116, 120, 127, 132, 134, 137, 138, 201, 214

Pairetto, Pierluigi   79–82, 87, 89
Palermo   7, 30, 70, 71, 102, 103, 112, 139, 157, 158, 165, 199

Palio   16
Palio Marinario   16
Papin, Jean-Pierre   4, 59, 60, 221
Paris Saint-Germain   64, 65, 222
Parks, Tim   69, 204
Parma   4, 42, 61, 66, 69, 72–4, 78, 84, 87, 103, 116, 117, 133, 173, 174, 181, 199, 200, 203, 204
Parmalat   69, 73–4, 84
Partito Comunista Italiano   19, 20, 23, 25, 31, 32, 33, 36, 42, 149, 214
partitocrazia   19, 20, 34, 37
Partito Democratico   31, 207
Partito Socialisto Italiano   20, 25, 29, 30, 33, 41, 72, 79, 82, 92, 118, 134, 214
patrimonialism   7, 10, 11, 14, 19, 20, 22, 24, 25, 29–31, 39, 41, 42, 43, 45, 46, 50, 60, 65, 66, 68–80, 85, 87, 92, 93, 95, 105, 107, 108, 109, 113, 124, 126, 127, 137, 139, 141, 163, 165, 179, 182, 183, 184, 189, 194, 199, 202, 204, 206, 209, 210
Pavarotti, Luciano   1
Pele   1
Perugia   54, 63, 71, 77, 84
Pescara   28, 118
Piacenza   95, 103, 104
Pirelli   21, 22, 26, 48, 71, 88, 89
Pisa   16, 111, 11, 145, 149–51, 154, 184, 215, 218
Pisanu Laws   86, 110–21, 127, 131, 133, 136, 160, 171, 175, 176, 177, 179, 185, 200, 201, 207
Platini, Michel   205
Platt, David   4
plus-valenze   74, 214
Plymouth Argyle   104, 187, 191, 208
police   7, 18, 23, 26, 40, 86, 91, 95, 98, 107, 110–15, 118, 119, 121, 122, 123–39 *passim*, 142, 144, 148, 152, 153, 165, 166, 167, 168, 169, 171–6, 179, 194, 197, 199, 200, 201, 202, 206, 210, 211, 213, 214, 219, 223
Portugal   9, 61, 86, 198, 222
postmodern populism   38–43
Premier League   2, 3, 5, 6, 8, 9, 10, 58, 59, 63, 67, 100, 107, 160, 192, 198, 203, 205, 208
Progetto Ultrà   156, 160, 161, 201, 217

Provera, Marco Tronchetti  21, 89
Pro Vercelli  48

racism  5, 6, 148, 151, 155–63, 171, 176, 177, 179, 188, 189, 211, 217
Raciti, Filippo  7, 110, 111, 112, 114, 117, 142, 167, 168, 173, 174, 175, 176, 199, 200
RAI  20, 27, 28, 33, 34, 55, 71, 82, 214
Real Madrid  10, 52, 61, 99, 165, 205, 221
Reggina Calabria  87, 89, 213
Riedle, Karl-Heinze  4
Rijkaard, Frank  2, 4, 59, 68
Risorgimento  13, 15, 214
Roma  2, 4, 5, 14, 24, 37, 53, 54, 59, 60, 62, 63, 66, 69, 71, 72, 74, 76, 77, 78, 79, 80, 84, 85, 87, 92, 96, 102, 104, 107, 109, 111, 112, 115, 116, 119, 120, 130, 131, 137, 139, 149, 150, 152, 154, 155, 156, 157, 160, 164, 165, 169, 171, 172, 173, 174, 175, 147, 178, 184, 193, 195, 197, 200, 203, 207, 210, 216, 217, 218, 219
Rome  4, 15, 18, 24, 28, 30, 37, 42, 49, 72, 78, 99, 101, 104, 106, 109, 112, 117, 119, 120, 130, 131, 134, 135, 137, 138, 149, 150, 151, 152, 153, 154, 165, 166, 172, 173, 174, 176, 177, 178, 184, 218
Ronaldinho  70
Rosetta Case  48, 49, 54, 206
Rossi, Paolo  54, 66

Sacchi, Arrigo  59
Salerno  114, 218
Salva Calcio  75, 76, 108, 165, 204
Sampdoria  4, 7, 8, 53, 60, 87, 103, 106, 145, 146, 147, 148, 149, 154, 155, 161, 168, 178, 184, 197, 221
Sampdoria Rude Boys and Girls  154, 155, 161
Sandri, Gabriele  7, 173, 174, 199
scandal  6, 11, 29, 30, 31, 33, 34, 37, 38, 40, 48, 49, 50 ,51, 52, 54, 57, 61, 66, 67–93 *passim*, 112, 139, 179, 197, 198, 199, 204, 205, 206, 210, 213, 214
Schilllachi, Salvatore  2

Scotland  144, 186
Sculli, Giuseppe  92, 166
Sensi, Franco  62, 69, 71, 76, 77, 80, 84, 165
Sensi, Rosella  62
Serie A  4, 5, 6, 7, 8, 9, 10, 57, 58, 67, 68, 69, 71, 72, 76, 77, 81, 87, 88, 89, 90, 91, 93, 103, 104, 151, 170, 173, 174, 179, 181, 190, 191, 197, 198, 202, 204, 205, 206, 209, 211, 213, 214, 215
Serie B  95, 103, 104, 118, 191, 193
Settebello  148
settore ospiti  117, 123, 132, 214
Siena  16, 80, 83, 85, 86, 87, 92, 103, 109, 112, 150, 151, 166, 197
Signori, Beppe  91
Siniscalco, Dominico  86
Sky Television  2, 3, 71, 107, 203
social capital  24, 25, 44, 83, 86, 91, 93, 108, 183, 184, 185, 186, 204, 208, 209, 210
Spagnolo, Vincenzo  168–71
Spain  3, 4, 6, 8, 9, 10, 40, 62, 86, 203, 221, 222, 235
Speziale libero  167, 175
Spinelli, Aldo  69, 70, 80, 108, 109, 181, 189, 190, 221
stadiums  1, 2, 5, 6, 7, 8, 11, 49, 57, 93, 95–122 *passim*, 133, 135, 136, 137, 139, 148, 155, 157, 164, 168, 174, 175, 176, 187, 192, 194, 199–210, 213, 216
stewards  71, 98 116, 117, 123, 131, 133, 136–8, 166, 189
Stoichkov, Hristo  4
striscione  143, 146, 151, 153, 155, 177, 214
Supporters Direct  192
Supporters in Campo  192–4, 211
Supporters Trusts  11, 179, 182, 191–5, 208, 211

Tafferel  4
Tangentopoli  24, 29, 30, 31, 33, 36, 37, 38, 39, 41, 78, 213, 214
Tanzi, Calisto  73
Tanzi, Francesca  84
Tanzi family  69, 73, 84
Taranto  193
Tardelli, Marco  1
Taylor report  2, 6, 97, 98, 100, 105, 108, 109, 110, 136, 198, 199, 200, 201

Telecom Italia   71, 88–90
Telelombardia   56
Telemontecarlo   69
Tessera del Tifoso   120, 188, 201, 202, 210, 214
Thatcher, Margaret   26, 42, 100
Thohir, Erick   63
Topophilia   99, 144
Torino   47, 48, 49, 51, 53, 60, 65, 66, 74, 76, 78, 103, 149, 161, 162, 175, 197, 206, 221
Totti, Francesco   165, 166
Trasformismo   17, 18, 19, 214
Trieste   49, 101, 104, 209
Turin   21, 22, 27, 28, 48, 49, 50, 51, 64, 65, 68, 78, 106, 112, 149, 154, 159, 184

UEFA   3, 9, 46, 61, 62, 67, 71, 76, 78, 80, 82, 90, 91, 102, 137, 160, 161, 190, 191, 198, 205, 217, 221, 222
ultras   7, 11, 23, 71, 92, 106, 115, 118, 119, 120, 123, 124, 127, 129, 130, 135, 137, 139, 141–79 *passim*, 182, 183, 184, 188, 189, 190, 191, 194, 195, 199, 201, 202, 208, 210, 211, 216, 217, 218, 219

Van Basten, Marco   2, 4, 59, 68
Vatican   19, 69
Venezia   45, 70
Verona   53, 79, 88, 103, 107, 115, 116, 145, 148, 149, 151, 153, 155, 156, 158, 193
Vicenza   145
Viola Club Viesseuax   148
violence   5, 7, 51, 80, 81, 82, 110, 111, 120, 122, 124, 127, 128, 129–31, 132, 134, 135, 138, 139, 142, 148, 151–62, 165, 171, 172, 173, 174, 175, 182, 184, 189, 198, 199, 205, 207, 210, 218
Völler, Rudi   1–2

Walker, Des   4
Winter, Aaron   4
World Cup   1, 4, 8, 10, 18, 45, 49, 50, 54, 55, 57, 61, 62, 64, 66, 67, 68, 74, 80, 85, 91, 99, 103, 130, 154, 205

Year Zero   11, 197–211 *passim*

Zamparini, Maurizio   70, 157
Zebina, Jonathan   159
Zemen, Zdenk   60
Zidane, Zinédine   68
Zoro, Marco   159, 160